SKYSCRAPER GOTHIC

SKYSCRAPER GOTHIC

Medieval Style and Modernist Buildings

Edited by
KEVIN D. MURPHY
and
LISA REILLY

University of Virginia Press
CHARLOTTESVILLE AND LONDON

University of Virginia Press

Printed in the United States of America on acid-free paper

First published 2017

9 8 7 6 5 4 3 2 1

Library of Congress Cataloging-in-Publication Data
Names: Murphy, Kevin D., editor. | Reilly, Lisa A., editor.
Title: Skyscraper gothic : medieval style and modernist buildings / edited by Kevin D. Murphy and Lisa Reilly.
Description: Charlottesville ; London : University of Virginia Press, 2017. | Includes bibliographical references and index.
Identifiers: LCCN 2016053410| ISBN 9780813939728 (cloth : alk. paper) | ISBN 9780813939735 (ebook)
Subjects: LCSH: Skyscrapers—United States. | Architecture, Gothic—Influence. | Architecture—United States—Medieval influences.
Classification: LCC NA6232 .S515 2017 | DDC 720/.483—dc23
LC record available at https://lccn.loc.gov/2016053410

Cover art: Drawing of Chicago's Tribune Tower, from the cover of Electrical Supplies Co. trade catalog, 1932. (Building Technology Heritage Library, contributed by Canadian Centre for Architecture, http://creativecommons.org/licenses/by-nd/3.0/)

To my parents, Brendan and Claire Reilly, who first introduced me to the joys of New York and its skyscrapers — L.R.

To the memory of Judith Haley Murphy — K.D.M.

CONTENTS

ACKNOWLEDGMENTS

Over the years that this project has been in preparation, the editors have accumulated debts to many organizations and individuals. The initial research for the project was supported by the School of Architecture at the University of Virginia, following a graduate seminar on the topic we taught together. We are grateful to our students in that seminar, who inspired our further work on the project. A short-term fellowship from the Hagley and Winterthur Museums supported further collaborative research. The Andrew W. Mellon Chair at Vanderbilt University underwrote the acquisition of illustrations.

Useful suggestions on an earlier version of the manuscript were provided by two anonymous readers recruited by the University of Virginia Press. Wherever possible we have attempted to respond to their insights. At the Press, Boyd Zenner was a patient editor; we also benefited from the work of Mark Mones and Cecilia Sorochin. Victoria Young's research assistance and Sally O'Driscoll's assistance in the preparation of the final manuscript were invaluable.

Many librarians and archivists from Atlanta to Maine assisted with our own research as well as with that of our contributors. We are grateful to them for their generosity and expertise.

Lastly, we are thankful for the patience of the contributors to this volume, who maintained faith in the project over the long haul.

SKYSCRAPER GOTHIC

INTRODUCTION

Skyscraper Gothic from Nineteenth-Century Origins to Postmodern Expressions

Among the most visually compelling and popular American urban monuments are Gothicized skyscrapers such as the Woolworth Building in New York (fig. 1), the Tribune Tower in Chicago, and the Cathedral of Learning at the University of Pittsburgh. Their ornate details and period decorative schemes are eye-catching and often amusing: for instance, the sculpted corbel portrait of F. W. Woolworth with nickels and dimes supports the ceiling of the lobby in the Gothic skyscraper that bears his name. Despite the popularity of these monuments among the general public and with the many artists who have depicted them, scholarly examination of them has been limited; in particular, scant attention has been paid to their relationships with the medieval buildings they invoke.

Skyscrapers have been studied from a variety of points of view, even if the Gothic examples have not received focused analysis until recently. Much skyscraper literature has dwelt on the question of where the type originated: New York or Chicago.[1] Recently, however, skyscrapers have been considered from diverse cultural, social, and economic perspectives.[2] This literature has demonstrated the dynamic roles that skyscrapers played in the lives of the cities—large and small—in which they were built. The significance of the skyscraper to the imagery of the modern city, and of modernity more generally, has been long

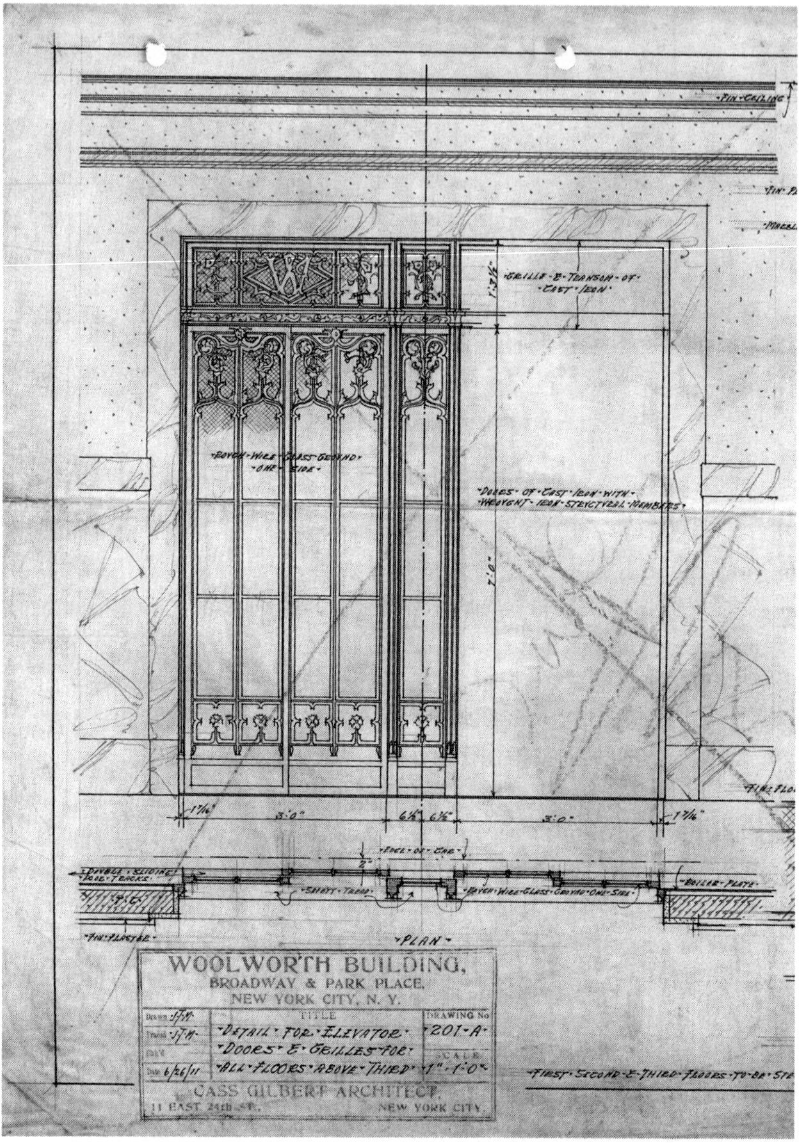

Fig. 1. *Detail for Elevator Doors & Grilles for All Floors*, Woolworth Building, New York, June 26, 1911, Office of Cass Gilbert, architect. (Vanderbilt University Fine Arts Gallery)

recognized, while its place in the development of modernist architecture has always been emphasized in histories of the movement. For example, in his influential account of the development of architectural modernism, *Space, Time, and Architecture* (1941), Sigfried Giedion drew attention to the key role played by Chicago's skyscraper architects in resolving what he saw as some of the fundamental issues in nineteenth-century architecture: "The importance of the [Chicago] school for the history of architecture lies in this fact: for the first time in the nineteenth century the schism between construction and architecture, between the engineer and the architect, was healed. This schism marked the whole of the preceding part of the century. With surprising boldness, the Chicago school strove to break through to pure forms, forms which would unite construction and architecture in an identical expression."[3]

Gothic skyscrapers, by virtue of their historicist claddings, may have failed to realize the unification of construction and architecture to which Giedion refers, but they nonetheless occupied important places in the cityscapes to which they belonged. Although most of the examples under examination here and others like them date from the early twentieth century, the connection between medieval and modern architecture was made considerably earlier. Late nineteenth- and early twentieth-century architects invoked the Gothic, in particular, for a wide variety of reasons that included its moral authority, structural honesty, flexibility, communal idealism, political freedom, and ties with the imagined origins of the northern Europeans responsible for settling the United States.

Themes relevant to the conceptual grounding of Skyscraper Gothic can be identified in nineteenth-century theoretical discussions. Enormously scaled works by engineers such as Gustave Eiffel prompted a discussion of the appropriate style for modern architecture that led theorists such as Eugène-Emmanuel Viollet-le-Duc to liken modern engineers to medieval builders, as both were seen as having effectively exploited the materials at their disposal—iron and stone respectively—to create daring, tall structures, leading to the common comparison of the Eiffel Tower (1889) with a Gothic nave or spire. The cubist sculptor Raymond Duchamp-Villon, for example, compared "engineers working in steel" and "medieval masons," asking, "Do we not find in both the same boundless ambition always to achieve the greater, the taller, the more daring? Across from Gothic Notre-Dame, the true tower of modern Paris [the Eiffel

Tower] rises on the Champs de Mars. Both works, the tower and the nave, are born of the same desire to build and both fulfill a similar dream of superhuman exaltation."[4]

In this passage, Duchamp-Villon echoes the view of the Gothic that had been expressed earlier by Viollet-le-Duc, whose theoretical writings continued to be influential well into the twentieth century. For example, much the same point was made by G. H. Edgell in 1928: "There is, indeed, a close analogy between Gothic and steel. The Gothic system is a skeleton of masonry, the modern designer attains much the same expression in steel. The constant ideal of the Gothic designer was to push his building higher and higher to the limit of financial resources and structural safety. The designer of the skyscraper does much the same. In short, the Gothic ideal and even the Gothic vocabulary is well adapted to steel construction and has been proven so in a number of great monuments."[5]

For Viollet-le-Duc, the Gothic was not intended as a stylistic model but rather as a theoretical one for modern architecture. The Gothic, like modernism, was seen as a style that represented a break from the past. In both this idealized view of the medieval past and the modern present, the truthful use of materials and the clear expression of structure were considered to have been fully realized.

The theories of structure promulgated by Viollet-le-Duc, as well as his writings on iron construction, and the influential drawings that accompanied them in his publication of the *Entretiens sur l'architecture* have been considered decisive for the development of the skyscraper in general, not just those articulated with medievalizing details. For instance, David P. Billington writes that "the aesthetic ideas of Viollet-le-Duc came to Chicago through the publication of his *Entretiens* (*Lectures*) in 1863 and 1872 and their translations into English in 1875 and 1881. The timing was uncanny and the influence profound."[6] In 1883, as Joanna Merwood-Salisbury observes, the Chicago architect William Le Baron Jenney published an article in the *Inland Architect* that "incorporated American architecture into Viollet-le-Duc's system of tectonic and ethnographic classification." In this system there were four principal racial groups, according to Jenney: the "Turanians, Semitics, Celts and Aryans." Plainness and simplicity were among the hallmarks of Aryan architecture, to which contemporary Chicago architecture was seen to correspond. Thus the ethnographic interpretation of architecture provided a conceptual grounding for the skyscraper in the early phase of its development.[7]

That stage in the history of tall commercial buildings began with their first appearance around 1882 and waned after the World's Columbian Exposition in Chicago in 1893, the financial crisis of the same year, and the growth of the City Beautiful movement at the end of the century, which entailed a critique of what some saw as the purely and crassly economic basis of contemporary American urban architecture.[8] Later, Edgell could look back to the development of the Skyscraper Gothic in which the relationship between medieval and modern architecture had been made explicit through the choice of historicist decorative forms. Moreover, by the time of his writing in the mid-1920s, the skyscraper had been revived, in part through an even more explicit reliance on the medieval metaphor in such highly publicized projects as the Woolworth Building and the Chicago Tribune Tower as well as in regional landmarks like Detroit's Buhl Building (1925, fig. 2).

Fig. 2. *Buhl Building and the Detroit Cityscape*, ca. 1915–25. (Detroit Publishing Company Collection, Library of Congress, Prints and Photographs Division, Washington, D.C.)

Another highly influential writer, the British critic John Ruskin, also understood the Gothic as a flexible style readily adapted to modern use but one with clear stylistic characteristics applicable to contemporary architecture. Ruskin, along with fellow British writers William Morris and A. W. N. Pugin, addressed what they saw as the moral poverty of modern building—characterized by shoddy construction with machine-produced elements—by prescribing a return to medieval building practices. Each of these influential figures saw medieval architecture somewhat differently, and Ruskin was unique among them for celebrating the Venetian Gothic above all other examples of the style.[9] Ruskin was also one of the thinkers who contributed to the development in the United States of what Merwood-Salisbury calls "architectural organicism." In this context, Ruskin's insistence on nature—God's creation—as the basis of aesthetic beauty was particularly influential. Ruskin stressed, in such widely read tomes as *The Seven Lamps of Architecture* (1849), and his American followers reiterated the point in published essays, "the importance of expression over imitation in design, arguing that man is infinitely creative, continually adapting himself and his artifacts to new environments in an organic manner."[10] Eventually, this conceptualization of organicism would be used to legitimate the Chicago school of commercial architecture, understood as a logical adaptation of building to the requirements of a burgeoning capitalist center.

However, the appearance of Ruskin's writings at midcentury sparked a theoretical debate about the appropriateness of medieval architecture as a model for modern building that predated the development of the skyscraper as a building type as witnessed by the extensive use of a Gothic vocabulary for commercial buildings employing both cast iron and masonry for their facades. One significant example is the seven-story Jayne Building in Philadelphia, the design of which was begun by William L. Johnston in 1849 and completed after his death by Thomas U. Walter two years later. Notable, especially in light of the later development of the skyscraper type, was the articulation of the shaft above the first-story commercial space with piers that terminated at the top of the facade with pointed-arched windows surmounted by Gothic-style quatrefoil windows. The architectural historian Winston Weisman showed that there were a number of commercial buildings, albeit of lesser height, constructed in Philadelphia at midcentury in which the facade designs expressed the structural system, some of which likewise used Gothic detailing. A notable example of this phenomenon was the Masonic Temple (1853–55) by Sloan & Stewart, which had "a pronounced Gothic flavor," "vertical emphasis," and "rational spirit," all evident in the facade piers and colonnettes that separated the paired lancet windows in the Gothic style. For Weisman, the facade was rational "despite its Gothic garb."[11] However, it might also be argued that the Gothic was an appropriate stylistic choice given that it was considered by some theorists and critics to represent a rationalist approach to tall buildings, or at least to be associated with impressively tall monuments.

These early attempts at adapting the Gothic to what were at the moment relatively tall structures was followed by the Civil War and a curtailing of construction. Following the war, however, there ensued a spurt of commercial building at increasing height, sparked in part by the development of the passenger elevator. For example, "between 1865 and 1875 buildings in New York shot skyward in rocket-like fashion." The Western Union Telegraph Building designed by George B. Post and the New York Tribune Building by Richard Morris Hunt (both 1873–75) mark the culmination of this rapid escalation in height. The former was ten-and-a-half stories; the latter, nine stories tall. Both made use of metal frames, elevators, and other technical advances capitalized on by skyscraper builders; both were publicly lauded for their height.[12] Although neither of these buildings was Gothic in feeling, they did feature the towers and mansard roofs characteristic of the High Victorian Gothic public architecture of the moment.

In the following decade, however, the Irish architect Isaac Hodgson's Minnesota Loan and Trust Building of 1885 featured a sandstone facade composed of a series of pointed arches and detailing reminiscent of late medieval forms although without being clearly associated with any particular source or style (as its frequently invoked label of English-Venetian Gothic suggests). This reference to the Venetian Gothic also underscores Ruskin's important place in nineteenth-century American architectural discourse. While it has been called Minneapolis's first skyscraper and it was indeed the city's tallest building for a year, at seven stories it is still a relatively small structure.[13]

But within the following decade, two Chicago buildings by Burnham and Co., the Reliance Building (1890–95), and the Fisher Building (1895–96), combined metal frames with a Gothic ornamented terra-cotta cladding with the height of a skyscraper at fifteen and twenty stories respectively. While the ornament applied to the entranceway and panels between floors is certainly Gothic in its details, the spiky quality associated with Gothic architecture is missing from these early examples.

The affiliation between late medieval architecture and the skyscraper is not simply a matter of applied decoration, however. The soaring height and verticality of the classic High Gothic structures made them an obvious source for the development of a new building type that similarly emphasized height and verticality. In part, the recognizable decorative scheme lends an air of familiarity to a type that some regarded as threatening and unsafe.[14] Its height was also couched in the forms of an architectural style widely associated with Christianity and moral goodness; indeed, the virtuous resonance of the Gothic may have been appealing to architects and their patrons in the first phase of skyscraper development, one that coincided historically with labor unrest in Chicago, where the Haymarket Riot and other working-class uprisings took place in the 1880s, as well as in other cities, and with a widespread criticism of capitalist greed. In New York City, the dedication of the Woolworth Building in 1913 was followed shortly by a major strike by the city's garment-district silk workers as well as by those in nearby Paterson, New Jersey, silk factories. On June 7 of that year, they collectively staged "The Pageant of the Paterson Strike" at Madison Square Garden. In such a charged social context, argues Sarah Watts, "Woolworth's Gothic design sought to codify [a] vision" of corporations as "seemingly anonymous and politically inert." She continues, with regard to the Renaissance-style Metropolitan Life Tower (1905) and the Woolworth Building: "Properly stylized in formal architectural detail and seemingly cleansed of class associations, the skyscrapers ascended to a silent plane of civic generosity, stability, and progress that, by default, branded contention, diversity, and critique as its antithesis."[15] In this way the Gothic style was put in the service of a conservative political agenda that sought to tamp down resistance to substandard working conditions and to capitalism more generally.

At the same time, theorists promoted the association between the perceived structural honesty of the Gothic and that of modern architecture. Indeed, as the skyscraper form evolved, particularly in response to the New York set-back laws of 1916, the Gothic form with its tapering spires dissolving against the skyline became even more popular as a source for the modern skyscraper. This model, which partially emerged due to the requirements of New York zoning, became a metaphor for modernity. Throughout the United States, in cities as diverse as Detroit and Atlanta, the set-back Gothic skyscraper first developed in New York was used repeatedly with the often-stated aim of lending an up-to-date and progressive appearance to its urban context. As Keith D. Revell writes:

> The New York zoning formula thus accomplished what flat height limits could not: it protected the city against some of the worst features of tall buildings while permitting architectural experimentation with great height and yet encouraging a unified urbanistic effect. That balancing of public needs and private liberties proved to be a formula worth emulating, inspiring both Chicago and Boston to forego their flat height limits for setback formulas as a way to satisfy developers' demands for increased rentable space and to emulate the architectural experimentation that had been so successful in New York.[16]

Although the Gothic vocabulary of some skyscrapers is most often associated with medieval ecclesiastical architecture, in fact this was not always foremost in the minds of the designers and patrons, despite the fact that some saw the style as lending the moral authority of Christianity to the commercialism of the modern age. The roots of capitalism were understood to be medieval, with the commercial cites of the late Middle Ages seen as the sites for the origins of America's economic system. Hence, late medieval buildings such as cloth halls and guildhalls, as well as ecclesiastical structures, are often the direct sources for these commercial structures. As Lisa Reilly argues in her essay "Design and the Study of the Past," the study of historic monuments was an integral part of architectural education in the United States until the introduction of the Bauhaus curriculum during and after the Second World War. The emphasis on such study continued in professional practice as architects frequently traveled abroad to study appropriate models often with specific meaning, such as the Ghent cloth hall, which was associated with the beginning of capitalism, the latter exemplified by early commercial skyscrapers such as the Woolworth Building.

Equally important to this development of a particular historical style for the new building type is the frequent discussion of historic monuments in periodicals such as *Architectural Record,* the *American Architect and Building News,* and the *Journal of the Institute of American Architects.* The First World War gave added impetus to the study of examples from northwestern France and the Low Countries. The widespread destruction of medieval monuments in these areas during World War I lent a particular urgency to their study as architects in the military often wrote to journals from the front lines recording historical architecture immediately prior to its demolition through shelling. Although the Beaux-Arts curriculum, which dominated architecture schools of the time, is most often associated with classical models, its basic instructional principle was not in fact tied to a particular style, classical or otherwise. The premise was that through the study of historic structures, the correct model and form would be found, the appropriate design solution for new building types made possible by the rapidly changing technologies of the nineteenth and twentieth centuries.

While structural honesty, verticality, and an emphasis on height are all invoked in the argument supporting Gothic as the appropriate style for these new structures transforming the scale and density of American cities, and despite the fact that they could sometimes be seen as disturbing the urban landscapes around them, context nonetheless sometimes played a role in their conceptualization as well. In his essay "The Gothics of Francis Kimball," Kevin D. Murphy articulates the multiple ways in which late medieval architecture is at work in the design work of "the father of the skyscraper." Although the Trinity Building (1904–5) and the U.S. Realty Building (1906–7) in Manhattan were not the first instances in which Kimball employed a Gothic Revival style, they do use a particular form of the Gothic relevant to their site. Whereas Kimball had used Venetian Gothic for the palazzo-type Montauk Club in Brooklyn of 1889–91, his two skyscraper designs refer directly to their neighbor, the renowned Trinity Church of 1846 designed by Richard Upjohn. The Gothic style is clearly seen here and elsewhere as a viable solution to the problem of articulating the massing of the skyscraper, but Kimball has also selected elements and motifs such as the paired windows that refer directly to the adjacent church. His concept of how to apply this ornament to the structure of the skyscraper does relate to Ruskin even if the specific vocabulary he has selected does not. Just as Ruskin understood the Gothic wall to be a kind of membrane or veil wrapped around the structural elements of the building, Kimball has created a layer of ornament that essentially functions as a membrane separate from the structural frame of his skyscraper. Thus, for Kimball the use of Gothic reflects both a desire to refer specifically to the architectural context of his building as well as a way of expressing the structural skeleton of his building as separate from its ornamental veil.

This same conceptual understanding of the Gothic underlay the design of one of the most famous of Gothic skyscrapers, the Woolworth Building (1910–13) as well as the ultimate shift toward modernism in skyscraper design. Gail Fenske also argues that the subject of her study is the product of a particular context, although her focus is more specifically on the intellectual and cultural setting for the Woolworth Building rather than on its physical environment. The distinctive form and extensive publicity associated with the "Cathedral of Commerce" guaranteed the type of high-profile corporate promotion Woolworth and his advertising director, Hugh McAtamney, sought and thereby established the role of commercial architecture as a corporate icon as well as the defining feature of urban skylines rather than the public buildings and spaces of the City Beautiful movement. Indeed, the prominent, and potentially disruptive, place of the skyscraper in the ensemble of buildings on urban skylines had been debated since the time of Chicago's World's Columbian Exposition, which threw into stark contrast the commercial architecture of the downtown "Loop" and the white, neoclassical idiom of the fairgrounds.[17]

Cass Gilbert, architect of the Woolworth Building, was aware of this debate over the place of the skyscraper in the city and in 1915 argued that the aesthetic freedom accorded American architects and their patrons worked against the achievement of visual harmony in urban ensembles.[18] Fenske argues that his designs for the Woolworth Building and its predecessor, the West Street Building, represent the integration or synthesis of differing views of medieval and modern architecture. On the one hand, Louis Sullivan (following the theoretical principles of Viollet-le-Duc) saw the Gothic as a conceptual model for the skyscraper, which he considered an exemplar of modernity. Rather than drawing on medieval prototypes for decorative motifs, Sullivan understood the importance of the Gothic as a model for the concept of articulating the height and verticality of the new building type without its stylistic associations. This was in contrast to the Beaux-Arts interest in the associative value of the Gothic as a stylistic source for the skyscraper. As Fenske makes clear, Gilbert draws on both of these approaches for his Gothic skyscraper designs. He effectively integrates his belief in Sullivan's principle of "form ever follows function" by emphasizing the verticality and height of his buildings and thus the structural skeleton of the building together with the invocation of historical precedents, selected through his own travel and study of Gothic models.[19] Together these approaches combined with Gilbert's Beaux-Arts pictorial sense to create a true landmark in the Woolworth Building that enhanced its urban setting.

While New York apparently embraced the Gothicism of the Woolworth Building in some buildings that followed, critics in Chicago argued as early as the 1920s that the city's first skyscrapers were not tied to a historical style, despite considerable visual and written evidence to the contrary. Beginning with the city's rebuilding after the 1871 fire, the Gothic style was in evidence in the city's commercial structures with a particularly strong emphasis on its positive moral associations. As Joanna Merwood-Salisbury's essay makes evident, however, the understanding of the Gothic and the reasons for its use were not static but dynamic during this period of political upheaval and rapid architectural change in Chicago. The spiritual authority and racial superiority of the style as well as its connection to communal idealism and craftsmanship were emphasized in the late nineteenth century by architects such as Peter B. Wight and William Le Baron Jenney, who used Gothic stylistic elements freely in their buildings. However, by the turn of the century the situation changed dramatically. As the structural system employed for skyscrapers shifted from masonry to steel-framed construction, the reasoning for the association with medieval architecture also altered. No longer were the fine stylistic details of Gothic Revival commercial buildings admired as a new approach shaped by the need for profitability, efficiency, and productivity in skyscraper construction. Gothic proved its flexibility, explains Merwood-Salisbury, as it was reinvented in Chicago as a style of structural honesty, one in which the support or buttress rather than the wall was the key element, and clarity in its use of materials. The rationalist understanding of the Gothic as articulated by Viollet-le-Duc came to the fore as the Chicago school implemented the curtain wall as a construction principle with its articulation of the skeletal support system. Gothic was no longer a stylistic prototype but rather a theoretical model for construction principles. While Gothic decorative elements continued to be used as in the Reliance (1895) and Fisher (1896) Buildings, they were now part of a promotion of modernity and industrialization with the opportunity for social freedom they represented rather than of the collaboration and craftsmanship of the preindustrial era. In contrast to later critics, contemporary writers saw this localized version of the Gothic as offering a new architectural vision of American democratic ideals.

Interestingly, this same connection between architecture and American ideals was made by the *Chicago Tribune* with regard to its highly publicized tower of 1922. As Katherine M. Solomonson establishes, the *Tribune* used the Gothic vocabulary of its building with its particular associations with the First World War to evoke both memories of the heroism associated with the recent military conflict and an image of a triumphant future now led by the United States and Chicago. Although architect Howells argued for the Gothic as an appropriate theoretical model for the skyscraper in its structural expressiveness, the building's owners portrayed it as an appropriate source on the basis of its historic affiliation with the higher ideals of communal effort and sacrifice for the greater good as articulated by the recent writings of Henry Adams and Ralph Adams Cram. In the hands of the *Tribune,* the medieval past now became the inspiration for an American future. Once again, the medieval had been reinvented by its users for their own purposes.

Both New York and Chicago provided powerful prototypes for skyscrapers throughout the country, and not just for commercial buildings. When the City of Atlanta undertook the construction of a new city hall in the 1920s, it looked to the Woolworth Building and the *Tribune* competition for models of progressive modern architecture that also embodied the commercial vitality of the age. As Carrie Albee demonstrates, the building's architect, G. Lloyd Preacher, turned his back on the traditional neoclassical forms used throughout the South for civic architecture to give Atlanta a new type of city hall that expressed the city's identity as a center of commerce and modernity. Despite the low density of its site, the building employed the now familiar setback forms of its New York models. Setbacks were now widely used outside New York as an emblem of modernity and a means of emphasizing the height and verticality of the skyscraper rather than a response to stringent zoning requirements. Preacher's employment of horizontal bands of Gothic detailing to divide the building into base, shaft, and crown; use of buff terra-cotta cladding; and alternation of strong and weak vertical elements are all drawn from Gilbert's building. Atlanta's self-image was strongly tied to its identity as a commercial center from its very beginnings. Contemporary local publications, particularly the *City Builder,* reinforce this message of civic pride in Atlanta's role as the economic leader of the New South. The new city hall building is closely tied to the "Forward Atlanta" campaign of the same time that promoted the region as a modern, industrialized hub of commercial enterprise well connected to a regional network of urbanized southern cities. The design of the new city hall fostered this image through its association with the most prominent commercial in building in the nation's business capital.

Much as Preacher looked to the Woolworth Building as a model, he also refined elements of its design for his building. Similar to Gilbert, Preacher quoted literally from late medieval, particularly Flamboyant Gothic sources, in some places for his applied ornament while also abstracting Gothic details in others such as the tapered caps of the entrance piers and bases of the lampposts.

In the 1920s, as the case of the Atlanta City Hall demonstrates, the functions that a skyscraper could serve expanded beyond the purely commercial. Thus, the University of Pittsburgh could contemplate a new skyscraper campus in that decade, as Anke Koeth demonstrates. The architect Charles Z. Klauder worked closely with the university's administration to design a building that would incorporate a variety of schools and departments within a structure that, in its overall massing, recalled the set-back Manhattan skyscrapers of the period. Whereas in New York and Chicago, the skyscraper was necessitated by the high cost of land, and the intensive development of the cities' commercial cores, in Pittsburgh those factors did not play into the decision to employ the type. Instead, the skyscraper carried associations that the university was keen to signal with its building, such as being up-to-date and modern. In Pittsburgh, a city with a thriving steel industry, the skyscraper also had an additional significance.

The Gothic style also had a particular appropriateness for the Cathedral of Learning as an educational building, allowing it to be compared visually with other contemporary Gothic campus buildings at Yale and Northwestern Universities and elsewhere. The Collegiate Gothic was, by the early twentieth century, a stylistic mode that had a long history of use in the United States and that referred also to the venerable educational institutions of Great Britain: the universities at Oxford and Cambridge. Nonetheless, Klauder's version of the Gothic was not archaeological and can be compared to contemporary skyscrapers in which the historical mode was becoming more abstract and embraced elements of the 1920s Art Deco style.

This type of abstraction, used increasingly in skyscrapers that retained the outline and massing of the Gothic models, is evident in Raymond Hood's Radiator Building of 1924. The Radiator Building in Midtown Manhattan, like the Woolworth Building in Lower Manhattan, was immensely popular as soon as construction was completed. Designed to house the showrooms and offices of the American Radiator Company in most of its space, it immediately became associated visually with the company and was in fact, frequently used in corporate advertising, with the company president, Clarence Mott Woolley, commenting in 1926 that good architecture was "an economic asset." The strong and immediate connection between the building and the products it housed was largely due to Hood's use of color, specifically black and gold, to articulate the massing of the building as well as its dramatic nighttime lighting scheme. The glowing black and gold building was immediately understood as an image of heat as generated by the radiators on display in the ground-floor showrooms. But, as Christine G. O'Malley demonstrates, this overt connection between product and architecture was not intentional on Hood's part. Although the decoration on the Radiator Building was more highly abstracted than the more literal forms and overt historicism of his slightly earlier work with Howells on the Tribune Tower, Hood cited, among other sources for his use of black on gold, the late medieval hôtel de ville in Brussels. Once again, as at the Woolworth Building, a late medieval secular structure with mercantile associations provided the architect with a model for his modern, commercial skyscraper. The medieval connection is even more forcefully demonstrated by the medieval revival showrooms. All of this historicizing vocabulary was ignored by both critics and the general public, a reaction no doubt facilitated by its more abstract nature, in favor of a more literal and vivid association between architecture and commercial company, one which made the Radiator Building a compelling advertisement for its product.

The discussion of the Gothic as a source for the new architectural forms of the nineteenth century began as one invested in both its moral associations and its role as a theoretical model that celebrated its flexibility and structural honesty. Both of these modes of thinking continued to be invoked throughout the early twentieth-century history of Gothic skyscrapers, although the specific interpretations associated with each vary according to the circumstances of the building's creation and in some cases its reception. The Gothic was used to represent, among other things, structural honesty, communal ideas, heroism, craftsmanship, and the history of capitalism or modernity. Indeed, the Woolworth Building in particular was seen to embody the "energy" of contemporary urban life, which had itself been equated with the experience of modernity since the nineteenth century. Among the modernist artists who attempted to capture the sheer height of the Woolworth Building as well as its effect on viewers was the painter John Marin, who had a "passion" for the tower, as well as the painter Charles Sheeler and the photographer Paul Strand, who incorporated it into their 1921 film *Manahatta* (alternatively known as *Manhatta*) as part of a sequence depicting skyscrapers and their construction.[20] Adnan Morshed argues that the artistic production of modernists was often connected with the novel perspectives they gained by living in or visiting skyscrapers.[21]

Modernist visual representations of the Woolworth Building, as well as of other skyscrapers, constituted one strain of their reception. For the artist Marcel Duchamp, the Woolworth Building epitomized the commercial culture that he interrogated through his "readymades," mass-produced objects—a bicycle wheel, a bottle rack—that he promoted to the status of art objects. It was in New York that he began to speak of these things as readymades and in 1916 scrawled on a piece of paper: "Find inscription for Woolworth Bldng as readymade—."[22] Modern artists' interpretations of the Woolworth Building, then, ranged from celebration of its embodiment of the dynamism evident in the modern city, to subtle exposure of its place in the consumer economy. Late in his life, the American impressionist Childe Hassam (1859–1935) painted *The Skyscraper Window* (1934, fig. 3), in which he depicted a solitary figure in a highly aestheticized environment replete with Asian objects. Through the window, just a sliver of the surrounding urban environment is shown to demonstrate the figure's elevated perspective. For her, unlike most office workers of the period, the skyscraper provides a space of reflection insulated from the commercial world beyond it. Despite divergent interpretations of the historicizing forms of such monuments as the Woolworth Building, on the parts of both designers and audiences, one aspect of the Gothic remains consistent: its flexibility, as both its meaning and its formal application could apparently be molded to any situation—commercial, sacred, or secular.

Fig. 3. Frederick Childe Hassam, *The Skyscraper Window*, 1934, oil on canvas, 59¼ × 47¼ in. (Vanderbilt University Fine Arts Gallery, The Peabody College Collection, 1979.0228P)

Despite its aesthetic flexibility and associational malleability, not to mention its association with the experience of urban modernity, the Gothic fell out of favor as a mode for skyscraper design by the late 1920s. In part, this decline can be attributed to the criticism of the winning design for the Chicago Tribune Tower that was voiced by the architects Louis Sullivan, Thomas Tallmadge, and Irving K. Pond, among others, who saw its flying buttresses and medievalizing masonry forms as inexpressive of the building's actual structure.[23] George H. Douglas describes a dilemma facing architects in the period of active skyscraper construction between 1927 and 1931. On the one hand, they shied away from the Gothic of the Woolworth Building and Tribune Tower; "at the same time, they rejected the starkness and abstractness of the extreme moderns. They were interested in decoration, ornament, perhaps too, in hedonistic values; they certainly wanted to offer buildings that would appeal to the giants of commerce and industry who were paying the bill and who wanted buildings that were in some sense glamorous. So they developed a competing style that they called modernistic."[24] This approach is embodied in the work of Hood and Howells as well as other firms examined here that shades into the Art Deco. This stylistic phenomenon would become more pronounced with two canonical New York skyscrapers: the Chrysler Building (1930) by William Van Allen and the Empire State Building (1931) by Shreve, Lamb, and Harmon.

The attempt at balance between a modernist expression of structure and materials, on the one hand, and decoration, on the other, was abandoned after

World War II, when a starkly modernist idiom for American corporate office buildings was widely favored. In connection with this critical ascendancy of modernism, the role of émigré European architects in the United States has often been cited as crucial, especially the architect Ludwig Mies van der Rohe, whose canonical Seagram Building on Park Avenue in New York City was completed in 1958. In the postwar period, the Miesian "glass box" skyscraper proliferated across the United States, forming what the architecture critic Ada Louise Huxtable characterized as "a superb vernacular, probably the handsomest and most useful set of architectural conventions since the Georgian row houses."[25] This enthusiasm for the modernist corporate office tower was not ubiquitous, and it would not prove long-lasting.

By the 1970s an emergent postmodernist sensibility sparked receptivity on the part of some patrons, but certainly not all critics, to the design of commercial buildings that reflected back on the Skyscraper Gothic, and ultimately on the medieval Gothic. For instance, the forty-story tower of PPG Place in Pittsburgh, designed by Philip Johnson, for which ground was broken in 1980, employs glass and steel in the manner of the postwar office tower but simultaneously bristles with ribs and turrets. Earlier and notably, in 1962, the architect Minoru Yamasaki had invoked the Gothic in his design for the twin World Trade Center towers, very near the Woolworth Building and Trinity and U.S. Realty Buildings in Lower Manhattan. As David L. Salomon has observed, "The buildings that earned [Yamasaki] a reputation large enough to be considered for the World Trade Center job were a series of relatively small, simple, box-like buildings that were often placed adjacent to, if not surrounded by, shallow pools of water and were augmented with an individual interpretation of Gothic ornament made from aluminum and/or precast concrete." In the World Trade Center towers, Yamasaki's evocation of the Gothic took place primarily at the lower levels, where pointed arches were suggested by ribs that tapered together above the street-level entrances and then soared more than one thousand feet up the facades. This design strategy found a mixed reception: "Although many disdained [Yamasaki's] personalized, pseudo-Gothic forms, committed modernists had to admire his commitment to and experimentation with technologically advanced methods and materials to produce these forms."[26]

The destruction of the World Trade Center towers in the terrorist attacks of

September 11, 2001, brought renewed attention to New York City's skyscrapers and indeed to the building type as a whole. With the Twin Towers gone, the Woolworth Building dominated, once again, the skyline of Lower Manhattan. The events of 9/11 led Stephen Jay Gould to reflect on this recovered prominence of the Woolworth Building: "When I was young, the Woolworth Building rose above all its neighbors, casting a warm terra-cotta gleam over lower Manhattan. But I have not seen this optimally tempered glory since the early 1970's because the Twin Towers, rising in utter metallic verticality just to the southwest, either enveloped my love in shadow, or consigned its warmer glow to invisibility within a metallic glare." Returning to Manhattan after 9/11, with the Twin Towers gone, Gould reflected: "But then I looked eastward from the shores of the Hudson and saw the world's most beautiful urban vista, restored for the worst possible reason, but resplendent nonetheless: the Woolworth Building, with its gracious setbacks, its gothic filigrees, and its terra cotta shine, standing bright, tall, and alone again, against the pure blue sky. We cannot be beaten if the spirit holds, and if we celebrate the continuity of a diverse, richly textured, ethically anchored past with the excelsior of a properly tempered reaching towards the stars."[27]

In an entirely new global context, the Skyscraper Gothic was pressed to new service. As in the early decades of the twentieth century, after 9/11 the Woolworth Building—like other examples of the style—was celebrated for its tapering shaft silhouetted against the sky. Moreover, the building was made to bear great symbolic and ideological weight as it stood for a continuity with the past, with the kind of metaphysical striving toward the beyond that the churches and cathedrals of the Middle Ages were sometimes thought to represent. In these senses, at least for Gould, the meaning of Skyscraper Gothic had come nearly full circle to its turn-of-the-century origins. The essays that follow explore the process by which medieval architecture—perhaps paradoxically—was adapted to one of the building types that was most closely identified with the modern age.

NOTES

1. See, for example, Rosemarie Haag Bletter, "Invention of the Skyscraper: Notes on Its Diverse Histories," *Assemblage,* no. 2 (February 1987): 110–17.

2. The bibliography is large, but especially useful sources for the study of Skyscraper Gothic from social, economic, and cultural points of view are Thomas A. P. van Leeuwen, *The Skyward Trend of Thought: The Metaphysics of the American Skyscraper* (Cambridge: MIT Press, 1988); Daniel Bluestone, *Constructing Chicago* (New Haven: Yale University Press, 1991); Carol Willis, *Form Follows Finance: Skyscrapers and Skylines in New York and Chicago* (New York: Princeton Architectural Press, 1995); Sarah Bradford Landau and Carl Condit, *Rise of the New York Skyscraper, 1865–1913* (New Haven: Yale University Press, 1996); Katherine Solomonson, *The Chicago Tribune Competition: Skyscraper Design and Cultural Change in the 1920s* (Chicago: University of Chicago Press, 2003); Roberta Moudry, ed., *The American Skyscraper: Cultural Histories* (New York: Cambridge University Press, 2005); Gail Fenske, *The Skyscraper and the City: The Woolworth Building and the Making of Modern New York* (Chicago: University of Chicago Press, 2008); and Joanna Merwood-Salisbury, *Chicago 1890: The Skyscraper and the City* (Chicago: University of Chicago Press, 2009).

3. Sigfried Giedion, *Space, Time and Architecture: The Growth of a New Tradition,* 5th ed. (1941; Cambridge: Harvard University Press, 1977), 382.

4. Raymond Duchamp-Villon, "The Eiffel Tower," in *Raymond Duchamp-Villon 1876–1918,* ed. William C. Agee and George H. Hamilton (New York: Walker, 1967), 115–16. The essay was originally published in part as "L'architecture et le fer," *Poème et Drame* 7 (January/March 1914): 22–29.

5. G. H. Edgell, *The American Architecture of Today* (New York: Charles Scribner's Sons, 1928), 73.

6. David P. Billington, *The Tower and the Bridge: The New Art of Structural Engineering* (Princeton: Princeton University Press, 1983), 100.

7. Merwood-Salisbury, *Chicago 1890,* 25–26.

8. Ibid., 1–3.

9. Michael W. Brooks, *John Ruskin and Victorian Architecture* (New Brunswick, NJ: Rutgers University Press, 1987), 276–98.

10. Merwood-Salisbury, *Chicago 1890,* 23.

11. Winston Weisman, "Philadelphia Functionalism and Sullivan," *Journal of the Society of Architectural Historians* 20, no. 1 (March 1961): 3, 14.

12. Winston Weisman, "New York and the Problem of the First Skyscraper," *Journal of the Society of Architectural Historians* 12, no. 1 (March 1953): 18.

13. Larry Millett, *Lost Twin Cities* (St. Paul: Minnesota Historical Society, 1992), 135, 173.

14. Ernest Flagg, "The Dangers of Tall Buildings," *Cosmopolitan* 21 (May 1896): 70–74.

15. Sarah Watts, "Built Languages of Class: Skyscrapers and Labor Protest in Victorian Public Space," in *The American Skyscraper,* ed. Moudry, 185, 192.

16. On the aesthetic implications of the 1916 zoning ordinance, see Keith D. Revell, "Law Makes Order: The Search for Ensemble in the Skyscraper City, 1890–1930," in *The American Skyscraper,* ed. Moudry, 53.

17. Ibid., 38–62.

18. Ibid., 38.

19. Louis Sullivan, "The Tall Office Building Artistically Considered," (1896), qtd. and discussed in Willis, *Form Follows Finance,* 14.

20. Merrill Schleier, "The Image of the Skyscraper in American Art, 1890–1931 (PhD diss., University of California, Berkeley, 1983), 107–11; Jan-Christopher Horak, "Paul Strand and Charles Sheeler's *Manhatta,*" in *Lovers of Cinema: The First American Film Avant-Garde, 1919–1945,* ed. Horak (Madison: University of Wisconsin Press, 1995), 267–86.

21. Adnan Morshed, *Impossible Heights: Skyscrapers, Flight, and the Master Builder* (Minneapolis: University of Minnesota Press, 2015), 38–39.

22. Qtd. in Ecke Bonk, "Marcel Duchamp: The Woolworth Building as Readymade, January 1916 (An Approximation)," in "New York," special issue, *Grand Street,* no. 51 (Winter 1995): 174.

23. Solomonson, *The Chicago Tribune Competition,* 174–75.

24. George H. Douglas, *Skyscrapers: A Social History of the Very Tall Building in America* (Jefferson, NC: McFarland, 1996), 87.

25. Ada Louise Huxtable, *The Tall Building Artistically Reconsidered* (New York: Pantheon, 1984), 52.

26. David L. Salomon, "Divided Responsibilities: Minoru Yamasaki, Architectural Authorship, and the World Trade Center," in "On 9/11," special issue, *Grey Room,* no. 7 (Spring 2002): 90.

27. Stephen Jay Gould, "Duchamp and September 11," *tout-fait* 2, no. 4 (January 2002), www.toutfait.com/issues/volume2/issue_4/news/gould/gould.htm. The article incorporates an earlier essay by Stephen Jay Gould, "Restoration and the Woolworth Building," *Natural History* 110, no. 10A (Winter 2001/2002): 96–97.

DESIGN AND THE STUDY OF THE PAST

The Gothic Skyscraper

Lisa Reilly

The Gothic gets away. No two men think alike about it, and no woman agrees with either man. The Church itself never agreed about it, and the architects agree even less than the priests.
—Henry Adams, *Mont-Saint-Michel and Chartres* (1905)

Henry Adams's assessment of the elusiveness of the word "Gothic" captures the difficulty of defining this term with its long and complex history. His remarks suggest that the term is original to its period, roughly defined as lasting from the mid-twelfth century to approximately 1500, although perhaps the one thing that can be said with certainty and agreement is that this is not the case.[1] In fact, the term was applied retrospectively to the architecture (and less frequently, the art) to which it referred. Its malleability, as we will see, was useful as American architects adapted forms drawn from medieval architecture for their contemporary design at the end of the nineteenth century and the beginning of the twentieth.

While its origins and meaning are problematic, the Gothic is generally understood to have emerged during the late Renaissance as a binary in opposition to the classical with its connotations of reason and rationalism. Typically associated with later medieval architecture and a set of particular formal characteristics, the Gothic becomes associated with romanticism and emotion as evinced by Horace Walpole's 1762 remark, "One must have taste to be sensible of the beauties of Grecian architecture; one *only* wants *passions to feel Gothic.*"[2] Thus it becomes a term related to intense feelings and emotions and sometimes horror, as represented by the writings of Johann Wolfgang von Goethe and the Gothic novel.

For the Middle Ages themselves the term "Gothic" is deeply problematic. It is clearly not a term of medieval making, and its application to late medieval architecture has come under close scrutiny and criticism. Historically, Gothic architecture has been defined according to the characteristics of Île-de-France cathedrals such as Reims and Amiens, which are characterized not only by pointed arches but also by flying buttresses, quadripartite vaults, tremendous height, and expansive stained glass windows. In the recent past, this focus has led to the near exclusion of secular examples, as well as the marginalization of churches that do not conform to this model, such as the Florence Duomo or Albi Cathedral. The architecture commonly referred to as Gothic today was sometimes called *opus francigenum* during the Middle Ages and *lavori moderni* in the Renaissance.[3] As Marvin Trachtenberg has suggested, a more appropriate term for the architecture of the later Middle Ages may be *medieval modernism,* an acknowledgment of this Renaissance term for late medieval architecture.[4] This term, in place of "Gothic," acknowledges the less historicizing nature of the Gothic (in fact, as some would say, it is actually antihistorical in the case of the Île-de-France), in contrast to the previous Roman-like or Romanesque period of medieval architecture.

Until the early nineteenth century, there was little clear sense of the chronology of what was being described as Gothic, and the fact that these examples were not contemporary with the Goths who destroyed the Roman Empire in late antiquity.[5] A taxonomy and terminology as well as chronology was established in large part by Thomas Rickman's study *An Attempt to Discriminate the Styles of Architecture in England from the Conquest to the Reformation* (1817), which disassociated late medieval architecture from the Germanic tribes known as Goths. During this same period, the Gothic became enmeshed in the quest for national identity throughout Europe as numerous countries laid claim to it as a particularly national style. The association with positive moral and spiritual values promoted by writers like A. W. N. Pugin and John Ruskin supported the use of Gothic in ecclesiastical and domestic architecture of the period. Ruskin emphasized the idea of the Gothic as the architecture of a communal and egalitarian society as well as a flexible and adaptable style.[6] Related to this understanding of the Gothic is William Morris's promotion of the Middle Ages as a time that valued craft, handwork, and the individual craftsman—in opposition to the anonymity and uniformity of the modern age, with its increasing industrialization and reliance on machinery. In this view, it was also a period of social cohesion and harmony, in contrast to the modern age of rapid change and divisiveness. In 1883 Morris joined the Social Democratic Federation and ultimately solely dedicated himself to his political work.[7] He construed an understanding of the Middle Ages that supported his political beliefs.

While many architectural writers during the nineteenth century (in England in particular) favored a moral interpretation of Gothic architecture that focused on its ethical and spiritual qualities, French authors, Eugène-Emmanuel Viollet-le-Duc in particular, promoted an understanding of the Gothic that focused on its structural rationalism. Marie Frank argues that by the 1890s, American aesthetic thought focused on form as the critical issue, rather than the moral and historical value of art emphasized by the British critic John Ruskin, whose writings were extremely influential in the United States.[8] This represents a shift in how American designers thought about the Gothic.

To summarize, then, views of the Gothic in the late nineteenth and early twentieth centuries centered on the following issues: structural aspects such as verticality, skeletonization, and rationalism; picturesqueness; moral and spiritual associations; the importance of the craftsman and his work; and a longing for social cohesion and stability.

For the Gothic Revival of the nineteenth century, which was predominantly used for churches, educational institutions, and houses, both the importance of a return to the craftsmanship of the preindustrial age and also the moral and spiritual associations (with their social implications) were important aspects of the style for both designers and clients. With the advent of a new, distinctly American building type, the skyscraper, a new and more complex set of associations emerged, often seemingly at odds with one another. Although the soaring forms of Gothic cathedrals such as Amiens and Reims seem obvious points of departure stylistically for the emerging skyscraper type of the late nineteenth and early twentieth centuries (which emphasized height and verticality), the use of medieval forms for such profoundly modern buildings is not as straightforward as visual comparisons of the two types bring to mind. A range of different and sometimes competing reasons led to the invocation of the medieval past by architects concerned with designing a distinctly new and modern building type for the United States, a nation without its own medieval past. The perceived suitability of the Gothic for the skyscraper was further enhanced by New York's enactment of the first zoning law in the United States. Known as the setback regulation, this code required that if a building reached the lot lines of its site, as it rose in height it had to be set back from the edge in order to allow light and air to reach ground level. This regulation led to the distinctive set-back or stepped profile of many New York skyscrapers. Early descriptions of how the new regulations would affect skyscraper design almost immediately drew upon the image of the Gothic cathedral: as Hugh Ferriss put it, "Our future buildings with their superimposed receding stages will produce as definite a sense of strength and unity as did the medieval cathedral, which, with their clerestories rising above their bases, were a similar example of setback construction."[9]

This essay considers how designers, patrons, and users of these early skyscrapers understood the Middle Ages, generally the Gothic, more specifically. Their understanding and use of the Gothic is often puzzling to medieval architectural historians; what is identified as Gothic in much Gothic Revival architecture, including the skyscrapers under discussion here, may not seem historically accurate. Sometimes merely the presence of pointed arches seems to lead to the labeling of a building as Gothic. Given the chronological and geographical breadth of the use of the term "Gothic," it is not surprising that it results in a considerable range of architectural expressions. Often, the selection of a particular Gothic model by an architect or patron has to do with what late medieval buildings the architect has seen, whether through study or independent travel. Both patrons and designers often bring their own particular understanding of the medieval past to their architectural projects, making their use of the Gothic more about their needs and their times than about the Middle Ages themselves.

In most cases it is not simply one, but several of the associations enumerated above that lie behind the choice of a Gothic vocabulary. Some may influence the architect, others the patron, while still others may play into the reception of the building by critics and the general public. Still further issues may be at work as the skyscraper form develops that were not necessarily associated with the Gothic Revival previously. This includes the assertion of the late Middle Ages as the time of the birth of capitalism and the search for the architectural expression of its origins. American familiarity with the Gothic grew during the late nineteenth and early twentieth centuries for several reasons. One of these is, of course, increased opportunities for travel due to Americans' growing wealth and education. Another, specific to architecture, is the significant role of architectural history in architectural education. Finally, the years of World War I (1914–18) brought images of Europe's Gothic heritage home to Americans, particularly following the shelling of Reims Cathedral in 1914. Magazines such as *Collier's* published actual images of the shelling, and a new photographic history of the war followed the United States' declaration of war on Germany and its allies in 1917; in addition, U.S. recruitment posters featured images of bombed-out Gothic churches in an effort to encourage American military enlistment.[10] These images, as well as others recorded in architectural journals of the day, were often drawn from the area around the Western Front, a region that looms large among the sources for the Americanization of the Gothic in the service of the skyscraper. Architects often drew on medieval buildings in quite specific ways for their formal vocabulary, as the association with the buildings of northern France and Belgium suggests, but they also had a more conceptual approach to their Gothic sources.

Popular visual culture thus put images of Gothic buildings before the public, architects and aspiring architects included. At the same time, architects-in-training would receive information about the Gothic as part of their education. Indeed, prior to the advent of modernism and the arrival of émigrés like Walter Gropius and Ludwig Mies van der Rohe in American schools of architecture, architectural history played a prominent role in formal architectural education. Drawing courses in architecture schools focused on historic models, and students were expected to travel and record what they saw in sketchbooks.[11]

Harvard University's architecture program, for example, began under the leadership of H. Langford Warren, who was both a historian and a practitioner.

Warren designed a curriculum in which history figured prominently, based on the model of the French École des Beaux-Arts, with its emphasis on the study of historical precedents. Warren wanted his students, however, to apply universal principles to their design work in place of what he described as the École's formulaic laws.[12] Under Warren, Harvard students spent their first year studying the architectural history of "ancient styles," followed by a second year studying medieval, and a third studying Renaissance and modern buildings. Finally, their fourth year included the study of ancient and medieval art.[13] This emphasis on the study of history is common to many other American programs, not surprisingly given the powerful influence of the École as an educational model.[14] In grappling with the problem of developing designs for a new and distinctly American building type—the skyscraper—Americans continued to follow the Beaux-Arts process of studying the architectural past for their models.

Even as professional architectural programs were founded in American universities at the end of the nineteenth century, many architects continued to receive their training through an apprentice system rather than a formal education at a degree-granting institution. This method is described in literature from the first half of the twentieth century as linked to the medieval method of training craftsmen and the builders of the age's renowned cathedrals. Donald Drew Egbert links the medievalizing aspect of this system to the prominence of the Gothic vocabularies in the architecture of the late nineteenth and twentieth centuries, citing Bertram Goodhue and Charles Z. Klauder (whose Cathedral of Learning in Pittsburgh is discussed in the essay by Anke Koeth in this volume) as architects who trained under this system.[15]

As form and structural rationalism became increasingly important to modern architects, Viollet-le-Duc's narrative of the medieval past, rather than Ruskin's or Morris's, became the dominant model. His assessment of the Gothic as a style of flexibility, about space and line and structural rationalism rather than moral correctness and ornament, accorded with emerging modernist ideas about architecture, leading Frank Lloyd Wright to describe Viollet-le-Duc's *Dictionnaire raisonné de l'architecture* as "the only really sensible book on architecture."[16]

This application of the Gothic often, but not always, works both formally and conceptually on the same building, as Joanna Merwood-Salisbury discusses in her essay in this volume. Similar to earlier examples of the Gothic Revival, early skyscrapers may imitate Gothic elements and details formally. The more conceptual approach is in line with Viollet-le-Duc's view, in which structural transparency, verticality, and a skeletal framework are the paramount elements of the Gothic "ideals of the society in which it was built," and "the truth of its construction." Merwood-Salisbury argues that they are not mutually exclusive, at least not in late nineteenth-century Chicago.[17] Both aspects—the historicizing ornament and the modernizing structure—aim to represent truth, albeit of different kinds, about their times. The ideals of American democracy, in this view, are made manifest in late nineteenth-century Chicago by associating its business culture with the moral authority and historical weight of the late Middle Ages, which was an era also interested in celebrating the new in its architecture.

Cass Gilbert and F. W. Woolworth's choice of the Gothic for their renowned building of 1913 has an equally complex set of associations.[18] Like the lesser-known Chicago structures of the late nineteenth century discussed by Merwood-Salisbury, the Woolworth Building invoked the Gothic for commercial purposes. Gilbert developed a Skyscraper Gothic idiom for his earlier West Street Building, in which he drew on late medieval Flemish civic buildings, such as the Cloth Hall at Yprès, believed to be the birthplace of capitalism and free trade. Gilbert's preparation for his architecture career was multifaceted. He began as apprentice in 1876 in St. Paul, Minnesota. In 1878 he enrolled at MIT and completed one year of the two-year architecture course under William Robert Ware. In 1880 Gilbert embarked on a nine-month study tour of Europe, during which he visited and sketched many of the buildings that would later influence his design work.[19] While Gilbert identified secular buildings as his main sources, many of his details are also drawn from religious models such as St. Ouen, Rouen, with a pronounced preference for the vocabulary of the late medieval Flamboyant style.[20] In his choices, Gilbert was in part addressing his own interest in creating a picturesque building that articulated the historical traditions of free-market capitalism as well as his patron's interest in a building that announced his company's international presence and ethical business practices. For both of them, the historical associations of the style are again a means of legitimizing the business practices of their times. These practices are promoted as part of a long-standing tradition with its roots in a profoundly Christian and ethical society. The Woolworth Building's popular title "Cathedral of Commerce" only emerged in 1916, three years after the building's completion, in an advertising booklet produced under the direction of the Broadway-Place Company that managed the building.[21] Once again, the ethical and spiritual qualities of the Gothic are invoked to highlight the moral integrity of the Woolworth Company and also of the other elite tenants who occupied the building. Now, however, the building was firmly associated with the ecclesiastical side of Gothic architecture, and hence its spiritual qualities were made more apparent despite the fact that neither Woolworth nor Gilbert endorsed this religious association. The title stuck, which is not surprising given the more common association of the Gothic with religious architecture in the popular mind. By this point, images of Gothic cathedrals such as Reims, damaged by shelling in 1914, were being circulated in the United States, further reinforcing this common association.

At the same time, the handicraft evident in the carved figures surrounding the doors (such as the work of Jacques Coeur) and the glorious mosaics and elaborately carved tracery of the lobby proclaims the sense of craft and artistry associated with the Middle Ages by writers such as John Ruskin and William Morris. Such details lend a sense of authenticity to a monument that draws on the religious and secular traditions of the Middle Ages as well as on Viollet-le-Duc's modernist understanding of the Gothic as a period of structural rationalism. Gilbert in fact wrote, circa 1920: "At this time I was an enthusiastic follower of the Gothic and looked upon Viollet-le-Duc as its chief exponent. Hence the École des Beaux-Arts did not attract me. Richardson had broken away from the École and was doing great work in America. Street, Gilbert Scott, Pearson and Burges were leading the Gothic movement in England and Norman Shaw and Alfred Waterhouse were names familiar to the young fellows in America and I eagerly followed the romantic tendency of the time."[22] The analogy between the skeletal structure of the Gothic (as evinced by flying buttresses, slender *piliers cantonné,* and enormous clerestory windows) and the steel-frame construction of the skyscraper is well known. The tower, window mullions, and clustered piers at the corner of the building all use Gothic elements to accentuate the verticality of the new building type. Gilbert and his structural engineer, Gunvald Aus, developed a design of structural rationalism that demonstrated Aus's conviction at least that, "from an engineering point of view, no structure is beautiful where the lines of strength were not apparent, where one cannot follow the distribution of loads from the top of the structure to its foundations."[23] Thus the Woolworth Building is understood as Gothic for a host of reasons, some quite specifically developed by Gilbert for the expressed function of his famous buildings, others applied to capture the popular imagination of the Gothic as an age of intense spirituality, craftsmanship, and social harmony.

The Tribune Tower in Chicago is similarly complex in its invocations of the Gothic.[24] In this model, Viollet-le-Duc's celebration of the Gothic structural system as analogous to the animal skeleton and well suited to modern building types is well known. In his widely read *Dictionnaire raisonné de l'architecture,* Viollet-le-Duc crafts, as Martin Bressani argues, "a genuinely 'organic' portrait of medieval architecture."[25] As Katherine M. Solomonson points out in her essay "Tribune Tower: Medievalism and Memory in the Wake of the Great War," Viollet-le-Duc's analogizing of Gothic structure to the skeletal system of a living being is enhanced by the invention of the X-ray in 1895, which made it possible to see the skeleton under the skin—much as the steel frame of the skyscraper is apparent beneath its stone covering.[26] In the Tribune Tower, as at the Woolworth Building, the vertical emphasis the skyscraper shared with the Gothic cathedral made the association all the more desirable. More than a sympathy for Viollet-le-Duc's structural rationalistic view of the Gothic is at work with the Tribune Tower, as the late Gothic detailing of the building's ornamental crown and flying buttresses created a picturesque image in the Chicago skyline. But for a building such as the Tribune Tower that, like the Woolworth Building, was intended as an enormous marketing exercise by its patron, the historical and moral associations of the Gothic are in many ways paramount and operate on a variety of levels. For a city frequently accused of having no history, the historical references contained in the Tribune Building bring the historical past literally (in the case of the *spolia* the building contains) as well as metaphorically into Chicago, and the building inserts itself into that historical narrative.[27] In this way the Gothic becomes both a historical style and an expression of modern structural rationalism. While the designers asserted that the structural rationalist aspect of Gothic was the critical factor behind the choice of the Gothic, the patrons promoted their choice of style as the consequence of a wider range of associations.[28]

Unlike the Woolworth Building, the Tribune Tower did not invoke models connected with the rise of capitalism and a free-market economy. Hood and Howells's design cited ecclesiastical sources, although like many of those used by Gilbert, these too were from northern France and Belgium. This invocation of the spiritual aspect of the late Middle Ages, in the eyes of the *Tribune,* was intended to invoke medieval society as a model for the modern age. In this view the medieval society was a democratic one under the leadership of an enlightened elite.[29] Further moral associations were derived from its celebration of the United States' role in World War I. As mentioned above, the models for Skyscraper Gothic buildings were drawn from the region of northern France and Belgium in which much of the fighting took place, with the church towers from the area, which were the models for the Tribune Tower, serving also as emblems of the Great War and the terrible sacrifice made to preserve democracy. Images of these buildings were widely known through recruiting posters, newsreel images, and magazines. Following the war, their destruction and imagery was kept in the public eye through the publicity surrounding their restoration. While the Tribune did not explicitly promote this association, elements such as the fleur–de-lis found under each of the fourth-floor windows and planned memorial reliefs suggested the military association.[30]

Francis Kimball, designer of the Trinity and U.S. Realty Buildings discussed by Kevin Murphy in this volume, trained under the apprentice system, which may have enhanced his understanding of contemporary Gothic Revival architecture.[31] Kimball's selection of the Gothic style for his two skyscrapers was driven by their architectural context, which was dominated by Richard Upjohn's nearby Trinity Church of 1846, a renowned example of Gothic Revival architecture. Despite Kimball's gesture to the nearby church, many early twentieth-century critics saw the skyscrapers as having eclipsed the place of the religious building on the skyline. In 1913, for example, Montgomery Schuyler opined: "It is sixty-seven years since old Trinity was completed and consecrated. There it still stands, after two thirds of a century, at the head of Wall Street, looking down and still more looking up, upon how changed a world, cowering among the temples of Mammon above which it used to tower, but still vindicating by its beauty the cause it can no longer vindicate by its pre-eminence."[32]

The selection of Kimball for these two skyscrapers was in part due to his reputation as a noted architect of Gothic Revival structures, such as the Montauk Club in Brooklyn. Kimball's understanding and implementation of the Gothic is drawn from his experience as a more traditional Gothic Revival architect who was involved with projects such as the design of Trinity College in Hartford. He also espoused a Ruskinian approach to the Gothic, in which the wall is understood as a "veil," in contrast to the structural rationalist articulation of the Gothic by Viollet-le-Duc, which was frequently cited as a justification for its use in a modern setting. The wall-as-veil concept provides the opportunity to clad the shaft of the skyscraper in a membrane of greater visual interest than the simple shaft it masked. As Murphy argues, this approach was one used in earlier Gothic Revival structures with which Kimball was undoubtedly familiar. Kimball's skyscraper work provides an important link between the nineteenth-century Gothic Revival, with its emphasis on craftsmanship and ornament, and buildings such as churches and colleges that are seen as historically appropriate sites for the use of the Gothic.

Similarly the Cathedral of Learning, the skyscraper at the heart of the University of Pittsburgh's urban campus, draws on the Gothic in part for contextual reasons.[33] In this choice, it is following a long tradition of collegiate architecture reaching back to the first foundations of universities such as Oxford and Cambridge in the later Middle Ages. While the physical context of the campus is not Gothic, unlike the case of Kimball's skyscrapers, the historical context of college campuses was considered to be medieval, as witnessed by the countless examples of Gothic Revival collegiate architecture at campuses such as Trinity, Yale, and Vassar. In his selection of the Gothic style and the skyscraper building type, Klauder is connecting his collegiate building to both a long-standing tradition of higher education based in the Middle Ages and the modernity and technological sophistication of its site: Pittsburgh, the center of the steel industry that produced the structural framework for the skyscrapers springing up in New York and Chicago. In this case, two ideas are at work simultaneously: the notion of the Gothic as historically appropriate for a building type such as a collegiate building; and the structural rationalist notion of it as a style suitable to a modern age and a new building type due to its flexibility. This once again demonstrates the multivalence of the Gothic. Unlike Kimball's buildings, the Cathedral of Learning's physical context, which is largely classical in style, did not suggest the Gothic style. Nor did the economics of its site, as the Oakland section of Pittsburgh was not densely developed. The set-back style of the Cathedral of Learning relates it even more clearly to the commercial skyscrapers of the crowded streets of New York. The Cathedral of Learning, as Koeth discusses, was tied to a civic identity as well as that of the university; its skyscraper form with its distinctive set-back profile, like that of the Atlanta City Hall, brings a modern, urban, and elegant architectural form to a city known for manufacturing steel rather than for the sophistication of its architecture—despite the fact that the streets of Pittsburgh do not require such an arrangement.

In Atlanta, there is a direct connection between the identity of the city as the economic and business center of the South, and the choice of a Gothic-style skyscraper with setbacks characteristic of New York for a spacious site in downtown Atlanta.[34] Here Atlanta is seeking to invoke neither the structural rationalism of Viollet-le-Duc's Gothic nor the moral dignity of Ruskin's but rather the commercial success of New York as a world financial capital. By the time of the Atlanta City Hall, Skyscraper Gothic, particularly when combined with the distinctive setbacks required by the planning code of New York, becomes an emblem of progressiveness and commercial success. The reservations about the style's historicity undermining the modernity of this distinctly American building type are shed as it moves out from New York and Chicago to cities like Atlanta and Lincoln, Nebraska, where the Skyscraper Gothic as a type becomes identified with the modern. The Atlanta City Hall stands in contradistinction to the city's earlier commercial skyscrapers, which largely adhered to the Beaux-Arts vocabularies and rectangular massing of the late nineteenth century. With this commission, the city, rather than its businesses, is seen as identifying with the modernity and commercial success of New York in particular. In this view, a modern business center is best represented by the use of a set-back skyscraper in the Gothic style.

The association of the Gothic with skyscrapers changed in other ways as well. Eliel Saarinen, whose losing design for the Tribune Competition is often regarded as the best entry in the competition as well as the most forward looking, also cited the Gothic as the inspiration for his entry despite its less historicist detailing. Like many of his more modernist colleagues, he understood the Gothic as a style of structural logic with a typologically appropriate emphasis on the vertical. In his view, the use of the Gothic would provide a necessary step in the evolution of a new architectural vocabulary. In some ways, Raymond Hood's Radiator Building of 1924 may represent the next stage in this evolution of Gothic associations.[35] Despite the fact that its details and its overall profile draw on medieval precedents, these were largely ignored in favor of a more literal and commercial reading of the building. As at the Woolworth Building, the design's reception and intention differ—there, an intentional reference to the secular medieval and its commercial traditions was received as a spiritual expression of a morally cohesive society. While Woolworth understood his building, like the Tribune Tower, to be a visible expression of values with which he wished his company to be associated, the Radiator Building became understood as a visual expression of the American Radiator Company, in fact as a giant, glowing advertisement for its products in the most literal way. At this point it would seem that the Gothic forms of the building, so evident and apparently intentional for Hood, had instead become for the public more simply an expression of skyscraperness without the historical associations read into previous examples of Skyscraper Gothic. As Christine G. O'Malley points out in her essay in this volume, in part this may have to do with the more abstracted vocabulary employed at the Radiator Building as well as the public's greater understanding of architecture as commercial expression. While the shapes of the pinnacles as well as the overall building derive from Gothic or Gothicized models, the detailing in its streamlined and blocky handling does not. With this building, in the public's mind at least, the skyscraper has become separated from the Gothic despite Hood's reliance on Brussels's late medieval hôtel de ville for his use of polychroming and sculpture detailing. At the Radiator Building the tension between the Gothic and the modern is dissolved, as it is used to create a powerful commercial identity for its patron that is fully divorced from its medieval precedents.

The very flexibility of the Skyscraper Gothic form in terms of its stylistic vocabulary as well as its meaning enhanced its viability for this new American building type. Its elasticity further meant it could be invoked in a variety of ways. In some ways it is this very variety that has made defining the Gothic so difficult. Marvin Trachtenberg's suggestion of medieval modernism acknowledges the Gothic as a moment of change and newness, its separation from its own historical past. Although Gothic Revival skyscrapers may seem, and in many ways are, historicizing, their adaptation of this medieval vocabulary also reflects the modernity of the Gothic style, manifested in its verticality, linearity, skeletonization, and structural honesty/transparency. Rather than seeing Skyscraper Gothic as yet another historicizing revival, perhaps it should be considered as a return to the past, yes, but a return to a past focused on modernity and ahistoricism in its structural properties—a kind of modern medieval that celebrates the Gothic as a new direction rather than an old one. Perhaps in today's terms it is more postmodern than modern in its invocation of historic forms in new materials; and postmodern also for its use of new building types in sometimes witty comments on the original (as elements such as the corbel figures of Cass Gilbert on the Woolworth Building and F. W. Woolworth with his nickels and dimes suggest). Skyscraper Gothic is indeed an architecture of complexity and contradiction, reflecting both popular notions of the Gothic and more scholarly analysis of its structural systems and historical associations.

NOTES

1. Kevin D. Murphy and Lisa Reilly, "The Gothic," in *Medievalism: Key Critical Terms,* ed. Elizabeth Emery and Richard Utz (Woodbridge: Boydell & Brewer, 2014), 87–96.

2. Horace Walpole, *Anecdotes of Painting in England* (1762), i, 107–8, qtd. in Nick Groom, *The Making of Percy's Reliques* (Oxford: Oxford University Press, 1999), 241.

3. Paul Frankl, *The Gothic: Literary Sources and Interpretation through Eight Centuries* (Princeton: Princeton University Press, 1960), 55–56, 256, 858. This text is also discussed in Marvin Trachtenberg, "Gothic/Italian Gothic: Toward a Redefinition," *Journal of the Society of Architectural Historians* 50, no. 1 (March 1991): 22–37. However, E. S. de Beer, "Gothic Origin and Diffusion of the Term: The Idea of Style in Architecture," *Journal of the Warburg and Courtauld Institutes* 11 (1948): 143–44, cites a seventh-century text that describes the church of St. Ouen at Rouen as *constructa artificis gothis.*

4. Trachtenberg, "Gothic/Italian Gothic," 22–37.

5. See, for example, Christopher Wren's description of Westminster Abbey cited in Frankl, *The Gothic,* 364.

6. See Joanna Merwood-Salisbury, "The Gothic Revival and the Chicago School: From Naturalistic Ornament to Constructive Expression," n. 7 on page 108 of this volume.

7. A. L. Morton, introduction to William Morris, *Three Works by William Morris* (New York: International, 1968), 12.

8. Marie Frank, "The Theory of Pure Design and American Architectural Education in the Early Twentieth Century," *Journal of the Society of Architectural Historians* 67 (June 2008): 248.

9. Hugh Ferriss, "The New Architecture," *New York Times Book Review and Magazine,* March 19, 1922, 56.

10. Thomas W. Gaehtgens, "Bombing the Cathedral of Reims," *Iris,* January 23, 2015, http://blogs.getty.edu/iris/bombing-the-cathedral-of-rheims/.

11. Michael J. Lewis, "The Battle between Polytechnic and Beaux-Arts in the American University," in *Architecture School: Three Centuries of Educating Architects in North America,* ed. Joan Ockman (London: MIT Press, 2012), 76.

12. Frank, "Theory of Pure Design," 259.

13. Arthur Weatherhead, "The History of Collegiate Education in Architecture in the United States" (PhD diss., Columbia University, 1941), 62.

14. Ibid., 76–79.

15. Donald Drew Egbert, "The Education of the Modern Architect," *Octagon,* March 1941, 6; Anke Koeth, "Gothic with an American Accent: The Cathedral of Learning," pages 157–80 in this volume.

16. *Frank Lloyd Wright: An Autobiography* (London: Longmans, Green, 1932), 75, qtd. in Anthony Alofsin, *Frank Lloyd Wright—The Lost Years 1910–22: A Study of Influence* (Chicago: University of Chicago Press, 1993), n. 11. Alofsin points out that not everyone agrees with this interpretation; for example, Donald Hoffman thinks Wright actually means Viollet-le-Duc's volume *Entrietens sur l'architecture.*

17. Merwood-Salisbury, "The Gothic Revival and the Chicago School," pages 88–111 in this volume.

18. See Gail Fenske, "Medievalism, Mysticism, and Modernity in Early Twentieth-Century New York: Cass Gilbert's 'Skyscraper Gothic,'" pages 55–87 in this volume.

19. "Cass Gilbert History," Cass Gilbert Society, www.cassgilbertsociety.org/architect/bio.html.

20. Gail Fenske, *The Skyscraper and the City: The Woolworth Building in the Making of Modern New York* (Chicago: University of Chicago Press, 2008), 155.

21. Ibid., 265–70.

22. Handwritten autobiographical account, ca. 1920, Box 17: Speeches, Articles, Notes, Poems, OGP, LC/MS, qtd. in Patricia Anne Murphy, "Architectural Education and Minnesota Career," in *Cass Gilbert, Life and Work: Architect of the Public Domain,* ed. Barbara S. Christen and Steven Flanders (New York: Norton, 2001), 29–30.

23. Fenske, *Skyscraper and the City,* 145.

24. See Katherine M. Solomonson, "Tribune Tower: Medievalism and Memory in the Wake of the Great War," pages 112–33 in this volume.

25. Martin Bressani, *Architecture and the Historical Imagination, Eugène-Emmanuel Viollet-le-Duc, 1814–1879* (Farnham: Ashgate, 2014), 273.

26. Katherine M. Solomonson, *The Chicago Tribune Tower Competition,* Modern Architecture and Cultural Identity Series, ed. Richard Etlin (Cambridge: Cambridge University Press, 2001), 174–75.

27. See Annabelle Wharton, "The Tribune Tower: *Spolia* as Despoliation," in *Reuse Value: Spolia and Appropriation in Art and Architecture from Constantine to Sherrie Levine,* ed. Richard Brilliant and Dale Kinney (Farnham: Ashgate, 2011); and Solomonson, *Chicago Tribune Tower Competition,* 166.

28. Solomonson, *Chicago Tribune Tower Competition,* 172–73.

29. Ibid., 189.

30. Ibid., 281.

31. See Kevin D. Murphy, "The Gothics of Francis Kimball: From Nineteenth-Century Revivals to the Early Skyscraper," pages 39–54 in this volume.

32. Montgomery Schuyler, "The New St. Thomas's Church, New York," *Scribner's Magazine* 54 (December 1913), 791, qtd. in Denis Robert McNamara, "Modern and Medieval: Church Design in the United States, 1920–1945" (PhD diss., University of Virginia, 2000), 155.

33. Koeth, "Gothic with an American Accent."

34. See Carrie Albee, "Forward Atlanta: G. Lloyd Preacher and the Atlanta City Hall," pages 183–210 in this volume.

35. See Christine G. O'Malley, "Radiant Heat and Glowing Lights: Raymond Hood's American Radiator Building," pages 183–210 in this volume.

THE GOTHICS OF FRANCIS KIMBALL

From Nineteenth-Century Revivals to the Early Skyscraper

Kevin D. Murphy

Writing in 1927 what he considered to be the first book on the Gothic Revival since Charles Eastlake's 1872 history of the movement, Kenneth Clark aimed to recover for general appreciation a group of buildings that included "so little on which our eyes can rest without pain."[1] If Clark's approach had not been so avowedly Anglocentric, and had his survey extended beyond 1860, he might have taken up some very recent and extraordinary Gothic Revival buildings. These examples could possibly have redeemed the style as they were the two best-known Gothic skyscrapers of his era: the Woolworth Building of 1913 by the architect Cass Gilbert and the Chicago Tribune Tower by the firm of Hood and Howells, who were the winners of the famous competition of 1922.

Yet conceptually, for Clark, these buildings would have stood apart from the Gothic Revival architecture that interested him, and, indeed, they have continued to be thought of as quite distinct from the monuments of the nineteenth-century Gothic Revival. That term still carries with it strong associations in the United States with the work of architects such as Richard Upjohn, A. J. Davis, and others who adapted the soaring vaulted masonry construction of the Middle Ages to the American context. Moreover, the term "Gothic Revival" suggests an architecture informed by the Romantic movement of the late eighteenth and nineteenth centuries. In the United States, the image of the Gothic

Revival is preeminently that of the relatively small board-and-batten or local stone church or cottage, in which the medieval European idiom was translated into the materials familiar and available to American builders. Nonetheless, the works of the New York architect Francis Kimball (1845–1919) in a variety of Gothic idioms provide a conceptual link between the nineteenth- and twentieth-century Gothic Revivals. Despite the vast differences in scale, program, patronage, and historical setting that separate the work of Upjohn and his contemporaries from that of Kimball and his cohort, the earlier architects and builders actually established a way of thinking about such central issues as the character of a wall, and the relationship between historicizing cladding and underlying frame, that were influential for the later Skyscraper Gothic. While in other cases, the use of medieval forms in skyscraper design was chiefly motivated by perceived similarities between the structural ambitions of Gothic builders and modern engineers, in Kimball's case, the selection of these historicizing forms grew out of a desire to respond visually to nearby Gothic Revival architecture. This contextual Skyscraper Gothic is distinct from that of other nearly contemporary examples, including the Woolworth Building, located just a few blocks north on Broadway in Lower Manhattan from Kimball's Trinity and U.S. Realty Buildings (figs. 1 and 2), the focus of this essay.

Important to the development of his unique brand of Gothic architecture for tall commercial buildings was the fact that Kimball was born in Kennebunk, Maine, a town where, in the first half of the nineteenth century, maritime trade and shipbuilding had produced wealthy merchants who lined the main streets with ambitious houses in up-to-date styles.[2] His oldest sister, Caroline, married Josiah M. Littlefield, also of Kennebunk, in 1848. Littlefield moved with his family to Haverhill, Massachusetts, in 1851 and entered the office of the architect Albert C. Heath. Later, Littlefield functioned at various times as a contractor, architect, and civil engineer, and he trained his brother-in-law Francis Kimball from the time his wife's younger brother was fourteen (around 1859). Kimball credited Littlefield with having taught him all that he knew. Certainly, Littlefield imbued his brother-in-law with an interest in the technical aspects of building—something Kimball would later capitalize on in skyscraper design—since he was known as a "wonderful mathematician, figuring out problems by his own method."[3] Second Empire in feeling, Littlefield's

Fig. 1. Trinity and U.S. Realty Buildings, New York. (By Gryffindor, CC BY-SA 3.0, https://commons.wikimedia.org/w/index.php?curid=11250076)

Fig. 2. Trinity Church with Trinity Building at left, postcard, ca 1920. (Museum of the City of New York)

actual designs seem to have had relatively less impact on Kimball. Nonetheless, a biographer dated Kimball's first real architectural experience to the years in Littlefield's office when he "was designing the simple structures his employer erected."[4]

Kimball's architectural career was interrupted when he enlisted in the navy during the Civil War. When his service ended, he went to work for the Boston architect Louis P. Rogers, who soon formed a partnership with Gridley J. F. Bryant. Although Bryant is perhaps best known for the Second Empire–style Boston City Hall (1862–65) designed in collaboration with Arthur Gilman,[5] he was also responsible for the Gothic Revival Peabody Institute Library in Danvers, Massachusetts, which was under construction in 1868–69 while Kimball was working for Bryant and Rogers. The building was ecclesiastical in feeling, with paired lancet windows alternating with buttresses along its side elevations, and crenellation at the roofline and around a tower at the rear.[6] In 1869, Kimball travelled to Hartford, Connecticut, in connection with their project for the Charter Oak Life Insurance Building, for which he prepared working drawings. Among Bryant and Rogers's many works was the Connecticut Mutual Life Insurance Company Building in Hartford.[7] This project was important for Kimball since the stone contractor for the building was James G. Batterson. From Bryant and Rogers's office, Kimball went to work for Batterson in Hartford, specifically to help with the production of competition drawings for the new Connecticut State Capitol. Kimball's move to Batterson's establishment was opportune; there he worked alongside the architect George Keller, who was likewise employed by Batterson on the competition project. Keller commented of the entrepreneurial Batterson, who operated not only a design firm but also a marble works that provided materials for the projects that he won, that "Batterson . . . seemed to crave being more thought of as a classical scholar and an art connoisseur than for what he really was, a far seeing business man and organizer of profitable enterprises, with a faculty of seeing those best fitted to assist him in promoting his own ends."[8]

In Keller, Batterson found a designer who was conversant with Ruskinian Gothic. Keller had worked for Peter B. Wight in New York around 1860 and had roomed with Russell Sturgis Jr. Wight had just won the competition for the National Academy of Design at Fourth Avenue and Twenty-Third Street in Manhattan, and Keller worked on the contractor's drawings for that Venetian Gothic building. In the second round of the Connecticut State Capitol competition in 1872, Batterson and Keller produced two alternatives: a "Gothic" design and a "secular Gothic" one. Although Richard Upjohn won the competition, Batterson was made the general contractor. For Kimball, participating in the competition must have been a decisive experience for it entailed his collaboration with Keller, who had a familiarity with the Ruskinian Gothic, and who had a keen interest in the Gothic Revival generally. Keller read the works of George Gilbert Scott, Edmund Street, and Eugène-Emmanuel Viollet-le-Duc (in French).[9]

Kimball's time in Hartford brought him close to Keller—who was one avenue to the English Gothic Revival—and it gave him an opportunity to travel and to work closely with another architect associated directly with the movement. In the fall of 1873 Kimball became involved with the conceptualization of the new campus of Trinity College in Hartford, designed by the British Gothicist William Burges (fig. 3). In December of that year Kimball arrived

Fig. 3. Trinity College, Hartford, ca. 1905. (Detroit Publishing Company Collection, Library of Congress, Prints and Photographs Division, Washington, D.C.)

in London to work with Burges on the plans: "The year in London was an apprenticeship in Mr. Burges's version of the French Gothic, and an endeavor to give his American assistant such a knowledge of his way of working that he could meet the exigencies that might arise during the construction."[10] After the groundbreaking in 1875, it was up to Kimball to adapt the plans and continue drawing as construction progressed. The *Trinity Tablet* reported in February 1875 that Kimball was then at work in Seabury Hall, "assisted by a corps of able draughtsmen . . . carrying out the proposed changes in the plans, and adapting the designs to conform to the same. Upon the walls of the office are hung colored bird's eye views of the pile of buildings upon which future generations are to gaze with awe and reverence."[11]

As the architectural historian Christopher Drew Armstrong has described,

Burges's initial 1873–74 project for the college was an incredibly ambitious plan that contained numerous buildings around four quadrangles. Despite the fact that Trinity's president, Reverend Dr. Abner Jackson, had traveled to England to meet with the architect and had toured several British colleges, "the importance of any English model in Burges's early design for Trinity College was minimal. His reliance on French models was absolute, and even if Burges had chosen an English college as his prototype it would have been subjected to a complete overhaul in his thirteenth-century French Gothic manner. The influence of [A. W. N.] Pugin's writings alone can be found to have exact parallels in Burges's schemes for Trinity College."[12] As the four-quadrangle plan was scaled down in the execution of the drawings to become a "Long Walk" plan organized around one major quadrangle, Kimball remained in contact with Burges and responded, as Armstrong has argued, to contemporary developments in American architecture, particularly with respect to his use of rough-hewn ashlar for the exteriors, which reflected the emergence of a Richardsonian Romanesque idiom.[13]

One example rose nearby in 1875–76, H. H. Richardson's Cheney Block in downtown Hartford, which was constructed by the architect's favored contractor, Norcross Brothers.[14] The block had both the rough-hewn stone exterior favored by Richardson and also a polychromatic treatment of the masonry arches over the windows and doors that recalls Ruskin's preferred Venetian Gothic. Kimball returned from London and Burges's office in late 1874 with the ambitious plan for Trinity College that was subsequently redesigned under the direction of the overwhelmed trustees; the ground breaking took place in July 1875.[15] The Cheney Building was commissioned in September of that year.[16] Thus, the two projects took shape simultaneously and demonstrated the predominance of the European revival styles in the architectural culture of the United States at that moment. Significantly, Kimball would have gained from his experience in Hartford exposure to both educational and commercial buildings in which medieval elements were adapted to unabashedly modern functional requirements.

It was with his subsequent move to New York that Kimball attained the reputation he enjoyed as the "father of the skyscraper" and where he gave expression to his knowledge of Gothic Revival architecture in a variety of building types, including churches.[17] When his work on the Trinity campus was finished, Kimball entered the New York office of Thomas Wisedell, "an architect of Gothic predilection and training."[18] The first New York project with which Kimball is associated is the renovation of the Madison Square Theatre on Twenty-Fourth Street (now demolished) in 1879–80. After Wisedell's death in 1884, Kimball continued on independently, but he pursued the firm's interest in theater design with the Fifth Avenue Theatre on West Twenty-Eighth Street of 1891–92 (also demolished). This work has been seen as important with regard to Kimball's technologically innovative side: it was "possibly the first building in the city" to use caisson foundations, according to Sarah Bradford Landau and Carl W. Condit's history of the New York skyscraper. In this instance, the caisson was of the "open," or "well," type in which the footing area of the building was sealed, excavated, and the foundation prepared. With the pneumatic caisson system, used first at the Manhattan Life Insurance Company in New York in 1893, essentially the same method was employed, with the difference that the excavation was done "under air pressure equal to the surrounding fluid pressure" exerted by the material outside, which included quicksand and water. Some have credited Kimball with the development of pneumatic caissons in connection with that project; others attribute it to his partner at the time of the Manhattan Life Insurance Company design, George Kramer Thompson. Either way, Kimball was closely associated with technological innovation in skyscraper design.[19] The Manhattan Life Insurance Company building was also the first skyscraper in the city to employ an entirely steel frame, further solidifying Kimball's reputation for using advanced structures.[20]

Just prior to partnering with Thompson in 1892, Kimball designed a building that is an important monument to his ongoing engagement with the Ruskinian Gothic. The Montauk Club (fig. 4) in Brooklyn, which dates from 1889 to 1891, as the critic Montgomery Schuyler noted not long after its completion, "is an essay in that Victorian Gothic of which we have, considering our tendency to try all things architectural, surprisingly few examples." Schuyler admitted that the clubhouse type, which demanded "few and large apartments," recommended an adaptation of the palazzo, but he was disappointed by the fact that the "traceried arcade of the loggia" appeared in the lower portion of the facade, rather than at the top where by tradition it belonged, and by what he perceived as an overall lack of "unity" in the design.[21] Such negative criticism notwith-

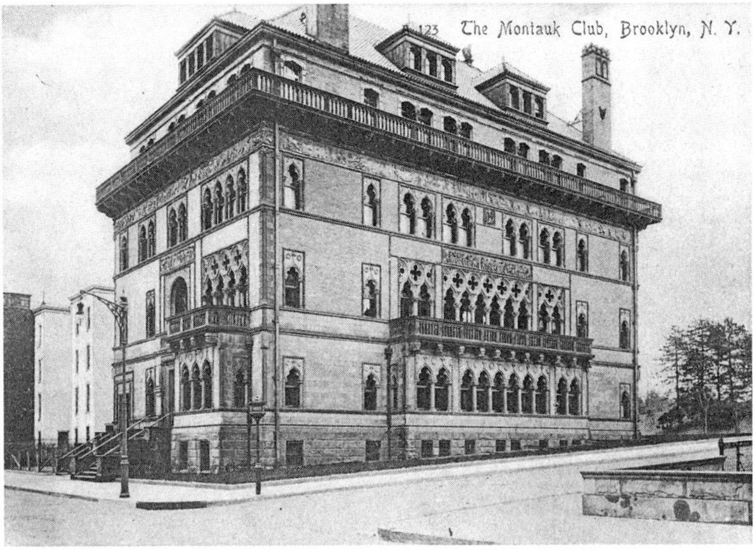

Fig. 4. Montauk Club, Brooklyn, Rotograph Co., ca. 1905. (Museum of the City of New York)

standing, the Montauk Club is notable as a demonstration of Kimball's interest in Venetian Gothic, which was undoubtedly spurred by Ruskin, and for its featuring of terra-cotta, a material that the architect used exclusively in other projects. Here, terra-cotta is employed for a frieze that ostensibly documents the history of the Montauk Indians. The club's headquarters thus asserted both its elite members' knowledge of European culture and their embrace of American history in its references to Native Americans.[22] The visual reference to Venice, a popular destination for American travelers at the end of the nineteenth century, would have telegraphed the urbanity of the club's members. In this instance, then, Kimball's use of the Venetian Gothic was justified by the nature of the institution that commissioned him.

By way of contrast, the particular choice of Gothic for the skyscrapers Kimball designed on lower Broadway in Manhattan was motivated by proximity to a midcentury Gothic Revival monument. These two "investment skyscrapers" built by the U.S. Realty and Construction Company during the first decade of the twentieth century, and designed by Francis Kimball, represent the assimilation of the earlier Gothic Revival to the new urban type. Both buildings are twenty-one stories tall on Broadway and an additional story in height at the west on Trinity Place. In 1904–5, Harry S. Black, president of Fuller Construction Co., which operated independently under the larger U.S. Realty and Construction Company, built on the site of the former Trinity Building (a five-story structure constructed in 1852) a new office block, 40 feet wide and 270 feet deep. The building consisted of "essentially one row of thirteen offices facing Trinity churchyard, with banks of elevators on the northern edge." The scope of the project was increased in 1907, when the City allowed Thames Street to be moved northward, thus adding 28 feet to the plot at that side. Thirty-five feet across Thames Street is the U.S. Realty Building, which was built in 1906–7.[23] As Landau and Condit have described, the depth of bedrock below the ground (80–85 feet) occasioned the use of pneumatic caissons for the two building projects.[24] Despite the technical challenges, the buildings were completed and fully rented quickly.[25] On the interior, the location of relatively narrow corridors and elevator lobbies toward the dark Thames Street side maximized rentable space. In these public spaces, the Gothic treatment of the exterior was carried through with metal tracery, ribbed vaults, and other details.[26]

Shortly after the completion of the two buildings, Robert E. Dowling, who stepped down as a vice president and director of the U.S. Realty Corporation in 1905,[27] stated: "I had known Mr. Kimball for a number of years before I had an opportunity of engaging his services as architect for the new Trinity Building. As I knew Mr. Kimball had had a great experience in Gothic style in London and in Hartford, Conn., and as we wished to have a building in harmony with the architecture of Trinity Church, I suggested Mr. Kimball be retained as the architect. The Trinity Building was such a success from an architectural as well as from a commercial point of view, that when I began to consider the building of the City Investing Building, I naturally turned to Mr. Kimball again."[28] Kimball's contextual response seen in these two buildings designed to complement Upjohn's 1846 Trinity Church received nearly immediate critical praise. The *New York Times* called the Trinity Building "a monument, a gigantic milestone marking the advance of ideas," and the critic Montgomery Schuyler thought of it as working, along with Kimball and Thompson's earlier Empire Building to the south of the church, to "frame" and "protect" what he called "the relic."[29]

Schuyler's commentary is especially significant for two reasons. First, he expresses a preservationist attitude toward an example of nineteenth-century Gothic Revival architecture and underscores the connection that Kimball's buildings established between the earlier phase of the movement and its twentieth-century expression. Second, Schuyler identifies a motivation for using Gothic forms in skyscraper design that is infrequently enumerated in other discussions of the style, specifically, the imperative to respond to the built environment surrounding the new building.

One of the features of Kimball's design that was especially singled out for praise was the long south facade of the Trinity Building, which addressed the church across the burial grounds. While that openness was one of the major attractions of the site (as most commentators agreed), it also offered a considerable challenge, one that was posed by any skyscraper: the detailing of a large expanse of masonry in a manner that avoided a bland and repetitious appearance. The Gothic elements break up the facade and directly echo the paired windows on the tower of Trinity Church. The physical proximity of Upjohn's building to Kimball's, and the requirements of his client were important, but in a more general way the Gothic Revival also offered an applicable solution to the design dilemmas posed by the skyscraper. The success of Kimball's response to Trinity is especially evident when his buildings are compared with the contemporary One Wall Street building by Barnett, Haynes, and Barnett of St. Louis (fig. 5). It is a brick box topped by what Landau and Condit hypothesize could be a gesture to Trinity Church across Broadway, with four finials of possibly "late Gothic or Jacobean" derivation.[30] Either way, the historical reference is awkwardly incorporated into the utilitarian design.

To understand the suitability of the Gothic Revival as a model for the skyscraper builder, it is necessary to return to Kimball's period of apprenticeship. Even before Kimball had the opportunity to work closely with Burges, he likely had the chance to observe the American Gothic Revival, an experience that could have prepared him to respond effectively to Trinity Church in his Trinity and U.S. Realty Buildings. At the time that Kimball was entering the world of architecture, around 1860, a most extraordinary Gothic Revival project was just completed in Kennebunk, Maine, from where he and his brother-in-law Josiah Littlefield both hailed. Between 1852 and 1856, George Bourne progressively

Fig. 5. One Wall Street building by Barnett, Haynes & Barnett. (Courtesy of Christopher Gray)

clad his house and barn in wooden details that he had personally drawn using images of Milan Cathedral as a guide. Almost like a figure from a Gothic novel, Bourne was apparently so guilt-ridden over an accident that had claimed his daughter's life on a family hike up New Hampshire's Mt. Washington that he became more and more peculiar, spiritual, and obsessed with covering his house with Gothic ornament.[31] The house was a well-known landmark, and although we do not have records of Kimball's travel back to Maine after his departure (assuming that he did return), it is certainly conceivable that as somebody who was interested in building, Kimball would have followed the project through friends and relatives, if not personally. The Bourne House (fig. 6)—or Wedding Cake House, as it is familiarly known—would have offered two important lessons reinforced for Kimball later: first, that the Gothic could be adapted for secular purposes; and second, that Gothic elements—fulfilling no structural role—could be wrapped around an independent frame.

Kimball could also have encountered a Gothic Revival house conceived in a similar way near Hartford during his tenure working on the Trinity College project. In Middletown, some twenty miles away, Charles R. Alsop, onetime mayor and state senator, altered an existing house built at 202 Washington Street by Chauncey Whittlesey around 1780. Like Bourne's renovation of his Kennebunk house, Alsop's project, undertaken around 1840, all but obliterated a Federal-style house with Gothic Revival details: in this instance, a Gothic-style veranda, bargeboards carved to look like tracery, windows with drip moldings, and others.[32] These decorative elements updated what by midcentury was seen as an old-fashioned house, and they had no essential relationship to the structure below.

Fig. 6. George W. Bourne House, Kennebunk, Maine; view from the southeast, photograph by Jack E. Boucher, August 1965. (Historic American Buildings Survey, Library of Congress, Prints and Photographs Division, Washington, D.C.)

This conception echoes Ruskin's idea of the "wall veil" presented in *The Stones of Venice* (1851).[33] The continuity in Kimball's conception of the wall with the nineteenth-century Gothic Revival resulted, at least in part, from the wide popularity of Ruskin's thought, most evident in his design for the Montauk Club. While the Venetian Gothic offered useable motifs in that case, Ruskin's whole way of thinking about the wall was also germane to skyscraper design. The way that he analogized the wall to a veil must have had resonance with skyscraper designers. If the Gothic wall were thought of as a kind of membrane, then its use as a source of inspiration for a skyscraper was all the more appropriate. Indeed, as the *Architects' and Builders' Magazine* commented of the Trinity Building, the "modernized Gothic" was a "new departure" in skyscraper design, but one that was more than just a response to the immediate site conditions: it represented "another interesting solution of the vexed skyscraper problem" with potential application to other projects.[34] In other situations, a response to a nearby Gothic Revival building might not be required, but certainly the need to break up a large expanse of a tower's shaft would remain important. In such instances, Kimball's use of Gothicizing elements would provide an instructive model, the critic implied. Indeed, when Cass Gilbert's Woolworth Building rose just to the north on Broadway within about a half dozen years, the new tower showed how the Gothic Revival—however briefly—provided a certain conceptual direction in the development of modern architecture. The terracotta Gothic exterior bore little relationship to the metal structure beneath it, other than a metaphorical one, but the medievalizing decoration created a degree of visual interest that a bare shaft never could have.

Francis Kimball contributed to one strategy to resolve the design challenge posed by the new skyscraper type, in the form of the medievalizing cladding he employed. He was also a champion of the skyscraper and fully embraced the economic and urban developments that its emergence represented. At a banquet given in his honor in 1908, he stated: "As to the artistic effect of tall buildings, I believe that when properly designed they are more impressive than low buildings that are ugly. There is no more impressive sight in the world than the lower part of New York, as viewed from the harbor. It is an evidence of the great growth of commerce, and the ability to meet the necessities when confined to a narrow strip of land."[35] Unlike that other commentator on the "artistic" aspects of tall buildings—Louis Sullivan—Kimball did not produce a full-fledged theory or philosophy of skyscraper design. He did, however, design two skyscrapers in Lower Manhattan that are of signal importance to the development of the type. The Trinity and U.S. Realty Buildings demonstrated a continuity between the nineteenth-century Gothic Revival and its twentieth-century permutation in the Skyscraper Gothic, and they showed how a historical model could help resolve the contemporary structural and decorative issues raised by the tall building.

NOTES

I would like to thank Drew Armstrong, Darren Vonstein, Victoria Young, and Susan Nowicki for their kind assistance with the research that led to this article. An earlier version of the paper was presented at the symposium "Francis H. Kimball and the Early New York Skyscraper," at the Skyscraper Museum in 2007, at the invitation of Carol Willis.

1. Kenneth Clark, *The Gothic Revival, An Essay in the History of Taste,* 3rd ed. (1928; repr., London: John Murray, 1962), 7.

2. Kevin D. Murphy, "The Historic Architecture of Summer Street, Kennebunk, Maine," *Magazine Antiques* 168, no. 2 (August 2005): 54–63.

3. "Many Callers Welcomed at the Home of Josiah M. Littlefield," *Haverhill Evening Gazette,* February 10, 1912, newspaper clipping, Haverhill Public Library, Special Collections. Suzanne Trottier kindly provided me with a copy of this article.

4. "Francis H. Kimball," *Town Topics* 69, no. 16 (April 17, 1913): 89.

5. David Watkin, *A History of Western Architecture,* 4th ed. (London: Laurence King, 2005), 516.

6. Earle G. Shettleworth Jr. kindly made this building and its history known to me. A historic photo of the building is in the collection of the Maine Historic Preservation Commission, Augusta. For Kimball's other work with Bryant and Rogers, see Roger Reed, *Building Victorian Boston: The Architecture of Gridley J. F. Bryant* (Amherst: University of Massachusetts Press, 2007), 192–95.

7. Montgomery Schuyler, "The Works of Francis H. Kimball and Kimball & Thompson," *Architectural Record* 7, no. 4 (June 1898): 479.

8. "Reminiscences of George Keller, Architect," 1932–33, transcript, Stowe-Day Memorial Library, Hartford, CT, qtd. in David F. Ransom, *George Keller, Architect* (Hartford: Stowe-Day Foundation, 1978), 10.

9. Ransom, *George Keller, Architect,* 4–17.

10. Schuyler, "The Works of Francis H. Kimball and Kimball & Thompson," 479.

11. "The New Buildings," *Trinity Tablet* 8 (February 20, 1875): 19. Drew Armstrong kindly provided me with this reference.

12. Christopher Drew Armstrong, "'*Qui Transtulit Sustinet*': William Burges, Francis Kimball, and the Architecture of Hartford's Trinity College," *Journal of the Society of Architectural Historians* 59, no. 2 (June 2000): 202–3.

13. Ibid., 208–13.

14. James F. O'Gorman, "O. W. Norcross, Richardson's 'Master Builder': A Preliminary Report," *Journal of the Society of Architectural Historians* 32, no. 2 (May 1973): 109.

15. Armstrong, "*Qui Transtulit Sustinet,*" 209.

16. Cynthia Zaitzevsky, "A New Richardson Building," *Journal of the Society of Architectural Historians* 32, no. 2 (May 1973): 164.

17. Kimball was frequently referred to as the "father of the skyscraper," both in the press and by his family, for instance, in Frances C. Littlefield to Miss [Edith Cleaves] Barry, March 30 [?], 1939, Kimball Genealogy Vertical File, Brick Store Museum, Kennebunk, ME.

18. Henry F. Withey and Elise Rathburn Withey, *Biographical Dictionary of American Architects (Deceased)* (1956; repr., Los Angeles: Hennessey and Ingalls, 1970), 344.

19. Sarah Bradford Landau and Carl W. Condit, *Rise of the New York Skyscraper, 1865–1913* (New Haven: Yale University Press, 1996), 316.

20. Edward A. Eigen, "Kimball, Francis," in *Encyclopedia of New York City,* ed. Kenneth T. Jackson (New Haven: Yale University Press, 1995), 766.

21. Schuyler, "The Works of Francis H. Kimball and Kimball & Thompson," 497–500.

22. Kiara M. Vigil, *Indigenous Intellectuals: Sovereignty, Citizenship, and the American Imagination, 1880–1930* (New York: Cambridge University Press, 2015), 72.

23. Gail Fenske and Deryck Holdsworth, "Corporate Identity and the New York Office Building: 1895–1915," in *Landscape of Modernity: New York City, 1900–1940,* ed. David Ward and Olivier Zunz (1992; paperback ed., Baltimore: Johns Hopkins University Press, 1997), 149.

24. Landau and Condit, *Rise of the New York Skyscraper,* 316.

25. Fenske and Holdsworth, "Corporate Identity and the New York Office Building," 149.

26. The interiors are extensively illustrated in "The New Trinity Building," *Architects' and Builders' Magazine* 6, no. 9 (June 1905): 383–401.

27. "New Realty Corporation," *Building Trades Employers Association Bulletin* 6, no. 2 (February 1905): 30.

28. "Mr. Dowling's Speech," *New York Architect* 2, no. 5 (May 1908): n.p.

29. "New York's Newest Downtown Skyscraper," *New York Times Sunday Magazine,* June 4, 1905; Montgomery Schuyler, "Some Recent Skyscrapers," *Architectural Record* 22, no. 3 (September 1907): 162–63; both qtd. in Elisa Urbanelli and Nancy Goeschel, New York Landmarks Preservation Commission, June 7, 1988, Designation List 204 LP-1558, TS, 3.

30. Landau and Condit, *Rise of the New York Skyscraper,* 317. The original conception of the building, published in 1906, was for a "beautiful bronze cornice richly decorated." The plan for the treatment of the roofline was likely changed to reflect Trinity Church, nearby ("No. 1 Wall St.," *Realty Record and Builder* 13, no. 7 [July 1906]: n.p.).

31. Thomas W. Murphy, *The Wedding Cake House: The World of George W. Bourne* (Kennebunkport, ME: Durrell, 1978).

32. Connecticut Historical Commission, Historic Resources Inventory Form, Wetmore-Weeks or Alsop-Weeks House, 200–202 Washington St., Middletown, comp. Barbara Ann Cleary, January1979, Department of Planning, Conservation and Development, Middletown, CT, available at www.middletownplanning.com/Committees/DRPB/historic propertieslist.html.

33. Vittoria Di Palma, "A Natural History of Ornament," in *Histories of Ornament: From Global to Local,* ed. Gülru Necipoğlu and Alina Payne (Princeton: Princeton University Press, 2016), 27.

34. *Architects' and Builders' Magazine* 6, no. 9 (June 1905): 383–401; ibid., 8, no. 9 (June 1907): 413–17.

35. "Mr. Kimball's Speech," *New York Architect* 2, no. 5 (May 1908): n.p.

MEDIEVALISM, MYSTICISM, AND MODERNITY IN EARLY TWENTIETH-CENTURY NEW YORK

Cass Gilbert's "Skyscraper Gothic"

Gail Fenske

For the American architectural community of the 1920s and beyond, Cass Gilbert's Woolworth Building of 1910–13 represented a decisive turning point in the development of the Skyscraper Gothic (fig. 1).[1] Architectural critics, Montgomery Schuyler prominently among them, applauded the design, and later the organizers of the Chicago Tribune Tower Competition, seeking "the most beautiful office building in the world," pointed to the Woolworth Building as the model to which competitors should aspire: "It should count as the Woolworth tower does in New York."[2] Still, Gilbert's Skyscraper Gothic idiom, which initially appeared in his West Street Building in New York of 1905–7, did not spring full-fledged and independent of a particular intellectual and cultural context (fig. 2). To the contrary, Gilbert showed that he had assimilated—albeit to varying degrees—the full range of contemporary criticisms, theoretical explorations, and aesthetic predilections associated with the Gothic. His Woolworth Building, furthermore, demonstrated that those meanings could take on a wholly contrasting character within the urban environment of early twentieth-century New York—the nation's capital of finance, showcase of consumer enticement, and center of news media publicity, a setting virtually tailor-made for the retailer Frank W. Woolworth's promotion of his "world's greatest skyscraper."[3]

Fig. 1. Cass Gilbert, Woolworth Building, New York, 1910–13. (Library of Congress, Prints and Photographs Division, Washington, D.C.)

Fig. 2. Cass Gilbert, West Street Building, New York, 1905–7. (Cass Gilbert Architectural Collection, PR-021, drawer 19, neg. 74165, New-York Historical Society)

Fig. 3. Cyrus L. W. Eidlitz, New York Times Building, New York, 1903–5, photograph by George P. Hall & Son. (George P. Hall & Son photograph collection, box 8, f:68, PR024_b-08_002-01, neg. 61226, New-York Historical Society)

In the mid- to late nineteenth century, noted architectural theorists such as Eugène-Emmanuel Viollet-le-Duc and Leopold Eidlitz singled out the Gothic past as a worthy precedent for a wholly original styleless, or "organic," modern architecture, establishing the theoretical direction that found full realization in Louis Sullivan's designs for skyscrapers, notably the Wainwright Building in St. Louis (1891).[4] Beginning in the mid-1890s, however, architects in Chicago and New York, among them Charles Atwood and Cyrus L. W. Eidlitz, focused on the visual character of the Gothic as a style. Although indebted to the modern theories of Viollet-le-Duc and the elder Eidlitz, they nonetheless viewed the tall office building in light of the Gothic cathedral, emphasizing the visual potentials of vertical structural elements and subordinate details, as shown in the Fisher Building (1895–96) and the New York Times Building (1903–5) (fig. 3). Around 1900, architects attuned to the day's broader context of thought began investing the Gothic with varied associative meanings as well. The antimodern viewpoint of Ralph Adams Cram; the Arts and Crafts teachings of Herbert Langford Warren at Harvard, inspired in turn by the criticism of John Ruskin and William Morris; the romanticism of Bertram Goodhue; and the mystical orientation of Claude Bragdon evidenced the power, depth, and kaleidoscopic richness of "Gothic."[5] That is perhaps why the day's Beaux-Arts critics and theorists, who had canonized the classical past, now made arguments on behalf of the Gothic. A. D. F. Hamlin, in particular, viewed the Gothic as an available style in the repertory of styles an architect might consult to invest a monumental composition with a distinctive character, still rich in associations with its original medieval source.[6]

It was within this intellectual context that Gilbert's West Street and Woolworth Buildings achieved instant renown as Skyscraper Gothic designs among architects, historians, and critics — for their modernity, memorability, and sheer visual drama: energetic and aspiring in their verticality, pictorial in composition, and fluid in their synthesis of Gothic motifs and details, they embodied the day's wide range of aspirations identified with the Gothic. Gilbert's designs also left an unforgettable impression on the urban spectator. Still, that impression, albeit strongly indebted to Gilbert's knowledge of his contemporaries' work in the Gothic as well as the pictorial force of his compositions, could not be extricated from the larger forces at work shaping the reception of his designs. In the case of the Woolworth Building in particular, those forces — the product of Frank W. Woolworth and the full-blown program of publicity by his director of advertising, Hugh McAtamney — rapidly took on a life of their own. Woolworth and McAtamney harnessed the Gothic's visual and iconographic possibilities to the end of crafting a tantalizing and memorable Gothic landmark, designed to resonate with New York's sidewalk crowds. More specifically, they exploited the Gothic's ethical underpinnings while at the same time severing the project from those underpinnings with the aim of advertising Gilbert's design. That design would, soon enough, serve as the F. W. Woolworth Company's most conspicuous commercial trademark.

During the 1920s, the Woolworth Building's Skyscraper Gothic transcended its milieu to reverberate in designs for major skyscrapers in cities across America and beyond. It served as the style of choice for builders of notable landmarks such as Howells and Hood's Chicago Tribune Tower of 1922–25 as well as lesser-known landmarks that graced the skylines of secondary urban centers, from Detroit to San Francisco, among them the architect Wirt C. Rowland's Buhl Building of 1925 in Detroit; Alfred C. Finn's Gulf Building of 1929 in Houston; and George W. Kelham's Russ Building of 1927 in San Francisco. The Woolworth Building, moreover — which Schuyler called a "higher power" of the West Street Building — served as the paradigmatic example of design for Gilbert's younger architect-contemporaries. It offered a full-fledged Gothic vocabulary ready-made for implementation in a range of individually unique designs.[7] Through their choice of the Skyscraper Gothic, the builders eager to advertise, by contrast, could hardly ignore the example set by Woolworth and McAtamney. But even in light of such contradictory aims, how and why, exactly, did the Woolworth Building capture the imaginations of so many architects, critics, builders, and appreciators of skyscrapers during the 1920s and 1930s?

That Gilbert should design his West Street Building in 1905, the year that the key debate over the Skyscraper Gothic exploded on the pages of the *Craftsman*—the respected journal of the American Arts and Crafts movement—points to his centrality as a catalyst in the creation of the style (see fig. 2). The debate—incited by Frederick Stymetz Lamb, an architect and medievalist as well as the lead designer in the New York decorative arts firm specializing in ecclesiastical mosaics and stained glass, J&R Lamb Studios—illustrated with poignant clarity the range of theoretical perspectives identified with "the Gothic" as well as with "the modern" in American architectural thought around 1900. In the *Craftsman*'s May issue, Lamb stated his own position in "Modern Use of the Gothic," then solicited viewpoints on the relationship of the Gothic to the problem of the skyscraper from the day's key critics and practitioners.[8] Noted among the replies were essays written by Bertram Goodhue, A. D. F. Hamlin, and Louis Sullivan.[9] All engaged in a vigorous round of criticism. In doing so, they defined with clarity the full array of contemporary positions on the significance—or lack thereof—of lessons from the Gothic past for the design of the skyscraper, which they viewed as the most perplexing and problematic of new building types.

Inviting his contemporaries' replies, Lamb argued in his "Modern Use of the Gothic" that, first of all, the architect might find lessons worthy of application to the skyscraper's "modern steel construction" in the example of the Gothic past, as opposed to the classical past, as illustrated by Cyrus L. W. Eidlitz's recently completed New York Times Building (see fig. 3). This, he thought, could be explained by the cathedral's chief characteristic, that of height. It could also be explained by features such as isolated points of support, walls or openings between supports that were screen-like and light-admitting, and the cathedral's characteristic subordination of ornament—based on its builders' close study of forms in nature—to structure. To substantiate his argument, Lamb emphasized the commonality between the society of the twelfth century and that of the early twentieth century. If the twelfth century had been characterized by the growth of the guilds, the liberty afforded the individual artist, and works of architecture in continual adaptation to the problem at hand, then in the twentieth century, Lamb explained, the Art Nouveau evidenced a comparable, highly individualistic responsiveness to change. The Art Nouveau, Lamb further argued, had shown an allegiance to the Gothic's structural principles and ornamental techniques, with the latter drawn from detailed observations of nature. For these reasons, according to Lamb, the best designs for contemporary skyscrapers showed parallels with the Art Nouveau.[10] Consequently, in Lamb's view, a theorist or critic could make a visual as well as a societally based argument linking the medieval cathedral to the modern skyscraper.

Among those who replied to Lamb in the *Craftsman*'s June issue, Bertram Goodhue countered Lamb to argue for a broader, more inclusive perspective on the Gothic that suggested a deeply rooted philosophical affinity between the medieval and the modern. Goodhue, who with his partners Ralph Adams Cram and Frank Ferguson had recently won the competition for the United States Military Academy at West Point, argued that the contemporary architect faced a question of far greater importance than that of Lamb's "mere style," noting that all architects could be divided into two categories: "conservative and radical, reactionary and revolutionist, satisfied and unsatisfied and . . . classicist and Gothicist." How to find true "originality," for Goodhue, constituted the essence of that question, and its answer called for courage on the part of the designer, particularly given that on account of travel, the diffusion of knowledge, and photography, "we all stand abashed before the greatness of the past." Most architects deferred to that past, he lamented, except when confronted with "some wholly novel constructive necessity." But fortunately, Goodhue further argued, such a constructive necessity had also managed to inspire in a few of his contemporaries a remarkable penchant for originality. This led Goodhue to conclude that "the true romanticist welcomes steel or concrete construction as his brother of the twelfth century must have welcomed the counter-thrusting arch or flying buttress. To this extent, he may be called a 'Gothicist.'"[11] To Goodhue's thinking, then, romanticism, Gothicism, and the modern could be considered variations of a shared and principled point of view, a uniquely contemporary position attuned to the early twentieth century and to the complexities of the moment.

A. D. F. Hamlin's reply to Lamb, by contrast, pointed to the virtues of the "historical styles" for solving the problem of the skyscraper, which he considered the most modern of the day's architectural challenges. Hamlin's emphasis on style in its own right was founded on his own *Textbook of the History of Architecture* (1896) and influenced by his position as professor of architecture at Columbia University's School of Architecture, a school noted for its Beaux-Arts–oriented curriculum, in which instruction in composition provided a basis for the choice of a historical style.[12] Hamlin added that within the historical styles there could be identified two markedly different "aesthetic systems," the first of which was classical and stressed certain predetermined combinations of proportion and form and the second of which was medieval and stressed the "principle of logic." In the hands of the cathedral builders the latter had produced "stupendous results." Such a "truly Gothic procedure," Hamlin further argued, had been more recently illustrated in the modern, or "Art Nouveau," office buildings of Louis Sullivan and D. H. Burnham & Company. That these contemporary skyscrapers demonstrated the logical satisfaction of structural requirements, however, did not preclude their architects' inspired application of authentic Gothic detail. Hamlin emphasized that the current age continued to be heir to all ages that came before it: "Eclecticism—a wise, reasonable, broad and artistic eclecticism—will mark the progress of artistic design in the twentieth century."[13]

Louis Sullivan presented the strongest counterargument to Lamb's proposition, rejecting outright the significance for the skyscraper of any reference whatsoever to the Gothic past. Already known for his modern skyscrapers, including, besides the Wainwright, his Guaranty Building in Buffalo (1896) and more recently, his Bayard-Condict Building in New York (1899, fig. 4), Sullivan pointed out that Lamb, in essence, had unconvincingly proposed that the skyscraper—regardless of its modern character as a building type—be understood as well as designed within the context of the historical styles. It mattered little to Sullivan whether Lamb's choice of style happened to be Gothic or classical, for Lamb had unfortunately proposed nothing less than an outright historical revivalism in arguing that medieval thought was "more American

Fig. 4. Louis Sullivan, Bayard-Condict Building, New York, 1897–99. (Illustration from *American Architect and Building News* 70 [October 6, 1900], courtesy of the Boston Public Library, Fine Arts Department)

than the thought of Greece or Rome." In doing so, Lamb had lost sight of "our twentieth century conditions and demands," and worse, had cast aside "the wonderful riches of modern thought," just so that "he may have dalliance with Gothic detail." Sullivan further questioned whether it was indeed possible for Lamb or others to "discuss American architecture and its possibilities" while ignoring the modern world with its "expansive force of democracy": "Our real, live American problems concern neither the classic nor the Gothic, they concern *us* here and now."[14] For Sullivan, the birth of modern architecture, as typified by the skyscraper, as well as the peculiar set of American conditions that engendered a "democratic" architecture, pointed to the overriding importance of making a complete and decisive break with any known style of the past.

Sullivan's rebuttal to Lamb in the *Craftsman* continued the line of thinking that he had established earlier in his "Tall Office Building Artistically Considered" of 1896.[15] More recently, in his "The Modern Phase of Architecture" of 1900, Sullivan had argued before a younger generation of architects at a meeting of the Architectural League of America that the architect should not consider himself an "artist, whatever that funny word may mean," but rather "a poet and an interpreter of the national life of his time." He added that "the clairvoyance of the age is steadily unfolding" and that "the only sign of dawn I can see" will make "for a day that shall regenerate an art that should be . . . the most intimate, the most expressive, the most eloquent of all."[16] Sullivan's Emerson-inspired words, with their emphasis on the regenerative capacity of youth, the importance of original thought, and an American architecture conceived in concert with the realities of the time, echoed those of the Vienna architect Otto Wagner in *Modern Architecture* (1896).[17] Ultimately, it was Sullivan's viewpoint as an architect that would have the greatest influence over Gilbert's designs for the West Street and the Woolworth Buildings, even though those designs also showed that Gilbert—who had studied in MIT's Beaux-Arts curriculum and apprenticed with McKim, Mead & White—remained indebted to the broader currents of thought articulated by Lamb, Goodhue, and Hamlin.

Gilbert and his office staff produced the first "Gothic" sketches for the West Street Building in early May 1905, coincident with the publication of Lamb's "Modern Use of the Gothic" in the *Craftsman,* and then refined the building's design during that June, at the same time the journal published Goodhue, Hamlin, and Sullivan's replies (fig. 5). As Gilbert later explained it in a lecture of May 1909 at the United States Military Academy at West Point, it was with the West Street Building's initial sketches that he brought together the modernist position of Louis Sullivan with his own position as a Beaux-Arts architect to craft a distinctive aesthetic for the skyscraper.[18] Gilbert's high regard for Sullivan's thought and work—influenced in turn by his own admiration for Eugène-Emmanuel Viollet-le-Duc's authority as a medievalist—is particularly evident in an early drawing for the West Street Building, produced during May or June 1905, showing that he and his assistants had made careful study of Sullivan's Bayard-Condict Building (see fig. 4, fig. 6).[19] Without Sullivan's example, Gilbert would have been hard-pressed to formulate the West Street Building's Skyscraper Gothic design, which featured a new and marked expression of verticality, that is, a forceful allusion in its powerful expression of height to the building type's modernity.

Gilbert had become well acquainted with Sullivan's skyscrapers and more generally with Chicago innovations in the design, engineering, and construction of tall office buildings during his early years of practice in St. Paul, between 1882 and 1889.[20] His knowledge of recent developments in Chicago showed in his early designs for office buildings, particularly the E. D. Chamberlain Building (St. Paul, 1895), the Brazer Building (Boston, 1896), and the Broadway

Fig. 5. Cass Gilbert, West Street Building, New York, sketch, 1905. (Library of Congress, Prints and Photographs Division, Washington, D.C.)

Chambers Building, the project with which he established his practice in New York (1898–99). But how deeply did Gilbert actually understand Sullivan's philosophical commitment to the skyscraper as an exemplary building type in modern architecture? In an interview with a reporter for the *New York Times* of 1908 and during his lecture of 1909 at West Point, Gilbert reflected on his decision to employ Sullivan's lessons of design to "the strictly modern" problem of the office building. In 1908, Gilbert emphasized that "the skyscraper offers a structural problem, a solution for which architects are seeking new lines. . . . Experience must in the end find some rational solution."[21] Then, in 1909 at West Point, he quoted Sullivan directly, showing knowledge of Sullivan's essay "The Tall Office Building Artistically Considered," indicating that "it has been well

Fig. 6. Cass Gilbert, West Street Building, New York, photograph of drawing, ca. 1905. (New-York Historical Society)

said that 'form follows function' . . . so in building, while there may be a few distorted examples, in the long run the form adapts itself to the use it is intended to serve." Gilbert concluded that as a consequence, "the inevitable logic of design now bids us lift these huge masses in the air with aspiring verticals, accenting rather than dissembling their height."[22] Still, for Gilbert, Sullivan's verticals, as well as their modern theoretical underpinnings, served as but a single feature, albeit a highly important feature, within what he considered the skyscraper's more significant Beaux-Arts composition.

Gilbert, already known as a Beaux-Arts architect for his highly "pictorial" Beaux-Arts compositions such as the Minnesota State Capitol and United States Custom House, sought a solution for the skyscraper that, as he wrote, "in the end may not be without *beauty,* too."[23] Consequently, Gilbert's earliest sketches for the West Street Building's composition—not unlike those for his Capitol—showed that in massing and outline, and in particular in the lavish ornamentation of the skyscraper's crown, he placed the greatest importance on views of his composition from afar. The skyscraper's waterfront site, bordering the Hudson River, was open to a sweeping panorama of the skyline shared by spectators aboard ships and ferries plying one of the world's busiest waterways (see fig. 5). Sullivan's Bayard-Condict Building, which he designed for Bleecker Street, had by contrast verticals that rose to conclusion in a decisive cornice (see fig. 4). For Gilbert, however, the West Street Building's picturesque termination in the sky rivalled in importance and expressiveness the skyscraper's energetic verticality. For that reason, early in the process of designing the West Street Building, he had included a tower, inspired by the hôtels de ville of medieval Flanders, among them Brussels, Middelburg, and in particular, the hôtel de ville in Audenarde. These he and his Beaux-Arts contemporaries associated with "municipal dignity," grandeur, and prosperity.[24] Even though his client Howard Carroll refused to build the tower, Gilbert conceived the West Street Building's picturesque crown as a rival attraction in the distant views. For that reason, he lavished study in sketch after sketch on the crown's details, turning to historical French châteaux, the recent "medievalizing" upper stories of Cyrus Eidlitz's newly completed New York Times Building, and more generally to the array of Gothic motifs documented in his own sketchbooks, along with the photographs, illustrations, and picture postcards that filled his office scrapbooks (see figs. 2 and 3).[25] Ultimately, the West Street Building's crown, with vigorously projecting canopies, corbelled colonnettes, crockets, gables, and finials, distinguished Gilbert's compositional strategy, more than any other feature, from the designs of Louis Sullivan.

Beyond any doubt, when imagining the West Street Building as a skyscraper, Gilbert had placed considerable emphasis on the project's highly visible waterfront site. But Gilbert's final design for the West Street Building—his very first essay in the Skyscraper Gothic—also suggested that he had gone beyond merely combining his own Beaux-Arts–inspired method of pictorial composition, which included his fluid syntheses of Gothic motifs and details, with the modern, theoretically inspired verticals of Sullivan. The design's key features suggest that he had also assimilated the critical perspectives on the Gothic that Lamb, Goodhue, and Hamlin had recently voiced in the *Craftsman*.

The West Street Building's verticals, first of all, showed a monumentality that Gilbert ascribed to the European medieval cathedrals he had studied on recent sketching tours and that Lamb had extolled as having parallels with modern vertical construction. Important among those cathedrals was St. Rombout in Malines, Belgium, the tower of which Gilbert characterized in 1897 as "remarkable for the effect of its *rise* or *uplift*—a sort of grand fling upward" with "many deep buttresses, giving vigorous vertical lines."[26] Second, the West Street Building's composition—and in particular, its crown—suggested in its evocative picturesqueness an affinity with Goodhue's romantic medievalism. Finally, Gilbert's handling of that composition, and especially his skills in making it fluid and imageable, hallmarks of its pictorial quality, showed that the West Street Building's design reflected Hamlin's Beaux-Arts convictions about composition as the basis for a choice of style. Gilbert had, in fact, recently written about such aspects of medieval architecture after visiting the cathedrals of Ely and Durham during his travels in England in 1906, describing Ely's "romantic" character by moonlight and Durham's "splendid effect of mass against the evening sky."[27] In the end, it could be argued that the West Street Building's Skyscraper Gothic design achieved its clarity and force from Gilbert's synthesis of the architecture of the Middle Ages, as he understood it, with his contemporaries' varied and wide-ranging perceptions, aspirations, and theories—all still fluid, disparate, and in their origins, even competitive, contradictory, and seemingly impossible to reconcile. Yet in Gilbert's hands, remarkably, the contextual disparities yielded nothing less than a remarkably coherent result.

Contemporary art and architectural historians and critics, attuned to the recent debates associated with the Gothic as well as with the skyscraper, showered the West Street Building with unanimous acclaim. In particular, they hailed Gilbert's synthesis of a Sullivan-inspired, soaring verticality with his own Gothic-inspired, ornamentally elaborate, and highly picturesque crown. The art historian John Van Dyke, tellingly, described Gilbert's design in his *New New York* of 1909 as a "more modern structure using the vertical instead of the horizontal line," calling it a first on the New York architectural scene—a scene previously dominated by Roman arches "drawn out of all recognition" and "Norman castles" rising to "phenomenal heights." Van Dyke further noted that as a consequence of Gilbert's design, "New York learned (or is in the process of learning) of its mistake from Chicago. . . . Instead of deprecating the height of the steel building, they emphasized it by using the vertical instead of the horizontal line . . . instead of fighting the height of the building, [they] accented it, gave it aspiration, dignity, and withal lightness and a semblance of honesty—the very things in which the first skyscrapers were lacking."[28] Van Dyke especially appreciated the West Street Building's crown, noting that "the effect of it is to carry the eye upward, to increase the height; and, finally, to allow definition to be lost in a mystery of ornamental wind caps, cornices, and terra cotta pinnacles."[29] Such a crown did not contradict Gilbert's emphasis on the skyscraper's modern verticality, for according to Van Dyke, the builders of skyscrapers in New York, who wished "their buildings to please the eye from without," aspired to such lavish ornamentation along with a richness of color; they aimed to catch the attention of the city's spectatorial crowds.[30]

In his essay "The West Street Building" of 1907, Montgomery Schuyler similarly called attention to Gilbert's verticals, which in his view triumphed over the designs of his New York contemporaries in their expression of the skyscraper's modern steel-framed construction. "Instead of concealing the fact" of such construction, those verticals had, to the architect's credit, suggested "mere envelopes and wrappages for a framed building."[31] Schuyler's perspective as a critic, as noted by William Jordy and Ralph Coe, found inspiration in the organicism of Leopold Eidlitz, and via Eidlitz, in the structural rationalism of Viollet-le-

Duc.[32] Even Schuyler himself noted that he was committed to "'Gothic principles' . . . without contradicting the contemporary fact" and to reality in art.[33] For these reasons, he had recently extolled Sullivan's Bayard-Condict Building in New York and would make the same argument in assessing the West Street Building: a skyscraper's steel frame lightly clad in terra-cotta accorded with "the facts of the case."[34] But as Jordy and Coe further noted, Schuyler also remained indebted to Ruskin's medievalism, which emphasized honesty in materials and a "painterly approach to picturesque massing."[35] It is not surprising, then, that Schuyler applauded the West Street Building's crown as "an inspiration" when glimpsed "from up or down the river," adding that only in the Gothic, "to recur to our Ruskin," might an architect discover the source for such "misty masses of multitudinous pinnacle and diademed tower."[36]

Claude Bragdon praised Gilbert's West Street Building in a similar fashion in his "Architecture of the United States III: The Skyscraper" of 1909, calling it "the last word in New York skyscraper architecture."[37] Bragdon had devoted most of his essay to explaining the skyscraper as a contemporary architectural and urban problem. In doing so, he emphasized Sullivan's theoretical position—"the shape, form, outward expression of the tall office building should, in the very nature of things, follow the function of the building, and when function does not change, the form is not to change."[38] Bragdon, furthermore, noted that "the commercial necessities of real estate" had not prevented Sullivan from "seeing the spiritual possibilities which lurk, undreamed of by most people in [the skyscraper's] inert mass of brutal materialism."[39]

Bragdon's sentiments about "spiritual possibilities" echoed those that he had earlier presented in talks for the Architectural League of America, "Mysticism and Architecture" of 1901 and "L'Art Nouveau and American Architecture" of 1903. In the latter, he argued that Sullivan's organic theories suggested a "Gothic" as opposed to "classical" temperament and, as such, showed a "freedom of individual expression . . . following the logic of the moment," as opposed to the more typical practice of falling back on a "predetermined formula."[40] "Beneath the dense materiality of American civilization," Bragdon added in his characteristically mystical vein, "there is fermenting a leaven of spirituality," which "may usher in a period of faith like that which Europe underwent in the Middle Ages, when Gothic architecture had its origin."[41] In

New York, Bragdon continued, only Gilbert's West Street Building had risen to the standard set by Sullivan, "that militant Goth," albeit within the waterfront's distinctive physical setting, highlighted by a favorable "background of city and sky." "In mass, in outline, in color, in detail," he concluded, "the building is the work of a mastermind."[42]

Cass Gilbert's Woolworth Building showed him advancing the West Street Building's Skyscraper Gothic idiom to a wholly new level of visual dynamism and picturesqueness (see figs. 1 and 2). First of all, the verticals, as the skyscraper's most striking architectural feature, suggested a quickened sense of energy and rhythm; now syncopated, they evoked the electrifying mood of a city caught up in the throes of modernity. Gilbert's chief design assistant, Thomas R. Johnson, had in early studies for the Woolworth's design shown those verticals—initially a synthesis of Sullivan-inspired colonnettes with the rising moldings of the Perpendicular Gothic style—reaching a new level of astylar abstraction. Johnson had previously associated such rhythmic and abstract structural sequences with the newest works of the European avant-garde.[43] But Gilbert also continued to argue for the importance to his work of Sullivan's modern functionalist theories. As construction of the Woolworth Building neared completion in February 1912, Gilbert emphasized Sullivan's aphorism "form follows function" a second time in a lecture he gave at Harvard, adding that "my logic and my judgment told me it was the right thing to do, and out of it grew a certain type, at least for me, and it was a decision fundamental to my practice."[44] Later, Gilbert recalled that if a skyscraper's chief attribute is its tallness, "its height should be recognized, insisted upon, and expressed by vertical lines."[45]

Second, Gilbert and Johnson employed in the Woolworth Building's design a still wider repertory of Gothic compositional motifs and details than they had in the West Street Building, utilizing that repertory to achieve in effect a still more fluid and imageable synthesis of style. In the final stages of the design, while integrating the West Street Building's primary Gothic and medieval sources—among them the Victoria Tower, Houses of Parliament, French châteaux, and the hôtels de ville and cathedrals of Belgium—they also ranged much further beyond those sources, to incorporate a still wider array of church and cathedral motifs, noted among them for the tracery and metalwork, French Flamboyant Gothic details.[46] In the process, they thoroughly collapsed the distinction between the sacred and the secular. As Gilbert later put it, "The Palace of Jacques Coeur at Bourges, the Hôtel de Ville at Rouen, the Hôtel de Cluny in Paris, the Town Hall at Middelburg, Hôtel de Ville, Compiègne," along with "the towers of Reims, Antwerp, and Malines, and many others all contributed their quota of precedent and suggestion in the development of the detail."[47]

Third, and most important, Gilbert infused the Woolworth Building's composition with a heightened level of intricacy, lightness, and ethereality. This showed especially in the tower, which he based on the spire of Antwerp Cathedral, subdividing the verticals of its upper stages with mullions to enhance the effect of a skeletal delicacy and loftiness. In the tower's highest stage, Gilbert skillfully synthesized the crossing tower of the Benedictine Abbey Church at Saint-Ouen in Rouen with the roof and spire of the Guild Hall in Cologne to the end of crafting and unforgettable crowning motif for the city's skyline (figs. 7 and 8).[48] Later he noted that "the mounting chords of the Stabat Mater kept sounding in my mind while I was piling up that building," adding that its pinnacle "is not isolated, but is accompanied by other secondary points surrounding it, and imparting a sense of the ultimate rhythm . . . gradually gaining in spirituality the higher its mounts." Thus, he hoped that such a skyscraper, prominent among the buildings that architects designed for commerce and industry, might also "inspire thoughts of a higher and more spiritual life."[49] Altogether, Gilbert's sophisticated—even scenographic—synthesis of such a wide array of Gothic motifs and details, many of them Perpendicular and Flamboyant, appeared stylistically unified only insofar as it recalled "late Gothic."[50] This, even more than his interest in the skyscraper's spiritual evocations, distinguished the Woolworth Building's design from the skyscrapers of Louis Sullivan.

For Montgomery Schuyler, Gilbert's Woolworth Building summed up the potentials for modern architecture inherent in the Skyscraper Gothic. Above all else, it signified the continuing primacy of Sullivan's functionalist theory to the new building type. It "most unmistakably denotes its skeleton. . . . [T]he uprights of the steel frame are felt throughout and everywhere."[51] In fact, Schuyler emphasized, a viewer might take the design "as the subject of a lecture on Mr. Sullivan's text: 'Where function does not vary, form does not vary.'" But Gilbert had also, to Schuyler's thinking, inflected as well as advanced upon Sullivan's

Fig. 7. Cass Gilbert, sketch of Saint-Ouen in Rouen, France, 1880. (Library of Congress, Prints and Photographs Division, Washington, D.C.)

method. As "an amplification, a clarification, and a perfection of the design of West Street," Gilbert had employed in the Woolworth Building the earlier design's "continuous reeded uprights," but now with each reed "so emphatically projected" and "so emphatically modeled" that in diagonal views from the side, the building's openings virtually disappeared: "Verticality is the character of the fronts."[52] Although Gilbert indeed remained indebted to the Gothic, Schuyler thought he had also, on account of Sullivan's example, triumphed over the earlier eclecticism, or "form-mongery."[53] In his "faithful following out of the indications of [the] problem," Schuyler concluded, Gilbert had become the sort of modern architect who intuitively understood the rational principles inherent in the Gothic, or "as Molière's hero talked prose without knowing it . . . a Gothic architect without knowing it."[54]

Perhaps most significantly, Schuyler's assessment of Gilbert's Woolworth Building as related to the earlier skyscrapers of Sullivan highlighted "the total disappearance of the 'cornice,' in the sense of a shelf." As if implicitly criticizing Sullivan's use of such a terminating shelf, Schuyler noted that the Woolworth's "elaborated upper stage," not unlike the Gothic "efflorescence" of the West Street Building's crowning feature, served as a "fitting crown and consummation" for the design's "slender reeds," which naturally like stalks, "prefigure buds and blossoms." Schuyler found the Woolworth's tower, moreover, with its "sudden, rocket-like shooting of the white and channeled shaft" and "dwindling bulk of the upper stages to the crowing finial" wholly worthy of "its conspicuousness and its preeminence" for "in its white spectrality it 'shines over city and river.'" With that "addition" to the building's composition, Schuyler concluded, "which is architecturally not an addition but a completion, it becomes such a triumph as is the rarest of achievements in modern architecture."[55] For Schuyler, then, Gilbert had taken Sullivan's theories as a starting point, but with the Gothic as his guide, had fulfilled a tantamount requirement: that of enhancing the views of the city.

Fig. 8. Cass Gilbert, Woolworth Building, tower, 1910–13. (Cass Gilbert Collection, box 562, folder 4, New-York Historical Society)

Schuyler's criticism of the Woolworth Building integrated the day's richness of perspectives on the Gothic—from the rational theories of Viollet-le-Duc to Goodhue's equation of medievalism and romanticism—with his own convictions about the modern. Among the most contemporary of those perspectives, Bragdon's mysticism had the least impact on Schuyler's point of view, but it is nonetheless clear that with the completion of the Woolworth Building, the complex array of ideas—medieval, mystical, and modern—circulating in the New York urban milieu around 1900 had consolidated as a rich body of thought among architects, historians, and critics, with Schuyler as their leading and most articulate exponent.

Consequently, Gilbert's design of the Woolworth Building as an exemplary landmark in the day's Skyscraper Gothic style—and especially to the critical acclaim of Schuyler—served in its own right to crystallize his aspirations as an architect, along with those of his architect-contemporaries. But the broader public reception of Gilbert's design turned out to constitute a separate matter entirely. That reception F. W. Woolworth powerfully shaped through his determination to publicize—in essence, to advertise—Gilbert's design as widely and as sensationally as possible. Working with his director of advertising, Hugh McAtamney, Woolworth conceived perhaps the first and most ambitious program of printed news publicity ever produced for a single work of architecture, aiming to achieve for his project no less than world renown.

Woolworth's earlier experiences as a merchant and retailing innovator—that is, as the founder of the famous chain of five-and ten-cent stores—had the highest importance for how he envisioned the Woolworth Building as what he called the "world's greatest skyscraper." Those experiences included Woolworth's fabrication of seductive consumer environments that highlighted his bargain-priced commodities—"remember our advertisements are in our show windows and on our counters," he told his store managers—in addition to contriving an array of visual strategies for still further advertising those commodities, comprising storefronts, trademarks, and signs. Equally important, they included his own in-depth study and observation of crowds of shoppers and settings for shopping with the aim of discerning as well as furthering the spatial, visual, and locational "logic" of consumption. Even though Woolworth had pointed to the Victoria Tower, Houses of Parliament, and to Gilbert's own West Street Building as models for the Woolworth Building, he also made it clear that he expected Gilbert's design to function like a "giant signboard to advertise around the world his spreading chain of five-and-ten-cent stores."[56]

In his determination to promote the Woolworth Building as widely as possible, Woolworth devised multiple strategies for making the skyscraper locally as well as internationally renowned. As he envisioned Gilbert's design, it would compete for the spectator's attention within the strident visual environment of the modern city. In the end, it would become deeply enough ingrained in the city's visual culture to make it a true mass cultural phenomenon. Even before workers began constructing the skyscraper's steel frame, for instance, Woolworth asked that Gilbert retain the noted architectural illustrator Hughson Hawley to "color" Johnson's perspective of the design; Hawley's illustration showed the tower in sparkling white with gilded roofs soaring triumphantly against a blue-and-rose-colored cloud-filled sky. Woolworth then copyrighted the design with the words "F. W. Woolworth Company," photographed it, and sent it to the city's major newspapers, the *New York Times, Herald, World, Tribune,* and *Post,* with instructions for simultaneous publication for the sake of impact in their Sunday editions.[57]

Once the Woolworth Building's steel frame began its incremental rise in the city, Woolworth officially employed McAtamney to launch a still more ambitious campaign of printed news publicity. In the end, McAtamney's advertising program resulted in the documentation of the skyscraper's entire process of construction, culminating in its spectacular opening ceremony of April 24, 1913: President Woodrow Wilson pushed a button on his desk in Washington, D.C., closed an electrical circuit, and the completed Woolworth Building leapt into full view before an expectant crowd of thousands—filling City Hall Park, lining the Jersey shore, and stationed aboard ships up to one hundred miles out at sea—as a brightly illuminated object against the evening darkness. McAtamney flashed news of the event by Marconi wireless to the Eiffel Tower and from there, to all European capitals. What one contemporary called "the premier publicity stunt of this or any other day" made the Woolworth Building "the most widely known office building in the world."[58]

McAtamney continued his program of publicity in a series of illustrated booklets, each designed to celebrate the Woolworth Building for a specific audience of appreciators. First, for those with a stake in the Woolworth Building as a construction enterprise, he conceived *Master Builders* (1913), which featured introductory essays by Woolworth and Gilbert. Woolworth compared his skyscraper to "the awe-inspiring cathedrals of the Middle Ages," and Gilbert called it "a worthy ornament to the great city of New York." Second, for the tourists who visited the Woolworth tower's observatory, he tailored *Above the*

Clouds and Old New York (1913) as an indispensable guidebook, presenting the skyscraper in the tradition of great European landmarks. McAtamney's publications starkly contrasted with *The Woolworth Building* (1913), a commemorative art book that Woolworth commissioned himself for another audience entirely, and that featured an essay by Montgomery Schuyler and etchings by E. Horter: cultivated appreciators of the fine arts. A still later publication, *The Cathedral of Commerce* (1916), probably also suggested by McAtamney, featured a gilded cover resembling a prayer book and text by Edwin A. Cochran highlighting Gilbert's "Gothic lines and tracery." *The Cathedral of Commerce* further identified the skyscraper as an elite as well as ethical white-collar workplace housing "only tenants of the highest standard," each of whom met Woolworth's requirement for "personal integrity."[59] More than the preceding publications, *The Cathedral of Commerce* shaped the broader reception of the Woolworth Building for generations of the future.

McAtamney and Woolworth's program of publicity powerfully influenced contemporary as well as later perceptions of the Woolworth Building. But from the standpoint of sheer advertising, and in particular, advertising of the type that facilitated the sale of the F. W. Woolworth Company's commodities, Woolworth had much more ambitious aims. In achieving those aims, he aggressively deployed Gilbert's design as a trademark—in corporate literature; in advertising; and most important, as imprinted, engraved, and embossed on the commodities themselves—with the aim of strengthening and sharpening the brand identity "Woolworth." That the Woolworth Building resembled a cathedral—recalling at once the cathedral as a great feat of construction, a European landmark, and Christian masterwork—could not have any better served Woolworth's objectives during what amounted to a spectacular, far-reaching, and multifaceted advertising campaign.

Beyond question, Woolworth, McAtamney, and the F. W. Woolworth Company benefited greatly from what amounted to a certain reciprocity between their promotional schemes and the urban environment of New York around 1900. John Van Dyke perceptively assessed that environment in his *New New York* of 1909. He highlighted the city's concentration of capital, its historic emphasis on consumerism and fashion—and with it, the world of consumerist fantasy in which architecture served a supporting role. Equally important, Van

Dyke emphasized the city's pervasive atmosphere of technological modernization, newness, and constant change. "Always a city of commerce, of display, of wealth and luxury, of color and light," New York is, he wrote, "nothing, if not modern. . . . And its average citizen prides himself upon being up to the day, if not ahead of it."[60] Gilbert, appropriately enough, had described his own West Street Building as "for the moment, the latest word on the subject."[61] But Van Dyke went still further: "Half of the 'freak' buildings in New York are not well-meant architectural failures, but deliberate efforts to catch the eye and advertise someone or his wares."[62] To "advertise," regardless of Gilbert's critically acclaimed Skyscraper Gothic design, was, not surprisingly, Woolworth's primary reason for building his "world's greatest skyscraper."

Largely as a consequence of the Woolworth Building's popular acclaim, the journal *Architecture* featured an editorial in 1923 entitled "Who Was the Architect?" It noted that Gilbert's identity as an artist had been, in fact, eclipsed by the fame of his own creation.[63] This Gilbert had already to a certain extent recognized, having written to Ralph Adams Cram in 1920, "I sometimes wish I had never built the Woolworth Building, because I fear it may be regarded as my only work and you and I both know that whatever it may be in dimension and in certain lines it is after all only a skyscraper."[64] As Gilbert accurately sensed, no less than a collision of values, his own and those of F. W. Woolworth, had pervaded all aspects of the Woolworth Building's design, construction, and reception; that is, the values of a Beaux-Arts architect who idealized his role as an "artist" as opposed to those of a retailing innovator keen to spectacularize the skyscraper as an advertising cynosure, whether within the city or within the printed news media and thus the world at large. Gilbert had aimed to design a skyscraper that rivaled his earlier great works of monumental architecture, noted among them the Minnesota State Capitol and United States Custom House. But once he completed the Woolworth Building's design, it was Woolworth who had in fact triumphed, with that design projected as Woolworth's own creation, not to mention his own property, by means of his copyrighting it as a trademark and subsequently actually making it a trademark through a spectacular and far-reaching advertising campaign. Woolworth, furthermore, had discovered in New York's city culture around 1900 no less than the ideal environment—that is, a lively, colorful consumer emporium prizing spectator-

Fig. 9. Woolworth Building, photograph by John Wallace Gillies, ca. 1915. (Avery Architectural and Fine Arts Library, Columbia University)

ship among sidewalk crowds—in which to make such an impact with Gilbert's design.

Gilbert, as if in response to Woolworth's presumed ownership of his creative work, in 1918 privately commissioned the pictorialist photographer John Wallace Gillies to produce a group of views showing the Woolworth Building as *he* preferred to have it seen (fig. 9). Highlighting the beauties of the skyscraper's composition and detail from vantage points that isolated it as a Gothic monument on a snowy winter's day, Gillies's photographs could not have contrasted more with Woolworth's method of aggressively, flamboyantly, and mechanically mass-reproducing the skyscraper's design. Gillies's photographs wholly lacked, significantly, Hughson Hawley's earlier emphasis on brightness, whiteness, gilding, and color. The urban surroundings in which Gillies located the skyscraper, moreover, featured little in the way of "amusements" or competitive and cacophonous commercial display. To the contrary, the photographs linked Gilbert's design—via its public associations with New York's civic center at City Hall Park—to the progressive and dignified urbanity of the City Beautiful movement. The photographs also suggested that Gilbert rejected outright Woolworth's ambitious promotional agenda, which had the objective of fixing the skyscraper within the popular imagination as the newest, the latest, and the most extraordinary of consumer enticements.[65]

It is not known what Louis Sullivan thought about the Woolworth Building. He had completed his last skyscraper, the Bayard-Condict Building, over a decade earlier and more recently had designed a series of banks for small towns in the Midwest, among them the National Farmers' Bank in Owatonna, Minnesota (1906–8), continuing to practice quietly and seemingly at far remove from the center of the American architectural scene. As construction began on the Chicago Tribune Tower in 1923, however, Sullivan did not hesitate to make known his views about the Skyscraper Gothic. His essay "The Chicago Tribune Competition" appeared in *Architectural Record* shortly after the Tribune's jury awarded the competition's prizes. The competition's entries had featured a significant number of Woolworth-inspired Skyscraper Gothic designs, among them a Gothic design by Claude Bragdon.[66] Sullivan, however, focused his criticism on Howells and Hood's first-place Skyscraper Gothic design, and he made explicit his antipathy toward its pictorial, trademark-like crown: "If the monster on top . . . could be gently pried loose, the real building would reveal itself as a rather amiable and delicate affair with a certain grace of fancy." By contrast, Sullivan extolled Eliel Saarinen's second-place design—characterized by graceful, stepped-back massing allowing the verticals to terminate in the sky—as "sublime."[67]

During the same years, Frank Lloyd Wright refined the design of his most notable early skyscraper, the National Life Insurance Company Building, Chicago (1920–25). He dedicated the design to Louis Sullivan.[68] Wright's interest in the skyscraper echoed that of the many European modernists who entered the Chicago Tribune Tower Competition of 1922, among them Walter Gropius, Bruno Taut, and Ludwig Karl Hilberseimer. But Wright's National Life Insurance project, in his view, aimed to fulfill a larger, more intrinsically American "organic" objective, extending Sullivan's ideal of plasticity.[69] Wright's standardized but altogether unified design featured a cantilevered concrete frame and sheathing in copper and glass. Although unbuilt, it served as the starting point for his later St. Mark's Tower project of 1929. There, Wright integrated Sullivan's concept of plasticity within a complex but organic and structurally continuous three-dimensional scheme that utilized rotated, intersecting geometries while introducing his own concept of the tower as a "tree."[70]

Wright explained the principles behind his National Life Insurance Company and St. Mark's Tower projects in his lecture "The Tyranny of the Skyscraper" of 1930, one of the six "Kahn lectures" he delivered that year at Princeton. Importantly, he recounted his first experience with "the tall steel office building as architecture" while working for Louis Sullivan during the early

1890s: in observing Sullivan's process of designing the Wainwright Building, he noted that "the skyscraper as a piece of architecture had arrived." The skyline of New York in the 1920s, by contrast, had shown that "the true nature of this thing [had become] prostitute to the shallow picturesque." As a consequence, Sullivan's "light that shone in the Wainwright Building as a promise" had for a short time "flickered feebly" and was now "fading away." In conceiving those 1920s skyscrapers, architects did not think in terms of "organicism," that is, of investing their designs with the "integrity" he had sought in "standardized steel and glass and copper." They had instead chosen to think of those designs scenographically and, in doing so, developed "a clumsy imitation masonry envelope for a steel skeleton."[71] Wright's words proved to be the most incisive critique of the day's Skyscraper Gothic.

Regardless of Wright's criticism, much less his own remarkably innovative designs, by the end of the 1920s the Skyscraper Gothic did, in fact, carry the day. It had become the style of choice for builders of landmark towers in American cities across the country. Why did the boldly modern and highly innovative designs produced by Wright and others scarcely receive notice? Woolworth and his director of advertising Hugh McAtamney offer at least a partial explanation. Both at the forefront of change in New York, they had, in fact, counted among the first to exploit the commercial tendencies that would become increasingly prominent in the American business climate of the 1920s, when the day's big enterprises commissioned, as Katherine Solomonson has shown, spectacular "trademark towers" to serve the ends of advertising. Those businesses deployed, moreover, the Gothic's associations of "high culture" with the aim of creating through advertising a romantic world of elite fantasy, or "class appeal," for the masses.[72] The environment in which the architect produced such trademark towers, significantly, now incorporated a vivid and colorful array of new media, making it an increasingly competitive, "overheated visual world." Glossy magazines filled with suggestive advertising, along with "movies" and related spectacular entertainments comprised a "world of images" that could be "manipulated to increase business vastly."[73] Architecture, now even more than previously, had to compete within such a broader visual culture. Now it, too, functioned as a vehicle for fantasy and entertainment as well as a potent tool for advertising.

When Gilbert conceived his Skyscraper Gothic designs for the West Street and the Woolworth Buildings, the worlds of big business and big advertising were still in the process of formation. His primary task as a Beaux-Arts architect, as he viewed it, entailed finding a convincing solution for the skyscraper that resonated with the distinctive character of what constituted a startlingly new and prominent building type. But unless that solution met the City Beautiful movement's requirement for urbanity, it would fail to bring decorum and dignity to the city. As a consequence, Gilbert aimed above all else to synthesize Sullivan's modernist principles with the Gothic's capacity for evocatively enhancing skyline views.

By the early 1920s, however, Gilbert's Skyscraper Gothic had become instead, in the hands of the big business enterprises and their advertising agents, a very effective tool for fulfilling their overarching objective of eliciting consumer desire.[74] Given that the trademark towers of big business now defined the skylines of major cities—as opposed to the monumental public buildings and monumental public spaces of the City Beautiful—Cass Gilbert's Skyscraper Gothic, regardless of his own original intentions, had indeed triumphed. It seized the eye of spectators with an energetic verticality, tantalizing ornamentality, and the day's most evocative of historical styles.

NOTES

1. This essay expands a theme that I treated briefly in *The Skyscraper and the City: The Woolworth Building and the Making of Modern New York* (Chicago: University of Chicago Press, 2008).

2. *The International Competition for a New Administration Building for the Chicago Tribune MCMXXII* (1923; reprinted as *Chicago Tribune Tower Competition*, vol. 1 [New York: Rizzoli, 1980], 3); Egerton Swartwout, "Review of Recent Architectural Magazines," *American Architect* 123 (February 18, 1923): 209, as qtd. in Katherine Solomonson, *The Chicago Tribune Tower Competition: Skyscraper Design and Cultural Change in the 1920s* (New York: Cambridge University Press, 2001), 99.

3. "Woolworth Building Will Be World's Greatest Skyscraper," *New York Times,* May 7, 1911.

4. Viollet-le-Duc references "organic" in his entry "Style" in *Dictionnaire raisonné de l'architecture:* "This is what our school of lay architects of the end of the twelfth century actually accomplished: they devised a structural system that was free, extensive, and applicable to every kind of plan . . . they endowed that structural system with a form that was nothing less than a wholly organic expression of the system itself" (see "Style," in *The Foundations of*

Architecture: Selections from the "Dictionnaire raisonné," introd. Barry Bergdoll, trans. Kenneth D. Whitehead [New York: Braziller, 1990], 252–53). According to Eidlitz, forms arose "naturally out of the conditions of the structure, out of the idea which has given rise to it" (Leopold Eidlitz, *The Nature and Function of Art, More Especially of Architecture* [London, 1881], excerpted as "L. Eidlitz, Form and Function in Architecture," in *America Builds*, ed. Leland Roth [New York: Harper and Row, 1983], 276). On Eidlitz's *Nature and Function of Art*, see Kathryne E. Holliday, *Leopold Eidlitz: Architecture and Idealism in the Gilded Age* (New York: Norton, 2008), 141–66.

5. For recent scholarship on Cram, Goodhue, Warren, and Bragdon, see Douglass Shand-Tucci, *Ralph Adams Cram: An Architect's Four Quests: Medieval, Modernist, American, Ecumenical* (Amherst: University of Massachusetts Press, 2005); Maureen Meister, *Architecture and the Arts and Crafts Movement in Boston: Harvard's H. Langford Warren* (Hanover: University Press of New England, 2003); and Jonathan Massey, *Crystal and Arabesque: Claude Bragdon, Ornament, and Modern Architecture* (Pittsburgh: University of Pittsburgh Press, 2009). Gilbert's correspondence with Cram dates from at least 1906 (as documented in the Cass Gilbert Papers, Manuscript Division, Library of Congress; and the American Institute of Architects Office Files, AIA). He held in high regard Cram's St. Thomas's Church, New York, but Cram's antimodern viewpoint, indebted to the New England intellectuals Charles Eliot Norton and Henry Adams, had little influence over his designs for skyscrapers (see Michael Brooks, "New England Gothic," in *Studies in the History of Art 35: The Architectural Historian in America*, ed. Elizabeth Blair MacDougall [Washington, D.C.: National Gallery of Art and University Press of New England, 1990], 113–25; and Shand-Tucci, *Ralph Adams Cram*, 42–46, 234). On Cram's antimodernism, see T. J. Jackson Lears, *No Place of Grace: Antimodernism and the Transformation of American Culture, 1880–1920* (New York: Pantheon, 1981), 203–9.

6. On Hamlin's perspective as a critic, see A. D. F. Hamlin, "The Battle of the Styles," *Architectural Record* 1 (January/March 1892): 265–75; and A. D. F. Hamlin, "Twenty-Five Years of American Architecture," *Architectural Record* 40 (June 1916): 1–14. For his role as a professor of architectural history within Columbia University's Beaux-Arts curriculum in architecture, see Richard Plunz, "Reflections on Ware, Hamlin, McKim, and the Politics of History on the Cusp of Historicism," in *The History of History in American Schools of Architecture, 1865–1975*, ed. Gwendolyn Wright and Janet Parks (New York: Temple Hoyne Buell Center for the Study of American Architecture and Princeton Architectural Press, 1990), 56–58.

7. Montgomery Schuyler, "The Woolworth Building," in *American Architecture and Other Writings by Montgomery Schuyler*, ed. William H. Jordy and Ralph Coe (Cambridge: Belknap Press of Harvard University Press, 1961), 2:616.

8. Frederick Stymetz Lamb, "Modern Use of the Gothic: The Possibilities of New Architectural Style," *Craftsman* 8 (May 1905): 150–70.

9. Bertram C. Goodhue, "The Romanticist Point of View"; A. D. F. Hamlin, "Style in

Architecture"; and Louis H. Sullivan, "Reply to Mr. Frederick Stymetz Lamb on 'Modern Use of the Gothic: The Possibility of New Architectural Style," *Craftsman* 8 (June 1905): 325–38.

10. Lamb, "Modern Use of the Gothic," 160, 164, 169–70.

11. Goodhue, "The Romanticist Point of View," 332. Beginning in 1903, Goodhue was managing Cram, Goodhue, and Ferguson's project for the United States Military Academy at West Point from an office in New York (Shand-Tucci, *Ralph Adams Cram,* 67–71).

12. Plunz, "Reflections on Ware, Hamlin, and McKim," 57.

13. Hamlin, "Style in Architecture," 326, 329, 331.

14. Sullivan, "Reply to Mr. Frederick Stymetz Lamb," 336–38.

15. Louis Sullivan, "The Tall Office Building Artistically Considered," *Lippincott's,* March 1896; reprinted in *Kindergarten Chats and Other Writings* (1918; repr., New York: Dover, 1979), 202–13.

16. Louis H. Sullivan, "The Modern Phase of Architecture," *Architectural Annual* 1 (1900): 27.

17. See esp. Ralph Waldo Emerson, "Nature" (1836), in *Selected Writings of Emerson,* ed. Donald McQuade (New York: Modern Library, 1981), 5–42; and Otto Wagner, *Modern Architecture: A Guidebook for His Students in this Field of Art,* 3rd ed. (1902; repr., Santa Monica, CA: Getty Center for the History of Art and the Humanities, 1988). The first edition of Wagner's book was published in 1896. Wagner had, in turn, similarly directed his lectures toward a younger group of architects. Within a year, those architects founded the Vienna Secession.

18. Cass Gilbert, "The Architecture of Today," lecture at U.S. Military Academy at West Point, May 4, 1909, pp. 1–4, Box 16, Cass Gilbert Papers, Manuscript Division, Library of Congress. Gilbert began his lecture with a reference to the monuments of the "past ages" and their importance to the contemporary architect, emphasizing that "architecture is of all the arts of man the record of the civilization that produced it," that "architecture is not an inventive art" but rather "a progressive one and develops by evolution," and that "it is too much to expect that *Art* will keep pace with material changes of usage and of form." Then, quoting Sullivan's "form follows function," he noted that "no better example of this truth can be found than in the building of a skyscraper."

19. On Gilbert's high regard for the writings of Viollet-le-Duc, see Fenske, *The Skyscraper and the City,* 83, 333n16.

20. For Gilbert's connections with the architectural and construction cultures of Chicago during his early years of practice in St. Paul, see ibid., 93–99; and Sharon Irish, "West Hails East: Cass Gilbert in Minnesota," *Minnesota History* 53 (Spring 1993): 202.

21. Cass Gilbert, as qtd. in "Skyscrapers and the Skyline of the Future: Leading Architects of New York See Many Practical and Aesthetic Problems Created by the Present High Building Technology," *New York Times,* May 10, 1908.

22. Cass Gilbert, "The Architecture of Today" (1909), 4–5, 8–9. In his use of Sullivan's

"form follows function," Gilbert was referencing the following sentence in "The Tall Office Building Artistically Considered," 208: "It is the pervading law of all things organic, and inorganic, of all things physical and metaphysical, of all things human and superhuman, of all true manifestations of the head, of the heart, of the soul, that life is recognizable in its expression, that form ever follows function."

23. Cass Gilbert emphasized in "The Architecture of Today" (1909) that he composed designs such as the United States Custom House for "pictorial interest" (10). See "Cass Gilbert's New York Custom House Design," *Inland Architect and News Record* 35 (February 1900): 7; and Fenske, *The Skyscraper and the City*, 83–93.

24. Julien Guadet, *Eléments et théories de l'architecture,* livre 8 (Paris: Librairie de la construction moderne, 1901–4), 455–60.

25. On Gilbert's process of designing the West Street Building, see Fenske, *The Skyscraper and the City,* 106–14.

26. Unpublished essay written by Cass Gilbert on December 2, 1897, box 6, Cass Gilbert Papers, Manuscript Division, Library of Congress.

27. Cass Gilbert to Julia Finch Gilbert, August 1, 1906, box 8, Cass Gilbert Papers, Manuscript Division, Library of Congress.

28. John C. Van Dyke, *The New New York: A Commentary on the Place and the People* (New York: Macmillan, 1909), 123–24.

29. Ibid., 124.

30. Ibid., 126.

31. Montgomery Schuyler, "The West Street Building," *Architectural Record* 22 (August 1907): 109.

32. William Jordy and Ralph Coe, "Editors' Introduction" to *American Architecture and Other Writings by Montgomery Schuyler,* abridged, ed. Jordy and Coe (New York: Atheneum, 1964), 4–8.

33. Montgomery Schuyler, "Gothic Revivals," in "Notes & Comments," *Architectural Record* 19 (January 1906): 67.

34. Jordy and Coe, "Editors' Introduction" to *American Architecture and Other Writings,* 39. Not surprisingly, Schuyler called Sullivan "essentially the most Gothic of all" in his "Gothic Revivals," 67. In doing so, he references Ralph Adams Cram, adding that Cram understood the principles undergirding Sullivan's designs, by contrast to "the architect who regards his business as form-mongery, and a historical style as merely a storage warehouse of forms." Such an architect would find "nothing at all Gothic about Mr. Sullivan's work."

35. Jordy and Coe, "Editors' Introduction" to *American Architecture and Other Writings,* 22–23

36. Schuyler, "West Street Building," 109.

37. Claude Bragdon, "Architecture in the United States III: The Skyscraper," *Architectural Record* 26 (August 1909): 96.

38. Ibid., 92.

39. Ibid., 90.

40. Claude Bragdon, "L'Art Nouveau and American Architecture," paper presented at a meeting of the Architectural League of America, 1903, as qtd. in Massy, *Crystal and Arabesque,* 70.

41. Ibid. Bragdon continued: "a period in which the soul comes near the surface of life, sweeping away existing conventions and creating for its expression a new symbolism and a new art."

42. Bragdon, "Architecture in the United States III: The Skyscraper," 96.

43. Johnson's drawings for Gilbert's earlier projects, and in particular his study for the New Haven Railroad Station, 1906, suggest that he kept an eye on European avant-garde developments, among them those identified with the Art Nouveau and the Vienna Secession. The New Haven Railroad Station is illustrated in Janet Parks, "Avery," *American Heritage* 35 (April/May 1984): 69.

44. Cass Gilbert, "The Relation of the Architect to His Client, to the Builder, and to His Brother-Architect, and the Organization of the Architect's Work, lecture delivered at Harvard School of Architecture on February 20, 1912, box 16, Cass Gilbert Papers, Manuscript Division, Library of Congress.

45. Cass Gilbert, "The Tenth Birthday of a Notable Structure," *Real Estate Magazine of New York* 11 (May 1923): 344.

46. Cass Gilbert, "Regarding the Woolworth Building" (1927), box 17, Cass Gilbert Papers, Manuscript Division, Library of Congress, 1.

47. Ibid., 2.

48. Although Gilbert never mentioned the Cloth Hall, Yprès, it is likely that the spire of its central tower also served as a reference for the Woolworth's pinnacle observatory.

49. Cass Gilbert, as qtd. in Charles Moore, "Cass Gilbert, Architect, 1859–1934," *American Architect* 144 (July 1934): 20; Cass Gilbert to C. F. Vandervoort, March 1, 1913, personal letterbooks, Cass Gilbert Collection, New-York Historical Society. See also Fenske, *The Skyscraper and the City,* 268–69.

50. On Gilbert and his office staff's process of designing the Woolworth Building, see Fenske, *The Skyscraper and the City,* 126–60.

51. Montgomery Schuyler, "'The Towers of Manhattan' and Notes on the Woolworth Building," *Architectural Record* 33 (February 1913): 104.

52. Schuyler, "The Woolworth Building," 615, 617–18.

53. On "form-mongery," see Montgomery Schuyler, "Gothic Revivals," in "Notes & Comments," *Architectural Record* 19 (January 1906): 67.

54. Schuyler, "The Woolworth Building," 616.

55. Ibid., 606, 618–20. Jordy and Coe, "Editors' Introduction" to *American Architecture and Other Writings,* 40, note that Schuyler did not find in any design a "solution" to the

problem of the skyscraper. I would argue that instead Gilbert's skyscrapers came very close to fulfilling Schuyler's criteria as a critic, as is evident in his evaluations of them.

56. On Woolworth's experiences with architecture for the purpose of advertising his commodities to passersby, see Fenske, *The Skyscraper and the City,* 25–29; and for his vision of the skyscraper as a "giant signboard," see ibid., 25, 29.

57. On Woolworth's scheme for publicizing Gilbert's design, see ibid., 163–65.

58. Spark, "How Hugh McAtamney Put the Woolworth Building on the International Map," *Real Estate Magazine* 2 (May 1913): 48, 50. For a full account of McAtamney's program of publicity during the skyscraper's construction and for its opening, see Fenske, *The Skyscraper and the City*, 210–15, 218–23.

59. *The Master Builders: A Record of the Construction of the World's Highest Commercial Structure* (Baltimore: Munder-Thomsen, 1913), 5, 9; *Above the Clouds and Old New York* (New York: Hugh McAtamney, 1913); Edwin A. Cochran, *The Cathedral of Commerce: Woolworth Building, New York* (New York: Broadway–Park Place Company, 1916), n.p.

60. Van Dyke, *The New New York,* 168, 425.

61. Cass Gilbert to R. Clipston Sturgis, November 8, 1906, personal letterbooks, Cass Gilbert Collection, New-York Historical Society.

62. Van Dyke, *The New New York,* 8–9.

63. "Who Was the Architect?" *Architecture* 47 (December 1923): 407.

64. Cass Gilbert to Ralph Adams Cram, December 23, 1920, personal letterbook dated December 1920 to February 1922, Cass Gilbert Collection, New-York Historical Society, as qtd. in Mary Beth Betts, "Cass Gilbert: Twelve Projects," in *Inventing the Skyline: The Architecture of Cass Gilbert,* ed. Margaret Heilbrun (New York: Columbia University Press, 2000), 126.

65. *Woolworth Building, New York, NY, Cass Gilbert, Architect,* 1918 (photographs by Wallace Gillies), Avery Library, Classics Collection.

66. Bragdon's design received an "honorable mention" (Massey, *Crystal and Arabesque,* 257–58; *The International Competition for a New Administration Building for the "Chicago Tribune," MCMXXII,* 70).

67. Louis Sullivan, "The Chicago Tribune Competition," *Architectural Record* 53 (February 1923): 151–57. See also Katherine Solomonson, *The Chicago Tribune Tower Competition: Skyscraper Design and Cultural Change in the 1920s* (New York: Cambridge University Press, 2001), 175.

68. In his autobiography, Wright explained that he was fortunate to have developed preliminary drawings and to have shown them to Louis Sullivan before he died in 1924. According to Wright, Sullivan called the design "a work of great art" and added: "I knew what I was talking about all these years—you see? I could never have done this building myself, but believe that, but for me, you could never have done it" (Frank Lloyd Wright, *An Autobiography* [1932], as qtd. in *Frank Lloyd Wright: An American Architecture*, ed. Edgar Kaufmann [New York: Bramhall House, 1955], 120).

69. Joseph Siry, "Wright's Price Tower: Context, Clients, and Construction," in *Prairie Skyscraper: Frank Lloyd Wright's Price Tower,* ed. Anthony Alofsin (New York: Rizzoli, 2005), 70–71.

70. Ibid.; Hilary Ballon, "From New York to Bartlesville: The Pilgrimage of Wright's Skyscraper," in *Prairie Skyscraper,* 105.

71. Ibid., 108; Frank Lloyd Wright, "The Tyranny of the Skyscraper" (1930), in *Frank Lloyd Wright: The Future of Architecture* (New York: Horizon, 1953), 166, 177, 178–79.

72. Solomonson, *The Chicago Tribune Tower Competition,* 37–41, 99–105.

73. David Van Zanten, "'Twenties Gothic," *New Mexico Studies in the Fine Arts* 7 (1982): 21, 23. On advertising in the 1920s, and especially for the significance of the skyscraper in that advertising, see Roland Marchand, *Advertising the American Dream: Making Way for Modernity* (Berkeley: University of California Press, 1985), xv–xxii, 1–7, 77–80, 94–104, 115–27, 235–47, 255–59.

74. See esp. Marchand, *Advertising the American Dream,* 235, on "visual clichés," which induced individuals "to recapitulate in their own fantasies the shared daydreams of society."

THE GOTHIC REVIVAL AND THE CHICAGO SCHOOL

From Naturalistic Ornament to Constructive Expression

Joanna Merwood-Salisbury

While the Gothic skyscraper type popular in the United States in the early twentieth century is easy to identify, locating the first one built is as impossible a task as finding the first skeleton-framed building. Just as there is an almost infinite series of gradations between "masonry" and "iron" construction, there is also a great deal of variation in what has and might be considered "Gothic." For decades, starting in the 1920s, critics were adamant that the architecture of the Chicago school was defined by an absence of regard for style, that the new construction methods that made the skyscraper possible also made any reference to historical precedent irrelevant. "What Chartres was to the Gothic Cathedral, the Montauk was to the high commercial building," the architect Thomas Tallmadge wrote in 1941, referring to a ten-story building designed by the architects Burnham and Root in 1882–83.[1] In other words, both buildings represented the rejection of the past and the beginning of an entirely new tradition. However, attention to the buildings that make up the canon of the Chicago school, and analysis of the writing of contemporary architects, quickly reveal that the pragmatism associated with the Chicago school included the expedient adaptation of historical styles to new purposes. In the mid-1880s the Gothic cathedral was the obvious reference point for the creators of the twelve- and sixteen-story buildings appearing on the Chicago skyline. As American architects had learned from John Ruskin and Eugène-Emmanuel Viollet-le-Duc, the Gothic was not a static style but a flexible one, easily adaptable to modern uses. In this way it was an ideal precedent for the skyscraper, and variations on Gothic motifs were widely utilized into the 1880s. Although changing methods of construction made mid-nineteenth-century Gothic Revival forms difficult to maintain, and the popularity of the Romanesque Revival temporarily superseded them, Gothic themes persisted as a popular way to ornament the skyscraper into the 1890s. Remarkably elastic in its meaning, the style retained its prestige as a signifier of material truth and political freedom, even as it was attached to an ever-greater variety of signifying monuments. This essay traces the transformation of ideas of the Gothic in Chicago's commercial architecture from 1871 to the turn of the twentieth century, focusing in particular on the transformation of the Gothic from a morally correct style to a rational constructive principle, a transformation that enabled local architects to untether the Gothic Revival from its antimodern connotations and to embrace it as a suitable aesthetic expression for the architecture of an urbanized, industrial society.

THE COMMERCIAL GOTHIC

Chicago architects began adapting medieval building styles for commercial purposes during the period of rebuilding that followed the disastrous fire of 1871. At this time the Gothic Revival was at the height of its popularity in the United States, denoting high quality and good taste.[2] Businesses establishing regional offices in Chicago, the hub of the rapidly developing American "West" (as the territory west of the Ohio River was known), commissioned buildings in this style, including the American Express Company Building drawn up by the Boston-based architect H. H. Richardson.[3] Begun in 1872, the design for this prominent and influential building included a towering mansard with Gothic dormers. While the American Express Building is the best known from this era, the Gothic Revival became the default style for any commercial building with pretense to significance in downtown Chicago. Around 1875 the real estate pages of local newspapers described numerous four- and five-story buildings being constructed in the devastated downtown business area as being of the "modern Gothic order," in the "secular Gothic" or "English commercial Gothic" style.[4]

These experiments in the commercial Gothic reflected, both stylistically and intellectually, architectural ideas and precedents from the cultural centers of New York, Boston, and Philadelphia, and beyond, from England, France, and Germany. The postfire generation of commercial Gothic structures included buildings by the recent New York transplant Peter B. Wight and his firm, Carter, Drake, and Wight, including the Lenox Building (1872) (fig. 1); and by William Le Baron Jenney, the most prominent architect in Chicago at that time, including the Portland Block (1872) and Mason Block (1880) (fig. 2).[5] Eclectic rather than strictly imitative, these buildings all contained some combination of the characteristic Gothic features: narrow windows with pointed arches, naturalistic ornament, and polychromatic stone and brick surfaces. Together they illustrate the widespread adoption of the Gothic for secular purposes in the United States, the free way in which it was interpreted in the West, and the beginning of its adaptation to new functional needs and methods of building.

Wight's long-standing advocacy of the Gothic as the most appropriate way of building began with his early career in New York City, and his connections to the art journals the *New Path* and the *Crayon* during the 1860s.[6] Inspired by Ruskin, American architects like Wight believed the Gothic had social implications, as well as structural and material ones. For Ruskin the difference between the Gothic and the classical was stark. While the classical presented a dull and rigid set of aesthetic formulae, he saw the Gothic, and the Gothic cathedral in particular, as a living mode of expression, changeable and adaptable to new contexts and uses, new places and peoples. In political terms, it symbolized a communal art form representative of the ideal of equal and collaborative endeavor.[7] Ruskin's American disciples rejected buildings in the Greek neoclassical style such as the New York Customs House (1842), the Philadelphia Mint (1833), and the United States Treasury in Washington, D.C. (1842) as "pestilent" forms of "skeleton copyism."[8] In contrast, they considered Gothic Revival buildings to be characterized by "expression of purpose, honest construction or artistic decoration."[9] Experiments in this style by architects such as Jacob Wrey Mould

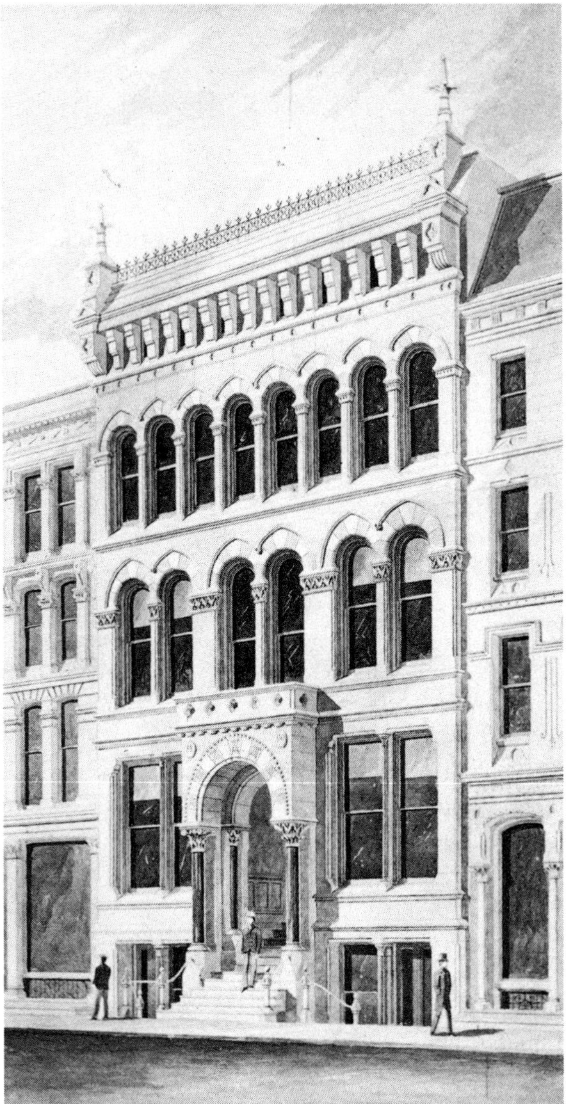

Fig. 1. Carter, Drake and Wight, *Lenox Building: Presentation Drawing, Perspective View of Front Facade*, ca. 1872. (Daniel H. Burnham Collection, Ryerson and Burnham Archives, The Art Institute of Chicago, digital file no.194301_110518-015)

Fig. 2. William Le Baron Jenney, Portland Block, SE corner of Dearborn and Washington Streets, ca. 1900, J. W. Taylor, photographer. (Historic Landscape and Image Collection, Ryerson and Burnham Archives, The Art Institute of Chicago, digital file no. 2261)

and Leopold Eidlitz were praised as robust and imaginative.[10] Wight himself employed the Ruskinian Gothic in his designs for the National Academy of Design in Manhattan (1865) and the Mercantile Library in Brooklyn (1867). In 1856 an anonymous review of Fergusson's *Handbook of Architecture* in the *Crayon* summed up the principles of the Gothic style: materials are used that are best suited to their purposes; construction is displayed, and nothing superfluous is added; as in the cathedral, every worker has a specific job to do; there is room in the building for "every art and every intellect."[11]

The moral associations of the Gothic Revival were particularly important in

Chicago. Even more so than New York, Chicago was considered the American Gotham, a city dedicated entirely to making money.[12] Established in 1833, the midwestern metropolis was constantly disparaged during the nineteenth century for lack of cultural feeling and spiritual sensitivity on the part of its citizens, and for the poor quality of its architecture. Here untrained local builders produced "the vilest architecture . . . extensive embellishments in forms never dreamed of by civilized architects," sniffed the *Crayon* in 1859.[13] In the wake of the fire that destroyed a great portion of the city, local architects aimed to undo this negative reputation. In the minds of architects like Wight (who moved to Chicago in 1871) and Jenney, the adaptation of the Gothic to commercial buildings was a fitting form of aesthetic evolution. In particular it lent the social cohesiveness of preindustrial northern European village life to a rapidly industrializing city on the western American frontier. The use of the Gothic Revival for office buildings that housed banks and insurance companies provided new and often financially precarious institutions with the moral authority previously held by sacred architecture.

Just as the moral distinction between "true" Gothic architecture, in the Ruskinian sense, and its modern counterparts became muddied, so did the formal distinction between Gothic and modern forms. Local architects like Wight and Jenney utilized Gothic Revival elements while at the same time adhering to a simplified planning method suitable to commercial programs and to their clients' demands for efficiency and economy. Though some of their clients were Chicago-based business owners, most were East Coast–based real estate interests, absentee landlords who cared little for worthy architectural ideals. Wight and Jenney employed a rational method of planning inspired by what they called the "French School" (meaning the Beaux-Arts), a method better adapted to the need for a regular structure, open-plan interiors, and large windows than the asymmetrical and idiosyncratic Gothic Revival popular in England.[14] For example, with its symmetrical facade and tripartite horizontal and vertical divisions, the three-story Mason Block is as classical as it is Gothic. The medieval influence was restricted to a row of narrow windows with pointed arches on the top floor. The six-story Portland Block is similarly regular in its form, Gothic only in the ornamented pediments over the doors and polychromatic brick and stonework.

Implying intellectual and spiritual correctness, if not strict stylistic authenticity, the commercial Gothic Revival style ensured prestige for the architect and, with luck, high returns for his patron and longevity for the building itself. Jenney's Portland Block, in particular, became a well-loved monument, one of the few buildings constructed immediately after the 1871 fire to survive longer than ten years.[15] On the occasion of its sale in 1889, the Portland was described as "one of the best and most favorably known in the city of Chicago" and "the patriarch among Chicago's office buildings."[16] However, with some exceptions, Gothic styling was not enough to save most of the postfire commercial buildings. Beginning in the early 1880s the land on which they stood was simply too valuable to support four- and five-story buildings, and the majority were demolished in favor of much taller ones. At twelve stories high, these were the first "skyscrapers." This new building type became the highly visible representative of rapid though erratic economic growth, and of dramatic social change, a symbol not universally embraced by Chicagoans or by foreign visitors. In the face of widespread ambivalence over the skyscraper type, Chicago architects continued to draw on Gothic symbolism to lend the new building form aesthetic and moral authority.

THE "AMERICAN ECLECTIC GOTHIC"

The center of skyscraper construction in Chicago was the south end of La Salle Street, the new financial district anchored by the Chicago Board of Trade, completed in 1885. The result of a controversial competition, W. W. Boyington's eclectic Board of Trade Building quickly became the most infamous building in Chicago, almost singlehandedly prompting a transformation of local ideas about the Gothic Revival (fig. 3). With its complicated massing, riotous color scheme, and elaborate ornament incorporating representations of Ceres, the Roman goddess of agriculture, holding shafts of wheat, we might categorize the Board of Trade as a classic example of Victorian Gothic, with all the negative associations that term has come to denote. With few exceptions, Boyington's educated contemporaries viewed it as a notorious example of bad taste. "[Boyington's] work is of no style," the New York critic Montgomery Schuyler proclaimed, "a proposition not invalidated by the probability that he himself

Fig. 3. W. W. Boyington, Board of Trade Building, 141 W. Jackson Blvd. at LaSalle St., ca. 1885–1900, J. W. Taylor, photographer. (J. W. Taylor Collection, Ryerson and Burnham Archives, The Art Institute of Chicago, digital file no. 16512)

would call it 'American eclectic Gothic.' We all know what the untutored and aboriginal architect stretches that term to cover."[17] The Board of Trade was politically as well as aesthetically contentious. Though it was designed to celebrate the collective wealth of the city, local working-class activists saw it as a powerful symbol of capitalism's tyrannical rule over labor. Dogged by strikes throughout its construction, its inaugural banquet was disrupted by the clamor of a loud demonstration outside. In a sardonic reference to this angry display, Schuyler observed: "It is difficult to contemplate its bustling and uneasy façade without feeling a certain sympathy with the mob of anarchists that 'demonstrated' under its windows on the night of its opening. If they were really anarchists, it was very ungrateful of them, for one would go far to find a more perfect expression of anarchy in architecture."[18] Though satirical, these comments reveal a parallel between the aesthetics of the tall office building and the social tensions dividing the city.

For Ruskin, the Gothic style represented an ideal of social harmony and cooperation, an antidote to the problems caused in England by industrialization. This ideal was no less appealing in Chicago, a city founded to process the agricultural products of the western plains for consumption back East. This processing occurred on a vast scale, requiring the labor of thousands of industrial workers. The rapid growth of the city was accompanied by social unrest. During the 1880s Chicago was wracked by a series of strikes that created deep antagonisms between capital and labor, between the middle and working classes, and between different ethnic groups, most particularly between native-born Americans and recent immigrants.[19] Culminating in the infamous Haymarket bombing of 1886, these strikes were the result of volatile economic conditions created by rapid industrialization and exacerbated by lack of regulation of prices or wages. Labor conflicts were cast in explicitly ethnic terms, pitting business owners with roots in the American Northeast against their labor force, recent immigrants from southern and eastern Europe. In this context, the Gothic Revival style became a useful ideological tool. Representative of social harmony and cooperation, the American version of the Gothic was to be the aesthetic expression of a unified culture, one that represented the strength and power of business as a common enterprise, healing the rift between immigrant labor and business leaders.

Despite these useful symbolic associations, Chicago architects soon began to wonder if the "American eclectic Gothic" was entirely suitable for the new commercial and industrial buildings springing up in and around the Loop, as the center of the city was known. They wondered if popular variations on the Gothic Revival might reflect an unbecoming obsession with fashion rather than eternal ideals of material truthfulness and social cooperation. Perhaps thinking of the Board of Trade, in 1889 Jenney criticized the high Victorian Gothic with its "thrust and counter-thrust of innumerable arches, pinnacles and buttresses" and "startling combination of colors or materials which flash upon and dazzle the sight, as the blare of trumpets deafens the ears."[20] In downtown Chicago, he argued, such violent aesthetic stimulation was undesirable. Architects should instead endeavor to achieve architectural "repose." "Business buildings should have a quiet dignity," he concluded, "a simple, massive grandeur that will not grow tiresome, that will, by the very sight of them, tend to rest men from the worry and turmoil of the struggle for bread."[21] The architect John W. Root echoed the same idea: the business block should be monolithic and plain, he wrote, since metropolitan dwellers are too busy to appreciate fine detail.[22]

Above all it was more and more difficult to reconcile the practical requirements of the skyscraper with the picturesque features of the Gothic Revival. The physical form and interior requirements of these large buildings, the practical conditions of their construction, and changes in fashion made overt Gothic styling go out of favor by the late 1880s. As Carol Willis has explained, the first skyscrapers were designed with mathematical precision, every detail dictated by precise real estate formulae that maximized profitability.[23] These rationalized buildings were erected by newly bureaucratic architecture practices and building trades organizations, each characterized by ever-increasing specialization. The significant changes in planning, structure, scale, and labor practices involved in building the skyscraper, what the critic Schuyler would later call "the general uniformity of the problem," made the eclectic, asymmetrical Gothic Revival style difficult to accommodate.[24]

THE ROMANESQUE REVIVAL

Prompted by changes in both fashion and programmatic need, eclectic Gothic Revival ornament and massing began to fall out of favor during the 1880s, superseded by the solid, square, and simply ornamented Romanesque Revival.[25] The adoption of the Romanesque in Chicago was due to two strains of influence. The first was the work of a group of German émigrés trained in the cubic, round-arched, Romanesque-derived *Rundbogendstil* (round-arch style) popular in Germany in the mid-nineteenth century. This group included Frederick Baumann, Augustus Bauer, and Otto H. Matz.[26] Though most of the buildings constructed in this style, such as Baumann's Marine Bank (1854), were destroyed in the 1871 fire, their memory lived on. The other influence came from H. H. Richardson, whose colossal Marshall Field Wholesale Store built just west of the Board of Trade in 1885–87 popularized his particular version of the Romanesque Revival in Chicago and across the country.[27]

The adoption of the Romanesque Revival for large-scale commercial work is most clearly evident in the work of Burnham and Root, later D. H. Burnham and Co., the most prominent firm in the city in the postfire era. Former employees of Peter B. Wight, Burnham and Root employed Gothic Revival motifs in many of their early buildings. However, in the mid-1880s, as they took on a number of important commercial commissions, the two architects began to experiment with the early medieval Romanesque style, creating a series of critically acclaimed buildings that served as model office blocks both locally and nationally. For Burnham and Root, the Romanesque Revival had two principal virtues when compared to the Gothic, one practical and the other symbolic. First, its simple massing, square bays, and heavy masonry walls were better suited to the rationalized plans and large scale of modern business buildings. Second, in the hands of Richardson, this style was popularly believed to represent the birth of an indigenous architectural style in the United States. According to professional lore, the Romanesque style had never been fully developed in Europe. In this way its rude and primitive vigor was ideally suited to the geography and climate of the American West, and to the robust character of the new American being formed there. For Chicago architects the local adaptation of the Romanesque was the solution to the intellectual struggle to find an indigenous style representative of a new "race" of Americans being born on the Western frontier.[28] With its simple forms, heavy massing, and understated ornament, it could best represent the pragmatism and strength of the western peoples, and convey the sense of "repose" sought by Jenney and Root. Burnham and Root's monumental Rookery Building (1886), combining a heavy masonry exterior with finely detailed iron interior structure and ornament, is celebrated as one of the finest products of the commercial Romanesque Revival.

However, when considering the origins of the Gothic skyscraper tradition in the United States, it is instructive to consider two slightly later Burnham and Root buildings, the Woman's Temple on LaSalle Street and the Masonic Temple on State and Randolph Streets, both completed in 1892. Starting in the early 1890s, new construction methods made the heavy exterior walls of the Romanesque Revival style more difficult to justify. With their monumental scale, emphatic verticality, and elaborately gabled roofs, the two temple buildings reconciled Gothic and Romanesque Revival ornament with the simple, block-like massing and veil-like facades of the contemporary tall office building (figs. 4 and 5).[29] These two buildings have not fared well in architectural

Fig. 4. Burnham and Root, Woman's Temple, 102–116 S. LaSalle St. on SW corner of W. Monroe St., 1892, J. W. Taylor, photographer. (J. W. Taylor Collection, Ryerson and Burnham Archives, The Art Institute of Chicago, digital file no. 199303_120806_052)

history. Modernist architectural historians including Carl Condit condemned their eclectic borrowing from the Gothic and Romanesque as fundamentally unsuited to the practical realities of skyscraper construction and function.[30] Yet as contemporary historians have recognized, the use of historic ornament in buildings of the Chicago school was essential to the effort to elevate the image of the tall office building.[31] Beyond simple capitalist machines, their architects imagined them to have significant parts to play in the creation of social cohesion.

Fig. 5. Burnham and Root, Masonic Temple, State and Randolph Streets, 1892. (Library of Congress, Prints and Photographs Collection, LC-USZ62–123683)

In the case of Burnham and Root's two temple buildings, the complex aesthetic treatment signified their cultural importance: both buildings were commissioned by organizations dedicated to civic reform. The Woman's Christian Temperance Union was a philanthropic organization dedicated to preaching abstinence from alcohol to workingmen. The Freemasons aimed to imbue an urban population with the values of independence, practicality, and Christian morality derived from the ancient fraternity of stonemasons. These organizations became the vehicles through which old class and ethnic ties could be dissolved and a new vision of social and urban unity projected. The headquarters of these two organizations reflected these values: they were designed to prove that the tall office building could have cultural as well as economic importance. Together they were intended to exemplify the redemptive potential of the skyscraper, reimagining its program as a truly public enterprise rather than one restricted solely to business interests.

Besides the symbolism of its ornament, the Masonic Temple illustrates the transformation from masonry to steel-framed construction for which the Chicago school became famous. Despite being commissioned by a group founded on the celebration of the craft of masonry, the Masonic Temple was constructed using the new method of "Chicago construction." This method involved erecting an iron or steel frame to support the weight of the building, and clipping on exterior walls afterward. It allowed for very tall buildings, twenty stories and higher (the Masonic Temple was twenty-two), with lightweight, porous curtain walls, flexible interior arrangements, and rapid construction. In most cases the frame was erected in just a few weeks and the whole building completed in one summer construction season. From the point of view of the architect and the building developer, the Chicago construction was especially desirable because it diminished the role played by traditional tradesmen, bricklayers, and stonemasons on the building site. These ancient trades were the most organized and powerful, and the most involved in strike action during the 1880s. To drastically reduce their importance on any building site meant a substantial saving of time and money. The transformation from masonry to frame construction resulted not only in increased efficiency and productivity; it also had significant implications for the interpretation of the Gothic as a suitable historical model.

THE "CHICAGO CONSTRUCTION"

In the pages of the *Inland Architect,* the professional journal published from 1883 to 1908, Chicago architects debated not only the details of the new Chicago construction but also the appropriate historical style with which to give it aesthetic expression. Some critics, including Kansas City–based Henry Van Brunt, believed the Chicago construction was incommensurate with the Gothic Revival style. "Such a problem does not call for the same sort of architectural inspirations as the building of a vaulted cathedral in the Middle Ages," he wrote in 1889.[32] "The one required a century of deliberate and patient toil to complete it; the other must be finished, equipped, and occupied in a year of strenuous and carefully ordered labor."[33] Others countered that, as a historical precedent relying on buttresses rather than masonry walls for its primary structure, the Gothic continued to provide a valuable example. In 1896 Schuyler argued for the ongoing suitability of the Gothic style to the new method of building: "Indeed we must own that the Chicago construction in its latest development, has not yet found its artistic expression," adding that "no designer has yet learned to deal successfully with a structural change so radical that it has abolished the wall, which is the chief datum of every one of the historical styles of architecture, *excepting only the developed Gothic.*"[34]

Influenced by the French architect Eugène-Emmanuel Viollet-le-Duc, Chicago architects increasingly made a distinction between Gothicism as a style with recognizable external form (as in the Ruskinian or Venetian Gothic), and Gothicism as a philosophy based on the principle of "constructive" expression in which materials were used "truthfully," that is, their structural capability was made visible. Viollet-le-Duc was to the *Inland Architect* what Ruskin was to the *Crayon,* the infallible expert on all things modern and all things Gothic. Crucially, he did not object to the use of iron in architecture, as Ruskin did, but saw in it the potential for a new modern style based on Gothic principles.[35] By the time he arrived in Chicago, Wight had come to adopt Viollet-le-Duc's rationalist understanding of the Gothic. The early nineteenth-century English Gothic Revival had led in two directions, Wight claimed: first, toward "the extravagant imitation of Gothic forms," and second, toward "the rational treatment on constructive lines, and the discarding of ornament in which there was little to suggest medievalism."[36] Wight and his Chicago colleagues placed themselves firmly in the latter camp. However, while adherence to this principle meant an emphasis on structural and material rationalism, it did not entail the complete abandonment of Gothic Revival ornament but rather its continued reinvention.

In their design of the curtain wall, the visual expression of the Chicago construction, some architects continued to utilize ornamental schema drawn from the Gothic Revival. Sometimes this appropriation was quite literal, as in the case of Henry Ives Cobb's Chicago Athletic Association Building on South Michigan Avenue of 1893 (fig. 6). With its ogive windows, decorative attic stories, polychromy, and Moorish details, this building imitated the Venetian palazzo style promoted by Ruskin. Here the Gothic, used as a costume, telegraphed certain symbolic ideas, not least of which was fashion. More memorably, the Gothic Revival was the basis for Louis Sullivan's extraordinarily inventive vegetal ornament.[37] In the same vein as Root, but with even more originality, Sullivan developed an elaborate system of ornamentation that built on an American tradition that Lauren Weingarden has described as "Gothic natural-

Fig. 6. Henry Ives Cobb, Chicago Athletic Association Building, 12 South Michigan Ave., 1893. (Detroit Publishing Company Collection, Library of Congress, Prints and Photographs Division, Washington, D.C.)

ism."[38] Developed by Wight and other architects associated with the *Crayon,* and refined by Root and others, this tradition reached its apogee in Sullivan's famous Wainwright and Guaranty Buildings (1891 and 1896 respectively).

Beyond their naturalistic ornamentation, Sullivan's skyscrapers are celebrated for the lightness of their facades and for their underlying geometric rigor. In contrast to Cobb's scenographic employment of the Venetian Gothic as a way to organize the facade, and to Sullivan's abstraction, Charles Atwood ventured a different version of the Gothic Revival, as a literal translation of the motifs of medieval carving into mass-produced ornament designed to elevate the simple and repetitive facades of modern office buildings. Working for D. H. Burnham and Co., Atwood achieved a hybrid of these two approaches in his designs for the Reliance and Fisher Buildings, completed in 1895 and 1896 respectively (fig. 7). As with other tall office buildings of the period, the proportions of their vertically oriented facades was largely determined by the dimensions of the steel frame within. In the manner of contemporary skyscraper architects, Atwood

Fig. 7. D. H. Burnham and Co., Fisher Building, 343 South Dearborn St, ca. 1900, Chicago Architectural Photographing Co., photographer. (Historic Landscape and Image Collection, Ryerson and Burnham Archives, The Art Institute of Chicago, digital file no. 77219)

filled most of the space between the vertical piers with plate glass, leaving a minimal amount of surface area to be clad in brick or terra-cotta tile. (A local review memorably described the Fisher as a "building without walls.")[39] In both cases Atwood decorated these startling and protomodern "window-walls" with motifs drawn from Gothic tracery, borrowing the ornament, proportions, and lightness of effect from medieval cathedrals.

Atwood's Fisher Building synthesized the Gothic Revival with the Chicago construction. His design was freely adapted and had no obvious precedent in any particular historical source. Contemporary commentators identified it as variously fourteenth-century French Gothic, sixteenth-century French Gothic, and even the "English Perpendicular Gothic."[40] Whatever its origin, this style was thought especially suitable to this type of building: tall, slender, with porous exterior walls. Critics emphasized the technical perfection of the cast terra-cotta work, which included aquatic-themed ornaments, including gargoyle-like fish around the main entrance vestibule (visual puns on the name of the building's owner), along with "trefoil and ogee arches, drapery, foliate patterns, salamanders, and even eagles" around the cornice.[41] In a departure from Ruskin's association between the value of the Gothic and perfection of handcrafts such as stone carving, these ornamental elements were not lovingly made by individual craftsmen but created by a semi-industrial process of casting. Critics saw this as a perfection of earlier building techniques rather than their diminution. With the aid of modern technology, the *Inland Architect* claimed, the Fisher not only matched but surpassed the artistry of the Gothic masons: "In the carvings of the enrichments of the large core moldings and finials we again see the spirit of the fourteenth century artists of France, not imitated, but reproduced with even greater effect (due to the plastic materials used) than in any old stone carvings."[42]

With the design of the Fisher, Atwood reclaimed the mid-nineteenth-century appeal to the potential of the Gothic Revival style, but in a completely new building form, one in many ways antithetical to the ideals of Gothic Revival of forty years earlier. While Atwood's version of the Gothic was true to the characteristics of its materials (iron, terra-cotta, and plate glass), to its structure (an internal steel skeleton), and to its method of production (semi-industrialized processes), the all-important Gothic Revival ideals of handicraft and collaborative effort had been replaced by an aestheticized representation of modern, rationalized building processes. The Gothic Revival had been transformed from a critique of modernity and industrialization into an expression of business itself as a moral endeavor. Standing tall on the horizon, the Gothic skyscraper was intended to symbolize a new era of industrial harmony.

By the 1890s the mid-nineteenth-century idealization of medieval handicraft as the physical embodiment of a harmonious premodern society was countered in America by a new ideal, the potential social freedom offered by industrialization. In 1896 Louis Sullivan famously claimed the modern business building as a monument to democracy.[43] He took as his ideal citizen not a romanticized vision of the medieval stonemason but the modern businessman. Along with many in the American middle class, Sullivan believed the divide between capital and labor was an artificial one. Any man could harness his skill and intellect to become a successful entrepreneur and to effect positive change in society, he thought. Echoing this idea, in 1901 Frank Lloyd Wright argued that the stonemason's chisel was the tool of the slave: only by embracing industrialized building methods could Americans free themselves and begin a new tradition of building and a new way of life. "The machine does not write the doom of liberty," he claimed, "but is waiting at man's hand as a peerless tool, for him to use to put foundations beneath a genuine democracy."[44] The transfer of the Gothic Revival ideal from handicraft to the Chicago construction, from preindustrial to industrial culture, was complete.

Atwood's experiment with mass-produced Gothic ornament in the Reliance and the Fisher Buildings was extended in the early twentieth century, most notably by Cass Gilbert's Woolworth Building (1913) in New York, and Howells and Hood's Chicago Tribune Tower (1925).[45] By the 1930s, modernist critics placed these modern Gothic towers in opposition to skyscrapers built under the influence of the European avant-garde, such as Howe and Lescaze's PSFS Building (1932).[46] They treated neo-Gothic skyscrapers as dubious exercises in spectacle, opposing them to the supposedly honest expression of modern construction and the modern business program, of which the architecture of the so-called Chicago school supposedly offered the earliest and finest examples. In the mythology of the Chicago school created in the 1920s and 1930s, the overt incorporation of historic styles was a failed experiment, a dead end in the linear evolution of modern architecture toward pure structural expressionism.[47] In this narrative the best outcome of the mid-nineteenth-century Gothic Revival was its focus on structural rationalism and "truth to materials." The modernist position rests on a familiar divide: that between structure and ornament, where structure is valued as the truth of building and ornament is denigrated as an unnecessary form of disguise. Neo-Marxist commentators like the architectural historian Manfredo Tafuri maintained a similar view: ornament, including the neo-Gothic gargoyles on the Fisher, was an attractive cipher meant to distract attention from the "real" economic bases of the skyscraper in the oppressive practices of capitalism.[48] (Indeed it was probably impossible to directly represent the sources of Fisher's wealth in the same way that Boyington had used shafts of wheat to ornament the Board of Trade.) Beautiful and intricate, the facade of the Fisher was an architectural spectacle, an aestheticization of capital designed to make modern business palatable to the crowds on the street outside.

For architects and critics in late nineteenth-century Chicago, however, there was no conflict between iron-framed structure and historicizing ornament. The Gothic version of the Chicago construction represented both the truth of its construction and the higher ideals of the society in which it was built. While Root's Gothic- and Romanesque-themed Masonic Temple was designed to convey the unification of business and social ideals, with the Fisher, Atwood aimed to communicate business *as* a social ideal. For Atwood, as for Sullivan, the ornamented curtain wall facade was an advertisement for an optimistic view of the future of American society under capitalism. The local adaptation of the Gothic and Romanesque Revivals to new building types and methods of construction had the potential to create an indigenous style, surpassing the neoclassical in its ability to convey the ideal of American democracy.

Modern architectural history rests on a binary distinction between the Gothic and classical styles, accompanied by an equally distinct view of their respective meanings. John Ruskin, for example, was as certain of the appearance of Gothic architecture as he was of its moral message: true Christian architecture meant the rejection of modern urban society along with its ugly, industrialized building forms. For him there was no distinction between sacred and secular buildings as long as both were created in the same spirit of faith and fraternity. American architects, passionate followers of Ruskin, tested that idea in Chicago, America's Gotham. In their adaptation of the Gothic Revival to the skyscraper, they sought to import the morality and authenticity of the Gothic style to a building form dedicated to modern business. In doing so, they transformed the Gothic from a historically distinct style to a constructive principle, one in which new materials and construction methods were valid as long as they were given truthful expression. In the process they removed the moral value from the handmade, from traditional materials, and from ancient craft practices, and attached it to new methods of industrialized building. The shifting interpretation of the Gothic Revival in Chicago between 1871 and 1896 reveals the utilization of the style to be extraordinarily fluid, at the same time as it was continually upheld as the exemplar of truth in architecture.

NOTES

1. Thomas Tallmadge, *Architecture in Old Chicago* (Chicago: University of Chicago Press, 1941), 142. The Montauk was for a long time considered by Chicago architects as the "first" skyscraper because of its height and formal cohesiveness. The architects made little attempt to divide the building into horizontal layers, as was the norm at that time. On the Montauk, see Thomas Leslie, *Chicago Skyscrapers, 1871–1934* (Springfield: University of Illinois Press, 2013), 20–22.

2. On the Gothic Revival in America, see Michael J. Lewis, *The Gothic Revival* (New York: Thames and Hudson, 2002).

3. The construction of the American Express Company Building was supervised by P. B. Wight. On the American Express Company Building, see Carl Condit, *The Chicago School of Architecture: A History of Commercial and Public Buildings in the Chicago Area, 1875–1925* (Chicago: University of Chicago Press, 1964), 22; and Sarah Bradford Landau, *P. B. Wight: Architect, Contractor, and Critic, 1838–1925* (Chicago: Art Institute of Chicago, 1981), 34–35.

4. "Real Estate," *Chicago Daily Tribune,* May 23, 1875, 7; "Real Estate," *Chicago Daily Tribune,* June 27, 1875, 6; "The Architects," *Chicago Daily Tribune,* July 11, 1875, 2; "New Trade Palaces: Two of the Most Elegant Office Buildings Yet Erected in Chicago," *Chicago Daily Tribune,* March 12, 1876, 5. Burling and Adler's Wrenn and Moeller Building, on Dearborn between Randolph and Washington Streets, was also described as being "a building in the Gothic Style" ("The Architects," *Chicago Daily Tribune,* July 11 1875, 2).

5. On these buildings, see Landau, *P. B. Wight,* 30–35; and Theodore Turak, *William Le Baron Jenney: A Pioneer of Modern Architecture* (Ann Arbor, MI: UMI Research Press, 1986), 166–72.

6. Wight described his own education and exposure to the Gothic Revival in New York circles in an 1884 essay, "The Development of New Phases of the Fine Arts in America," *Inland Architect* 4, no. 4 (November 1884): 51–53; 4, no. 5 (December 1884): 63–65.

7. On the influence of Ruskin's writing in the United States, see Michael W. Brooks, "Ruskin's Influence in America," in *John Ruskin and Victorian Architecture* (New Brunswick, NJ: Rutgers University Press, 1987), 277–97; and Lauren Weingarden, "Gothic Naturalism and the Ruskinian Critical Tradition in America," in *Louis H. Sullivan and a Nineteenth-Century Poetics of Naturalized Architecture* (London: Ashgate, 2009), 71–96.

8. "The United States Treasury Building," *Crayon* 3 (1856): 178.

9. "The Public Buildings of Washington," *Crayon* 3 (1856): 150.

10. "Medieval Gothic," *Crayon* 3 (1856): 288; "Church of All Souls," *Crayon* 5 (1858): 20; Leopold Eidlitz, "Christian Architecture," *Crayon* 5 (1858): 53.

11. "Architecture," *Crayon* 3 (1856): 288.

12. William Cronon describes the economic basis of Chicago's rapid growth in *Nature's Metropolis: Chicago and the Great West* (New York: Norton, 1991).

13. "Notes on the West," *Crayon* 6 (1859): 223.

14. "French Architecture in America," *Inland Architect* 3, no. 3 (April 1884): 38.

15. The economic viability of the Portland Block was extended when the owners, the Brooks estate of Boston, commissioned the architects Burnham and Root to add two stories to the building in 1880 ("New Buildings" *Chicago Daily Tribune,* September 26, 1880, 11).

16. "A Brooks Estate Deal," *Chicago Daily Tribune,* June 8, 1889, 8; "Chicago Real Estate," *Chicago Daily Tribune,* June 9, 1889, 27. The Portland Block was eventually demolished in 1933.

17. Montgomery Schuyler, "Glimpses of Western Architecture: Chicago" (1891), in *American Architecture and Other Writings,* ed. William Jordy and Ralph Coe (Cambridge: Belknap Press of Harvard University Press, 1961), 2:253.

18. Ibid., 2:254.

19. Richard Schneirov, *Labor and Urban Politics: Class Conflict and the Origins of Modern Liberalism in Chicago, 1864–97* (Urbana: University of Illinois Press, 1998); Eric L. Hirsch, *Urban Revolt: Ethnic Politics in the Nineteenth-Century Chicago Labor Movement* (Berkeley: University of California Press, 1998).

20. William Le Baron Jenney, "A Few Practical Hints," address delivered to the Chicago Architectural Sketch Club, January 1889, in *Industrial Chicago,* vol. 2: *The Building Interests* (Chicago: Goodspeed, 1891), 619.

21. Ibid.

22. John W. Root, "Architectural Ornamentation," *Inland Architect and Builder* 5, extra number (April 1885): 54.

23. Carol Willis, *Form Follows Finance: Skyscrapers and Skylines in New York and Chicago* (New York: Princeton Architectural Press, 1995).

24. Montgomery Schuyler, "Architecture in Chicago: Adler and Sullivan" (1896), in *American Architecture and Other Writings,* ed. Jordy and Coe, 2:383.

25. Kathleen Curran, *The Romanesque Revival: Religion, Politics and Transnational Exchange* (University Park: Pennsylvania State University Press, 2003).

26. Roula Geraniotis, "German Architectural Theory and Practice in Chicago, 1850–1900," *Winterthur Portfolio* 21, no. 4 (Winter 1986): 293–306.

27. James F. O'Gorman, "The Marshall Field Wholesale Store: Materials Towards A Monograph," *Journal of the Society of Architectural Historians* 37, no. 3 (October 1978): 175–94; James F. O'Gorman, *H. H. Richardson: Architectural Forms for an American Society* (Chicago: University of Chicago Press, 1987).

28. On the belief in the appearance of a new, American "race" in the frontier states, see Reginald Horsman, *Race and Manifest Destiny: The Origins of American Racial Anglo-Saxonism* (Cambridge: Harvard University Press, 1981); and Richard Slotkin, *The Fatal Environment: The Myth of the Frontier in the Age of Industrialization 1800–1890* (New York: Atheneum, 1985)

29. On the two Temple buildings, see Donald Hoffman, *The Architecture of John Wellborn Root,* (Chicago: University of Chicago Press, 1973), 193–94, 196–202; Rachel E. Bohlmann, "Our 'House Beautiful': The Woman's Temple and the Woman's Christian Temperance Union Effort to Establish Place and Identity in Downtown Chicago, 1887–98," *Journal of Women's History* 11, no. 2, (Summer 1999): 110–11; and Paula Lee, "The Temperance Temple and Architectural Patronage in Late-Nineteenth-Century Chicago," *Gender and History* 17, no. 3 (November 2005): 793–885.

30. Condit, *The Chicago School of Architecture,* 103–5.

31. Daniel Bluestone, "A City under One Roof: Skyscrapers 1880–95," in *Constructing Chicago* (New Haven: Yale University Press, 1991), 123–28.

32. Henry Van Brunt, "John Wellborn Root," *Inland Architect and News Record* 17, no. 8 (January 1891): 87.

33. Henry Van Brunt, "Architecture in the West" (1889), in *Architecture and Society. Selected Essays of Henry Van Brunt* (Cambridge: Belknap Press of Harvard University Press, 1969), 187.

34. Schuyler, "Architecture in Chicago: Adler and Sullivan," 387, my emphasis.

35. Eugène-Emmanuel Viollet-le-Duc, *The Foundations of Architecture: Selections from the "Dictionnaire raisonné"* (1854–68), trans. Kenneth D. Whitehead (New York: Braziller, 1990), 182–86, 190–91.

36. Peter B. Wight, "Modern Architecture in Chicago," *Pall Mall Magazine* 18 (July 1899): 299.

37. David Van Zanten and Lauren Weingarden have explored the ways in which Louis Sullivan carried on the Gothic tradition in his ornament: David Van Zanten, *Sullivan's City: The Meaning of Ornament for Louis Sullivan* (New York: Norton, 2000); Lauren Weingarden, "Ruskin's Reception in the Chicago School," in *Louis H. Sullivan and a Nineteenth-Century Poetics of Naturalized Architecture,* 183–212.

38. Lauren Weingarden, "Gothic Naturalism and the Ruskinian Critical Tradition," 88.

39. "Technical Review: The Fisher Building, Chicago—A Building without Walls," *Inland Architect and News Record* 27, no. 4 (May 1896), n.p.

40. Wight, "Modern Architecture in Chicago," 303.

41. Commission on Chicago Historical and Architectural Landmarks, *Fisher Building* (1977; repr., Chicago: The Commission, 1983), 9.

42. "Recent Chicago Tall Buildings," *Engineering News,* October 17, 1895, 250–52; "Newest Skyscrapers," *Daily Inter Ocean,* January 1, 1896, 20; "Technical Review: The Fisher

Building, Chicago–A Building without Walls"; *Fisher Building Souvenir: A Brief Review of the Distinctive Features of a Model Chicago Office Building: Profusely Illustrated by the Half Tone Process*, ed. William S. Dolbey (1896; repr., Chicago: Fisher Building Limited Partnership, 1980).

43. Louis Sullivan, "The Tall Office Building Artistically Considered," *Inland Architect and News Record* 27 (February 1896): 32.

44. Frank Lloyd Wright, "The Art and Craft of the Machine" (1901), in *America Builds: Source Documents in American Architecture and Planning Book,* ed. Leland M. Roth (New York: Harper and Row, 1983), 376.

45. Gail Fenske discusses the relationship between Gilbert's work and that of earlier Chicago architects in *The Skyscraper and the City: The Woolworth Building and the Making of Modern New York* (Chicago: University of Chicago Press, 2008), 106, 112; on the Tribune Tower, see Katherine Solomonson, *The Chicago Tribune Tower Competition: Skyscraper Design and Cultural Change in the 1920s* (Chicago: University of Chicago Press, 2003).

46. See, for example, Philip Johnson, "Skyscraper School of Modern Architecture," *Arts* 27, no. 8 (May 1931): 575.

47. This argument, formulated by critics and historians including Thomas Tallmadge and Henry-Russell Hitchcock, was canonized by Carl Condit in *The Chicago School of Architecture: A History of Commercial and Public Buildings in the Chicago Area, 1875–1925* (Chicago: University of Chicago Press, 1964). On the creation of the mythology of the Chicago school, see Robert Bruegmann, "The Myth of the Chicago School," in *Chicago Architecture: Histories, Revisions, Alternatives*, ed. Charles Waldheim and Katerina Ruedi Ray (Chicago: University of Chicago Press, 2005), 15–29; and Daniel Bluestone, "Preservation and Renewal in Post–World War II Chicago," *Journal of Architectural Education* 47, no. 4 (May 1994): 210–23.

48. Manfredo Tafuri, "The Disenchanted Mountain: The Skyscraper and the City," in *The American City: From the Civil War to the New Deal,* ed. Giorgio Ciucci, Francesco Dal Co, Mario Manieri-Elia, and Tafuri (Cambridge: MIT Press, 1979).

TRIBUNE TOWER

Medievalism and Memory in the Wake of the Great War

Katherine M. Solomonson

In the early 1920s, the largest and certainly the most diverse array of Gothic skyscrapers yet conceived was produced for the Chicago Tribune Tower Competition of 1922.[1] Given almost free rein to conjure visions of "the most beautiful office building in the world," 264 architects produced a spectrum of designs that ranged from Egyptian, Greek, Roman, Romanesque, Gothic, and Renaissance revivals to the most recent innovations at the Bauhaus. Generated at a time of productive ferment in architectural theory and design, the entries and their relative merits quickly became the subject of heated debate in both the popular and professional presses. By the 1930s, critics and historians would recast the Chicago Tribune Tower Competition as a contest between modernism and historical styles, dismissing the latter as deviations in the evolution of modern design. But during and immediately after the 1922 competition, the real contest was between differing concepts of the modern Gothic skyscraper. More than sixty of the entries were influenced by the Gothic style. Some transformed modern skyscrapers into well-known church towers. Others featured small Gothic touches, and a few radically reinterpreted the style, transforming it into something new but still recognizably Gothic. As the competition drew to a close, its jury narrowed the entries down to ten, most of them Gothic, and then to two: one, a design bursting with flying buttresses by the New York architects John Mead Howells and Raymond Hood; the other, a sparer, more abstract interpretation of the Gothic style by the Finnish architect Eliel Saarinen. In the end, first prize went to Howells and Hood, second prize to Saarinen (figs. 1 and 2). Not everyone agreed that this was the right choice. A small number of critics and a member of the competition's jury made it known that they believed Saarinen's design should have won, and the *Tribune* clearly admired it.

Why, then, did the jury choose Howells and Hood's design rather than Saarinen's or any of the others? There are two basic responses to this question, and a third more complex one that will be the focus of this essay. The first is that John Mead Howells had an inside connection with the *Tribune;* his wife was a Tribune Company stockholder and a member of the board of directors.[2] The second is that the *Tribune,* well known for its ardent nationalism, would not likely have selected a design by a foreign architect no matter how much its jury liked it.[3] The third concerns the ways Howells and Hood's design served the *Tribune*'s larger agenda—more fully, I would argue, than Eliel Saarinen's could have. The winning design's explicit allusions to famous European monuments, its ornamentation, and its elaborate top—the very features that would draw the most criticism—afforded a rhetorical resonance that reverberated across discursive fields. The *Tribune* made abundant use of this in the narratives it spun around both the competition and the new building that resulted from it.

This essay will explore the ways the *Tribune* enlisted and redeployed meanings associated with the Gothic style to produce a skyscraper that became a monument to American modernity and postwar ascendancy as well as a monument to the *Tribune* itself. This offers the opportunity to examine the ways both forms and long-standing meanings associated with the Gothic style were reinterpreted in the United States during and after the war, as well as the processes through which meanings and memories were evoked and constructed.

THE *TRIBUNE* AND CHICAGO IN THE WAKE OF THE WAR

The *Chicago Tribune* announced the competition for its new building on June 10, 1922, to celebrate its seventy-fifth anniversary. Starting as a small local newspaper, the *Tribune* had become the "World's Greatest Newspaper"

Fig. 1. John Mead Howells and Raymond Hood, entry to the Chicago Tribune Tower Competition. (*The International Competition for a New Administration Building* [Chicago Tribune Company, 1923], plate 1)

Fig. 2. Eliel Saarinen, with Dwight G. Wallace and Bertell Grenman, entry to the Chicago Tribune Tower Competition. (*The International Competition for a New Administration Building* [Chicago Tribune Company, 1923], plate 13)

(according to its own masthead) and one of the largest and most powerful media corporations in the United States if not the world. Under the direction of the *Tribune* coeditors Robert McCormick and Joseph Patterson, the company's reach extended nationally and internationally through radio, various publications, its own wire service, and offices all over the world. From beginning to end, McCormick and Patterson exerted as much control over the competition for the design of the *Tribune*'s new office building as they did over the newspaper and the company that published it. Both were former politicians; together they wielded newspapers and other media as powerful instruments in service of their views. For them, the competition became a means of promoting their vision of a future that would transcend the turmoil that had wracked the country since the end of the war. Millions of veterans were out of work. Race riots, strikes, and a Red Scare brought to the surface divisiveness and fear that had been partially masked or redirected by the call for common purpose during the war. By 1920 the United States had slid into a severe recession that lasted into 1921, bringing construction to a standstill.[4] Some Americans responded to these conditions with an ardor that recalled the sense of moral idealism, heroism, and common purpose that had drawn people together during the war. As the historian John Higham put it, "Men who had [experienced] the heat of national conflict had little difficulty supposing that the war had not ended, that the adversary had merely assumed another guise."[5] This aptly describes Robert McCormick and Joseph Patterson, the *Tribune*'s coeditors. They both served as officers during the war; and they used their newspapers to rally support for the Allied cause. As the war ended, they redirected their wartime militancy into the peacetime battles they fought through the *Tribune* as they railed against labor unrest, anarchy, and Bolshevism at home while championing American self-interest and ascendancy in a global arena. The competition and the new Gothic tower became instrumental in advancing their campaign.

COMPETITION AND CONTROVERSY

The Tribune Company publicized the competition widely, making good use of its global network of offices, newspapers, and other media. Eventually as many as 1,800 architects from all over the world requested programs; 264

ultimately delivered their entries.[6] As the designs arrived, the jury—which consisted of the *Tribune* editors Robert McCormick and Joseph Patterson, two Tribune Company subordinates, and just one architect—reviewed them and narrowed them down to a short list of twelve, ten of which showed some manner of Gothic influence. Finally, after weeks of deliberation, the jury reached its controversial verdict. First prize went to Howells and Hood of New York, second prize to Eliel Saarinen of Helsinki, and third prize to Holabird and Roche of Chicago (who had designed the building the *Tribune* occupied at the time of the competition). At the competition's close, the jury's report expressed the *Tribune*'s satisfaction with its outcome: "One gratifying result of this world competition has been to establish the superiority of American design." The report also acknowledged the virtues of Saarinen's entry: "Only one foreign design stands out as possessing surpassing merit, and this truly wonderful design did not come from France, Italy or England, the recognized centers of European culture, but from the little northern nation of Finland."[7] Germany, which submitted more designs than any nation outside the United States, did not even get a mention. The point here is that the "recognized centers of European culture," as the *Tribune* defined them, were no longer even contenders; America had triumphed.

Although many commended Howells and Hood's first-prize design, a small group of Chicago architects exploded in protest. The most vocal of these was Louis Sullivan, who saw Saarinen's design as embodying everything he believed in: the soaring vertical lines that made the most of the tall building's height; the consistent expression of structure from base to crown, displaying "a high science of design such as the world up to this day had neither known nor surmised"; the avoidance of historicism; and above all, the "aspiring" idealism the design represented.[8] What bothered Sullivan and his colleagues most about the winning entry was that crown of flying buttresses. Thomas Tallmadge dismissed them as "stage scenery to the last degree."[9] Sullivan, more colorfully, characterized them as "the monster on top with its great long legs reaching far below to the ground." He did admit that if they "could be gently pried loose, the real building would reveal itself as a rather amiable and delicate affair with a certain grace of fancy." How, he asked, could the *Tribune* abandon its own professed ideals, bowing beneath the "tyranny of fixed ideas" rather than accepting a "pearl of great price" that so fully captured the idealism of the American people?[10]

Howells also got his say. At the dinner celebrating the competition's awards he justified a design that is so clearly Gothic by referring to the well-established notion that the Gothic style is an effective means of expressing the skyscraper's steel-frame construction. But then he gave this a specifically nationalistic and war-related twist. He began by comparing the skyscraper to the "fighting machine built up by the German aristocracy." Just as this "needed a war for its expression, and so an excuse was found," the skyscraper, a specifically American achievement, "must express its use and its construction." This was a challenge that only an American could successfully resolve. Howells believed that he and Hood had achieved this through their design's expression of "the actual steel cage, with its vertical steel columns from top to bottom and its interpolated steel beams." To him, this naturally resulted in "something Gothic in line, because the Gothic architecture was also one of structural expression." Leaving unmentioned the buttresses flying at the top, he concluded that his entry was "meant to be a design expressing to the limit our American steel cage construction, and nothing else."[11]

But the design's Gothic style expressed far more than this. The architects' intentions were one thing. How the *Tribune* interpreted and presented what they produced was quite another. During the competition the *Tribune* had expressed its confidence that steel-frame construction would enable Americans to surpass European architecture. Europeans are amazed to "see what American architecture can do with the flexibility of steel," the *Tribune* reported. "We can raise a temple, a cathedral, or a great monumental building with ease and grace, with infinite effects of lace as desired, with towering height and majestic proportions."[12] Rather than taking years of toil, American technological ingenuity could now make it possible to erect buildings that were bigger, quicker to construct, and equal if not superior in their ornamental beauty. At the competition's conclusion, the *Tribune* was clearly delighted to present a design that (from its point of view) so successfully conveyed this. But the appropriateness of the Gothic style for the expression of "steel cage construction" was a more significant issue within architectural discourse than it was for the *Tribune,* which articulated a host of other ways their Gothic skyscraper expressed American ideals, not to mention the newspaper's own.

SPIRITUAL ASPIRATION AND UNITY

The Tribune Tower's style, form, embellishment, and significance were all deeply informed by the events and discourse of the Great War. The *Tribune* positioned its new building as a monument to the city's and the nation's ideals and to the United States' role in the war to defend them. To reinforce this, *Tribune* publications charged with symbolic significance the very features Sullivan condemned in Howells and Hood's design.[13] In the process, the newspaper's editorial writers and reporters enlisted, redirected, and secularized meanings that architects and historians had long associated with medieval society and the Gothic style. In the process, they also repurposed medieval imagery that had pervaded the discourse of the Great War on both sides of the conflict—though nuances of meaning and underlying purpose differed.

To transform an office building into a monument with higher, noncommercial ideals, the *Tribune* drew upon the Gothic style's long-standing associations with religious structures and spirituality. Inspired by Gothic church towers, Howells and Hood's design meshed well with the sacralizing metaphors that suffused the newspaper's descriptions both of its own mission as a newspaper and of the building that would house it. "Even steel has its spiritual quality," the *Tribune* proclaimed while the tower was under construction; it has "the restlessness and seeking of a Gothic tower."[14] When the tower was completed, the *Tribune* gloried in the building's vertical impetus: "there is inspiration in that tremendous sweep upward, and it ends in benediction."[15] The *Tribune* might have said much the same if it had selected Eliel Saarinen's competition entry rather than Howells and Hood's. Those who praised Saarinen's design found spiritual qualities, a sense of aspiration and exaltation, in the continuous vertical piers that carried the building's main structural lines up to meet the sky.[16] But what Saarinen's design did not have, for the *Tribune*'s purposes, was the Tribune Tower's concentration of Gothic-style ornament at the base and its dramatic shift in imagery from the shaft to the crown. The building's culmination in a burst of flying buttresses—its "embattled chapel"—enhanced and made more obvious its resonance with its Gothic ancestors.[17] "It has its feet firmly upon the ground. Its head looks starward," the *Tribune* explained, drawing attention to the building's mixed imagery. The design thus "brings home not thoughts of more dollars and more circulation . . . but thoughts of the obligations of a profession which to mean anything lasting, must mean service."[18]

As the *Tribune* presented it, the cathedral-like Tribune Tower would be a monument to the unified aspirations of Chicago's citizens as well as to ideals worth fighting for. During the competition the *Tribune* referred to the selection of the new building's design as a community matter and continuously solicited its readers' input, staging in print a fictive process of forging consensus and "imagined community."[19] The winning design's Gothic style helped to reinforce this. A number of recently published books on Gothic architecture characterized Gothic cathedrals as the product of the common effort of cohesive communities unified by spiritual ideals in a world not yet shaken by the disruption and divisiveness of industrialization. In *Mont-Saint-Michel and Chartres* (which went through several editions), Henry Adams evoked this particularly vividly as he described how people of all classes yoked themselves to carts to aid in the construction of Chartres Cathedral.[20] To Ralph Adams Cram, a well-known advocate of this view, the eleventh, twelfth, and thirteenth centuries defined a period when all classes were bound into an organic democratic social order in which individual liberty was balanced with community.[21] "The Medievals," he wrote, "produced the greatest unity, achieved by and expressed through liberty and individuality, history has thus far recorded. . . . It was the exact antithesis of anarchy."[22]

It is not surprising that Cram published this statement during the Great War. During the war, in England, France, and Germany, medieval imagery was instrumental in forging distinct and unified national identities by evoking continuity with deep national traditions, as Stefan Goebel, Jay Winter, and many others have noted.[23] In the United States, which had no medieval traditions of its own to call forth, newspaper reports and national propaganda used similar imagery to exhort a culturally diverse population to come together as Americans united by the ideal of service to a common purpose: to defend democracy and win the war. The *Tribune* participated in this. A particularly good example is the popular film *Joan the Woman,* which played in theaters throughout the

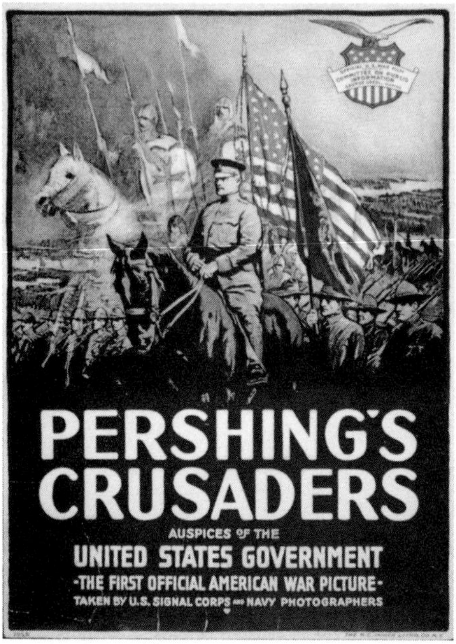

Fig. 3. "Pershing's Crusaders," sheet music for piano associated with the film by the same name, published by E. T. Paul. (World War I Posters Collection, Library of Congress, Prints and Photographs Division, Washington, D.C., LC-USZC4-1539)

United States in 1917, just as the United States was entering the war. A Cecil B. DeMille extravaganza with elaborate medieval-looking sets, it explicitly linked Joan of Arc's battles for France with the cause of the Allies against Germany. The *Tribune* promoted both the film and enlistment: "She Led Her Country to Victory. What Are You Doing for Your Country?" Joan of Arc was a powerful unifying image, appealing to American recruits who spoke more than forty different languages, one in five of them foreign born.[24] Their mission was often referred to as a crusade and a sacred cause. Nothing said this better than *Pershing's Crusaders,* a feature film produced by the Committee for Public Information (fig. 3). Promising an eyewitness view of "our own crusaders striding in legions on to victory," the film connected viewers in the United States—over here—with "our boys in action," "over there." Publicity for the film featured American troops on foot led forth by General Pershing and medieval knights on horseback. In a conflict often described as the first mechanized war, young men went into battle, figuratively, as medieval knights fighting for the ideals of liberty and democracy.

Medieval church towers also became important rallying points for troops on a "sacred" mission to save them from destruction.[25] During and after the war, the same church towers, many of them damaged, were represented as symbols of civic identity, unified resistance, and finally triumph. But whose triumph was it, really? To the *Tribune,* the United States was the war's ultimate victor. In making this claim, the *Tribune* was far from alone.

NARRATIVES OF DECLINE AND ASCENDANCY

During the competition, the *Tribune* created a context for its future building, both aesthetically and geopolitically, by informing the publicity that surrounded it with metanarrative of European decline and American ascendancy. In the process, it particularized this narrative, relating it to its own future building, and by implication, to its readers' own memories and associations.

The *Tribune* explicated its narrative of decline and ascendancy most explicitly in an editorial titled "The Twilight of Europe." Before the war, the editorial intoned, Europe was the "home of the world's greatest civilization." It was "the heart of the world's finance, commerce, and culture and the achievements were the greatest known to man." But then the German Kaiser extinguished the sun by reaching for it, leaving Europe "beggared" and central Europe menaced by sovietism. And so, the *Tribune* asked: "Is the twilight of kings to be followed by the twilight of civilization in Europe?"[26] In answering this for its readers, the *Tribune* drew upon the well-known and at that time prevalent conception of history as the rise and fall of a succession of empires moving ever-westward. From an American perspective, this process would inevitably culminate in the United States, which would attain the preeminence once held by Athens, Rome, Venice, Spain, and Great Britain. The *Tribune* took this one step further, asserting that Chicago would inevitably become the premier city.[27] Through the competition, the *Tribune* positioned its new building as a monument to that vision.

Although this editorial was not specifically about the competition, its message informed the series of pictorials that publicized the competition in the *Tribune*'s Sunday *Coloroto Magazine.* These featured what the *Tribune* billed as the most beautiful monuments in the world. Any of these, it said, could serve as the model for the most beautiful modern office building in the world. Most examples were predictably famous European buildings, including the Parthenon, the Pantheon, and St. Peter's in Rome. But the number of Gothic buildings would have left little doubt about the *Tribune*'s predilections. The cathedrals at Antwerp and Amiens, the Tower of St. Jacques in Paris, the hôtel de ville at Arras, and the Houses of Parliament, for example, were mixed in with the more recent Harkness Tower at Yale, and the Bush Tower and the Woolworth Building in New York. The Woolworth Building appeared no fewer than three times—a tribute to the Gothic skyscraper that was arguably the most famous tall building in the world at that time, as well as a challenge to design a Chicago skyscraper that could outdo it. The implication, throughout, was that the United States had inherited the best of European civilization, and that it would soon outdo it.

The narrative of European decline and American ascendancy surfaced most clearly in the pictorials that featured French and Belgian buildings that were endangered, damaged, or destroyed by the invading German army during World War I. The caption beneath an image of Amiens Cathedral, which sustained considerable damage, evokes beauty, loss, and the ravages of war with a calculated poignancy: "With its flame-like tracery, its complicated pinnacles, its glimmering niches, pierced parapets, dainty filigree work and sculptured lace, it was a marvel of imagination, dramatic sense and consummate craftsmanship"—qualities the *Tribune* clearly admired. "All now is gone—overwhelmed in indiscriminating ruin . . . the carved stones calcined and flaking hourly in a dreary rain on blood stained pavements."[28] In a pictorial that featured the hôtel de ville at Arras, the *Tribune* evoked memories of war while suggesting ways the beauty of European monuments could be transferred to America. A prewar image of the building intact dominates the page. Beneath it, the caption exclaims: "Ransacking the architectural Beauty Secrets of the old world!"—conjuring rather disturbing images of conquest, plunder, and appropriation.[29] After the war was over, ransacking continued, albeit at a small scale, as American troops and increasing numbers of tourists made their way through war-torn areas pocketing bits and pieces of devastated buildings as souvenirs.[30] One of them was the *Tribune* editor Robert McCormick, who stood among the ruins of Arras and collected a fragment of the hôtel de ville to take home with him—a petty version of *Tribune* competitor William Randolph Hearst's practice of extracting entire rooms and buildings from their original locations to put to new purposes in the United States.[31]

Although large-scale appropriation was not what the *Tribune* had in mind for its new building, the newspaper was clear in its intention to transform the splendors of Europe to new uses on American soil. In a feature on Antwerp Cathedral, the *Tribune* explained how best to draw upon European sources for the American skyscraper (fig. 4). Antwerp was not "something to be imitated or copied." Rather, it offered "inspiration by comparison." To explain this, a small sketch in the margin showed what the cathedral's tower would look like grafted onto the top of an office block.[32] Like the hôtel de ville at Arras, Antwerp Cathedral had special significance to the *Tribune.* Joseph Patterson was in Antwerp in 1914 covering the war when a *Tribune* photographer documented the fact that the cathedral's tower was being used as a lookout, making it vulnerable to attack. When the Belgian commander saw the photograph, he had the lookout removed and made an agreement with the Germans to spare the cathedral. In the end, the *Tribune* credited its photograph with saving the cathedral from ruin.[33] When Antwerp's cathedral—happily intact—reappeared as inspiration for a skyscraper in the pages of the *Tribune,* it demonstrated how the synthesis of old and new could produce a building that transcended its sources.

What do *you think* The Tribune's new building will be like?

As you know, awards amounting to $100,000.00 will be made by The Tribune for designs of the most beautiful building in the world. This offer has aroused much comment, which is not confined to the architects. "The subjects you reproduce," writes F. T. W., "are fine, but I foretell that The Tribune monument will easily surpass them all." Another Tribune reader, T. C. C., suggests the Cathedral of Antwerp as a model, so we reproduce it—at the right. What's *your* opinion? Do you think a perfect expression of journalistic achievement can be made architecturally? Write to the Architectural Editor. Give him your ideas on The Tribune's proposed new home!

The Cathedral *of* Antwerp

This building, one of the most beautiful in the world, is not presented as something to be imitated or copied, but for "inspiration by comparison." We review all the fine buildings in the world, and we say, "We shall endeavor to make ours more beautiful than any of them!" That is the spirit which inspired Jan Amel, when he began work on the Antwerp Cathedral in 1352, and thus was beauty achieved—in the sheer sweep of the tower as it fairly sings its way upward, in the exquisite handling of the decoration, in the superb mastery manifested in the design as a whole.

Fig. 4. Antwerp Cathedral. (*Chicago Tribune Coloroto Magazine*, July 30, 1922)

TOWERS OF THE WESTERN FRONT AND AMERICAN MEMORIALS

The church towers of northern France and Belgium—located in or near the Western Front—provided the most immediate inspiration for the Tribune Tower's design. Specifically, Howells and Hood adapted elements from the Butter Tower of Rouen Cathedral (fig. 5) and the cathedral towers of Antwerp and Mechlin (which the *Tribune* referred to as Malines). The design thus provided a tangible connection to McCormick's and Patterson's—and many others'—experiences during and after the war. For many, the towers of the Western Front—endangered, damaged, or destroyed during the war—were bound into recent memory. While American troops experienced them directly, those at home knew them through the many images that appeared in the magazines, newsreels, and newspapers that reported on their bombardment or salvation, and later, their potential for restoration. After the war, the American press reported on reconstruction efforts, presenting this as evidence that barbarism had been defeated and civilization had survived. Some proposed leaving some of the ruins in place as a form of memorial.[34] Many others focused on reconstruction and renewal. The Chicago architect Thomas Tallmadge, for example, rallied American architects to rebuild the damaged portions of Soissons Cathedral as an inspiration to the French and a message to the world that "the spoiler" had been defeated.[35] Ralph Adams Cram advocated reconstructing on American soil the monuments devastated during the war. "I am not very fond of replicas," he explained in *Architectural Record,* but he believed that the re-creation of these monuments would show that "the fine spirit of true civilization . . . has been preserved, that it may sow itself again."[36]

The towers of the Western Front soon were drawn into the debates about how best to commemorate the war. Some continued to advocate "votive" memorials that served commemorative purposes only. Others proposed utilitarian memorials that could serve some additional functional purpose for the community. Plans for both types tended toward monumental classicism.[37] France and Belgium's Gothic towers provided an alternative.[38] A month after Cram's article advocating the re-creation of medieval towers appeared, the *Tribune* published a proposal for a war memorial in the form of "a Gothic structure in the center of [Chicago's] Grant Park, with lofty ornate steeples to recall the

Fig. 5. Butter Tower, Cathedral of Notre Dame, Rouen. (Drawing by John R. Rowe, 1921, from *Pencil Points* 4 [February 1923]: plate 7)

many buildings of such construction destroyed in the war." Victor Falkenau, the contractor responsible for the Auditorium Annex/Congress Hotel and the Chicago Stock Exchange, among other works, was the force behind this idea. "To awaken public spirit in the enterprise Mr. Falkenau would have every Chicagoan contribute one day's work or the equivalent in money to finance the project," the *Tribune* reported. In this, Falkenau recalled the "cult of the carts," popularized by Henry Adams in *Mont-Saint-Michel and Chartres.*[39] In addition to the conventional tombs and tablets, Falkenau envisioned this as a functional memorial that would also include an auditorium and a publicly supported day-care center. Above all, it would be a "liberty temple" standing for "the spirit of all the high ideals this country has fought for."[40] This particular idea never gained ground, but a desire to evoke these towers persisted in a number of war memorial proposals—and also in the Tribune Tower Competition, through some of the entries and, finally, through the winning design.

Although the *Tribune* never formally described its own building as a war memorial per se, the newspaper shaped it into something akin to a functional memorial (albeit for its own use rather than for public purposes). The *Tribune* could draw upon popular knowledge and interest in the types of Gothic towers that provided precedents for its future building, and it made the most of this. But the winning entry and the subsequent development of the design were also connected with the editors' personal interests and experiences, and the ideals they defined on behalf of the community.

When the Tribune Tower was completed in 1925, the *Tribune* presented the Butter Tower of Rouen Cathedral as the building's "first cousin."[41] In some ways, it is surprising that they did not choose a design based on Antwerp Cathedral given the role the *Tribune* claimed to have played in its survival, and the way the newspaper featured it as a model for its new building. At one point, when the *Tribune* received permission to increase the tower's height, the architects produced scenarios for a taller tower with a pointed spire bursting out of a vestigial set of buttresses, turning Rouen into Antwerp, enlarged to 650 feet.[42] In the end, they stayed with a slightly enlarged version of the design they already had (no doubt expedient given that the building was already under construction). If the *Tribune* had really wanted a design based on Antwerp's tower, the competition entries offered them options, including James Gamble Rogers's design, which merged the Woolworth Building's massing with Antwerp Cathedral's tower, right down to the ornamental details and clock faces. A design based on a French church tower, however, suited the *Tribune,* especially Robert McCormick. McCormick had a profound admiration for the French military, which he lauded in *The Army of 1918,* a combined memoir and polemic concerning American military preparedness.[43] Rouen Cathedral was never seriously threatened or damaged, and it emerged from the war fully intact. There was thus no poignant narrative of decline, destruction, and resurrection associated with it. Rather, the *Tribune* described its symbolic significance in a much earlier war: it was "the supreme belfry that sprang up to commemorate the freeing of France from the English yoke."[44] This lent itself well to the triumphalist narrative that pervaded the competition.

Beyond this, the *Tribune* and others infused the design with military references, both metaphorically and tangibly. When they submitted their competition entry, Howells and Hood asserted that the building was designed to express the "journalistic ideal of battle and service"—an appropriate sentiment for a newspaper that conceived its mission in martial terms.[45] For example, not long before the competition the *Tribune* waged war on the recent recession by initiating a "1921 Will Reward Fighters" campaign, which offered awards for true stories of "Fighting Salesmanship." The advertising department participated in this maneuver as well: "The young men in that organization believe that at the present time they are the 'assault troops' in the attack to bring back prosperity."[46] When the Tribune Tower was completed, the *Tribune* transformed a Gothic church tower into a species of "military Gothic," crowned with "flying buttresses which, in their totality give the enormous power of battlements."[47] The Tribune Tower provided a new command post for Colonel McCormick and Captain Patterson, who had returned to fight their editorial battles in Chicago.

The Tribune Tower's design received considerable elaboration as time went on. The *Tribune* worked with the architects to build up a rich store of imagery in the building's ornamentation, much of which referred either to World War I or to journalism. These details offered the building's many visitors curiosities to linger over and decode with the help of the guidebooks the *Tribune* published to explain the building's craftsmanship, historical associations, and symbolism. Over the main portal, for example, a carved screen known variously as the Tree of Life or as Aesop's Screen is filled with allegorical carvings. At the top, two men in military garb represent McCormick and Patterson as World War I servicemen. Others are allegorical figures from Aesop's fables offering lessons that the *Tribune* tweaked to make a case for military preparedness and the importance of the freedom of the press. Above, the limestone grills that wrap around the fourth-floor news and editorial departments (the *Tribune*'s "nerve center") feature fleurs-de-lis meant to remind "us of the heroic deeds of our American boys on the battlefields of France."[48]

The *Tribune* also planned to introduce more traditional commemorative elements into the building's design. On each side of the entrance, the company planned to install a relief to recognize those who had fought in the Civil War and Great War, "to give the Tower symbols of militant America in periods covered by the *Tribune*'s existence." The *Tribune* went on to explain that these were to be "memorials to American soldier heroism and manhood," symbolizing "in heroic form the qualities we admire in men."[49] This rhetoric echoes McCormick's own description of heroism in his book *The Army of 1918.* Fighting, he said, is "the primeval purpose of the male. . . . The fact that it is the male mission is as true as in the stone age." In war, "men stand alone, the preservers, the admired of women. Here they glory in their masculinity and resent any suggestion that males of another race can excel them in technique."[50] For McCormick, the Tribune Tower was an intensely personal monument to masculine heroism. (How it must have rankled when Sullivan described Howells and Hood's design as so "helpless and defenseless" that it "savors of the nursery" compared with the Saarinen design's "controlled and virile power" and "native quality of manhood.")[51] Although the memorial reliefs were never realized, the *Tribune* did install a bronze tablet in the lobby with names of the 268 *Tribune* employees who fought in World War I; and later, another honoring World War II veterans. In the midst of all of the symbolic elements that require decoding, these are the most straightforward and traditionally commemorative.

Howells and Hood's design, as it was transformed into the building known as the Tribune Tower, became simultaneously a memorial and a monument to American triumph—especially to the *Tribune*'s role in it. But it was a memorial with no space for death, mourning, or loss. As Adrian Forty and others have observed, commemoration involves forgetting:[52] forgetting recent turmoil, divisiveness, and difference; and even forgetting the forced forgetting French and Belgian towns experienced as their monuments were destroyed. For Rouen's Butter Tower, the inspiration for the Tribune Tower, never fell to the Germans or sustained any damage. Inscribed tablets list the names of those who fought in the wars, not of those who died. Fleurs-de-lis and commemorative reliefs prompt memories of heroism, and other details advocate military preparedness.

Other elements were also incorporated into the triumphalist narrative that wove through the competition and the realization of the new building. In the lobby, adorned with "cathedral-like carving," a framed map of North America rises over the information desk like a reredos over an altar. The *Tribune* installed it in 1927 to demonstrate that it was geographically inevitable for Chicago and the Mississippi valley to supplant the Eastern Seaboard. Outside, one of the Tribune Tower's most popular tourist attractions was, and still is, the collection of fragments of historic monuments from all over the world cemented into the building's base. The collection began with two stones Robert McCormick picked up in Arras and Yprès during World War I (these fragments never actually made it into the tower's base). The collection continued to grow when he charged his foreign correspondents with gathering stones as they gathered news.[53] The great monuments of the world, some of them spoils of war, quite literally became the foundation of a tower designed to surpass them.

CONCLUSION

On the day it announced the competition, the *Tribune* wondered about the designs it would receive. "Will the drift be toward classicism or toward the ultra modern?" its writers asked, and then answered: "For itself THE TRIBUNE sees naught incompatible between ancient beauty and modern uses, for it believes that the ancient type can be so modified and adapted that . . . no incongruity will result. Its beauty will remain, but it will find a new expression."[54] For the *Tribune,* this "new expression" materialized in the form of a soaring steel-framed skyscraper clad in elaborate Gothic raiment. The *Tribune* spun an elaborate narrative around this design, one that drew upon and reinterpreted the medieval imagery that suffused the call to arms during the Great War. It celebrated the spirituality and sense of unified purpose the Gothic style evoked; and it transformed a skyscraper that recalled some of the great Gothic towers of the Western Front into a monument to masculine heroism and American ascendancy. The *Tribune* redeployed the meanings associated with the Gothic style to present its building as both memorial and triumphalist monument to an imagined past and more glorious future for Chicago, the United States, and the *Tribune* itself.

When it was completed in 1925, the *Tribune*'s Gothic tower was well received, despite Louis Sullivan's opinion to the contrary. By the early 1930s, however, many regarded Saarinen's design as the competition's real winner. In terms of subsequent influence, this is hard to deny. With its soaring lines, setbacks, and restrained use of ornament, it was a thoroughly modern reinterpretation of the Gothic style. Secularized and rinsed of allusions to specific Gothic church towers, it was also highly adaptable. Though Saarinen's design itself was never constructed, its progeny may still be spotted on skylines across the United States and as far away as Shanghai.

NOTES

1. See *The International Competition for a New Administration Building for the Chicago Tribune MCMXXII* (Chicago: The Tribune Company, 1923). See also Katherine Solomonson, *The Chicago Tribune Tower Competition: Skyscraper Design and Cultural Change in the 1920s* (New York: Cambridge University Press, 2001).

2. Abbey White Howells was the daughter of Horace White, managing editor and part-owner of the *Tribune* in the late nineteenth century. Her family had been involved with the *Tribune* for decades, though not as actively in recent years. Her name appears in the Statement of Ownership the *Tribune* published on October 5, 1919. See also "The Key to the *Tribune*'s Management," *Fortune* 9 (May 1934): 108.

3. The jury knew from the packaging that Saarinen's entry came from Finland, even if they may not have known the architect's identity.

4. Gail Radford, "New Building and Investment Patterns in 1920s Chicago," *Social Science History* 16 (Spring 1992): 2; Chicago Commission on Race Relations, *The Negro in Chicago: A Study of Race Relations and a Race Riot* (Chicago: University of Chicago Press), 1–52; Ernest W. Young, *The Wilson Administration and the Great War* (Boston: Richard G. Badger, 1922), 408, 414–19, 429–49; "Be Prepared, Is Plea on Armistice Day," *Chicago Commerce* 18 (November 18, 1922): 17.

5. John Higham, *Strangers in the Land: Patterns of American Nativism 1860–1925*, 2nd ed. (New Brunswick: Rutgers University Press, 1988), 222.

6. *Chicago Tribune*, November 2, 1922; *The Trib* 4 (September 1922).

7. *International Competition*, 44.

8. Louis Sullivan, "The Chicago Tribune Competition," *Architectural Record* 53 (February 1923): 151–57.

9. Thomas Tallmadge, "A Critique of the Chicago Tribune Building Competition," *Western Architect* 32 (January 1923): 8.

10. Sullivan, "The Chicago Tribune Competition," 156, 153.

11. Qtd. in the *Chicago Tribune*, December 4, 1922. *Architecture* reinforced Howells's position by paraphrasing it in its discussion of the design. ("John Mead Howells to Be the Architect of the New Chicago Tribune Building," *Architecture* 47 [1923]: 18).

12. *Chicago Tribune*, June 12, 1922.

13. For example, when the Tribune Tower was completed in 1925, the *Tribune* presented it as a monument "conceived, designed, and completed in a sense of trusteeship for the higher needs of a civilized community. It is in the highest sense a gift to the city of today and the city of tomorrow" (*Chicago Tribune*, July 6, 1925).

14. Ibid., May 25, 1924.

15. Ibid., December 3, 1922.

16. Sullivan, "The Chicago Tribune Competition," 151–57; Irving K. Pond, "High Buildings and Beauty, Part I," *Architectural Forum* 38 (February 1923): 42.

17. See Solomonson, *The Chicago Tribune Tower Competition,* chap. 6. With a few exceptions, prewar Chicago skyscrapers with more elaborate tops were constructed by noncommercial organizations.

18. *Chicago Tribune*, December 3, 1922.

19. On the *Tribune*'s construction of an imagined community (drawing upon Benedict Anderson's concept), see Solomonson, *The Chicago Tribune Tower Competition,* chap. 3.

20. Henry Adams, *Mont-Saint-Michel and Chartres* (Boston: Houghton Mifflin, 1915), 104. (The twelfth impression of Adams's work was released in December 1922, the month the *Tribune* announced the competition's winners.) Arthur Kingsley Porter discusses the cult of the carts in *Medieval Architecture: Its Origins and Development*, vol. 2 (New Haven: Yale University Press, 1912), 151. Porter cautions that this compelling image had more to do with mortification of the flesh and the desire for salvation than with the love of architecture.

21. Ralph Adams Cram, *The Substance of Gothic* (Boston: Marshall Jones, 1917), 38, 108.

22. Ibid.

23. Stefan Goebel, *The Great War and Medieval Memory: War, Remembrance and Medievalism in Britain and Germany, 1914–1940* (New York: Cambridge University Press, 2009); Jay Winter, "Sites of Memory," in *Memory: Histories, Theories, Debates,* ed. Susannah Radstone and Bill Schwar (New York: Fordham University Press, 2010), 312–24.

24. Robin Blaetz, *Visions of the Maid: Joan of Arc in American Film and Culture* (Charlottesville: University Press of Virginia, 2001); Leslie Midkiff DeBauche, *Reel Patriotism: The Movies and World War I* (Madison: University of Wisconsin Press, 1997), 18–21.

25. See, for example, William Gorham Rice, "The Carillons of Belgium after the Great War," *Art and Archaeology* 12 (August 1921): 51–73.

26. *Chicago Tribune,* August 18, 1922.

27. This was a familiar trope in the promotion of the 1909 Plan of Chicago (see, for example, Walter D. Moody, *Wacker's Manual of the Plan of Chicago/Municipal Economy,* 3rd ed. [Chicago: Chicago Plan Commission, 1920], 18).

28. *Chicago Tribune,* November 19, 1922.

29. *Chicago Tribune Coloroto Magazine,* August 13, 1922.

30. Numerous articles in popular periodicals discuss this. A few examples include "Coming of the War Tourist," *Living Age* 301 (June 7, 1919): 603–5; "Seeing Battle-Scarred Europe," *Forum* 64 (July 1920): 43–57; and the advertisement for the United States Shipping Board," "Visit the great battlefields before reconstruction obliterates all traces of them" (*Life* 79 [January 5, 1922]: 27).

31. Robert McCormick, "Memoirs, Part 12," broadcast November 22, 1952, transcript, Tribune Archives.

32. *Chicago Tribune Coloroto Magazine,* July 30, 1922.

33. "'Tribune' Photograph Saves Antwerp's Fine Cathedral," *Chicago Tribune*, October 21, 1914.

34. This was an idea that was less popular with those who lived with the ruins than with the outsiders who thought this would be a good part of the battlefield tour circuit (see Goebel, *The Great War and Medieval Memory,* 179).

35. Thomas E. Tallmadge, "The Destruction of Historic Buildings as Revealed by the Official French War Photographs. Part 1. The Cathedral of Soissons," *Architectural Record* 42 (September 1917): 258.

36. Ralph Adams Cram, "War Memorials," *Architectural Record* 45 (February 1919): 117.

37. See Charles Over Cornelius, 'War Memorials," *Architectural Record* 46 (December 1919): 535–55. For a perceptive analysis of living memorials (as utilitarian memorials were known by World War II), see Andrew Shanken, "Planning Memory: Living Memorials in the United States during World War II," *Art Bulletin* 84 (March 2002): 130–47.

38. Goebel, *The Great War in Medieval Memory,* focuses on the central role the Middle Ages played in World War I remembrance in Britain and Germany.

39. *Chicago Tribune,* March 23, 1919; Adams, *Mont-Saint-Michel and Chartres,* 104.

40. *Chicago Tribune,* March 23, 1919.

41. Ibid., July 6, 1925.

42. These schemes appeared in the *Chicago Tribune,* December 27, 1923.

43. Robert R. McCormick, *The Army of 1918* (New York: Harcourt, Brace, and Howe, 1920).

44. *Chicago Tribune*, July 6, 1925, roughly paraphrases the scholar Elizabeth Boyle O'Reilly, *How France Built Her Cathedrals: A Study in the Twelfth and Thirteenth Centuries* (New York: Harper and Brothers, 1921), 508.

45. *Chicago Tribune*, December 3, 1922. In this quotation, the *Tribune* paraphrases a statement by Howells that may have been submitted with his competition entry.

46. *The W. G. N.: History of the Chicago Tribune, 1847–1922* (Chicago: Chicago Tribune, 1922), 104–6; Robert McCormick to Joseph Patterson, Thorold, Ontario, February 1, 1921, Series 2, Box 51, folder 4, Joseph Medill Patterson Papers, 1901–1950, Lake Forest College Library and Special Collections.

47. *Chicago Tribune*, December 3, 1922.

48. *Glimpses of Tribune Tower* (Chicago: Chicago Tribune, n.d.), 30.

49. *Chicago Tribune*, August 17, 1925.

50. McCormick, *The Army of 1918*, 271.

51. Sullivan, "Chicago Tribune Competition," 153, 156–57.

52. Adrian Forty and Susanne Küchler, eds., *The Art of Forgetting* (Oxford: Berg, 2001), esp. Forty, "Introduction," and Alex King, "Remembering and Forgetting in the Public Memorials of the Great War."

53. Robert McCormick, Memoirs, Part 12, broadcast November 22, 1952, transcript, Tribune Archives.

54. *Chicago Tribune*, June 10, 1922.

FORWARD ATLANTA

G. Lloyd Preacher and the Atlanta City Hall

Carrie Albee

February 22, 1930, marked the grand opening of the newest addition to the downtown skyline of Atlanta, Georgia, the burgeoning "Gate City" to the Southeast. Designed by the successful local architect G. Lloyd Preacher (1882–1972), the fifteen-story skyscraper was of steel-frame construction clad in buff-colored terra-cotta and consisted of a twelve-story tower rising from a three-story base flanked by three-story block wings (fig. 1). Although not the tallest in Atlanta, the building stood out due to its location outside of the central downtown cluster in an area targeted for new development. In design and exterior articulation it was also the most modern constructed in the city. The new city hall incorporated elements from the cutting-edge skyscrapers of the nation's leading urban centers, New York and Chicago of the 1920s. These tall office buildings had not been embraced as models for commercial structures in the more conservative cities of the traditional Old South, but they nonetheless provided Preacher with a point of departure for the Atlanta City Hall. With setbacks at the twelfth and fourteenth stories, emphasized verticality, and Gothic ornamentation, Preacher's skyscraper bore closer kinship with Eliel Saarinen's revolutionary Chicago Tribune Tower Competition entry (1922) and Raymond Hood and John Mead Howells's American Radiator Building (1924)

Fig. 1. Elevated view showing north (main) and west elevations—Atlanta City Hall, Bill Wilson, photographer. (Kenan Research Center at the Atlanta History Center)

than with Atlanta's more typical skyscraper, which had changed little in form or expression since the late nineteenth century (fig. 2).

Antecedents such as the Candler Building (1906), Atlanta's tallest building until 1929, and the Rhodes Haverty Building (1929), the city's tallest from 1929 to 1958, were typical of these structures in their block-like forms and Beaux-Arts vocabularies. With the selection of the commercial skyscraper form and language as a model for their city hall, the citizens of Atlanta sent a powerful message to the region and the nation. Its massing and ornamentation proclaimed Atlanta to be a progressive, commercially minded city of opportunity that had rejected the backward ways of the old Confederate South in favor of the vision of the reconstructed New South espoused by the *Atlanta Constitution* journalist and orator Henry Grady.[1]

Grady's proud declaration to General Sherman that "from the ashes he left

The CITY BUILDER

Atlanta's Magnificent New City Hall

Will Cost a Million and a Quarter Dollars and Will Embody All Points of Beauty and Modern Convenience—Located on Capitol Square

By J. HENSON TATUM

ANOTHER skyscraper will pierce Atlanta's sky line within the next eighteen months when the new city hall building is erected. The structure, of semi-Gothic set-back design, monumental and imposing, will tower fifteen stories above ground, and its walls will enclose twice as much floor area as the present city hall provides.

The edifice will occupy and extend beyond the site of the old Girls' High School building at the corner of Washington and Mitchell streets, rising as a near neighbor to both the state capitol and Fulton county court house.

G. Lloyd Preacher & Co., Inc., of Atlanta, are the architects, and they announce that final drawings will be complete ready for the City to advertise for bids by May 15, which means that actual construction will probably start during June. It is estimated that fifteen months will be required to finish the building. Total cost of the structure, if existing plans are unmodified, will approximate $1,250,000.

Ground floor dimensions of the city hall will be 116 by 160 feet, with the longer dimension on Mitchell street. These dimensions will continue thru the fourth floor, at which elevation the structure will set back to a tower 54 by 82 feet and continue to the height of fifteen stories.

Frame work of the building is to be of structural steel, and the exterior materials, all Georgia products, are to be granite, marble, brick and terra cotta. Marble and tile will be used for portions of the interior finish.

According to the architects, monumental type of construction is distinctively American and has gained widely in favor in recent years, much modern construction in the large cities being of this type. Such design of structure lends itself to ample window spacing, it is stated, which is a decided advantage in a public building.

For a considerable time the architects have been working on studies and preliminary plans. It was necessary to have a detailed survey and study made of the municipal departments as they exist and computations made of their probable future expansion. Expert assistance was rendered by a committee from the Atlanta Association of Building Owners and Managers. This committee spent several days of constant work on the survey, submitted complete and comprehensive findings to the City, the architects, the Bond Commission and General Council, and charged nothing for its labors. During February experts of the National Association of Building Owners and Managers came to Atlanta, at the City's invitation, and reviewed the architectural drawings of the new city hall. This group, which made certain suggestions relative to portions of the plan, complimented highly the external appearance of the structure as designed by the architects.

On the ground floor, according to plans of the architects, will be located the health department, warden's office, work space for the water works department and record rooms. A refreshment stand will have space on the ground floor also.

On the first floor will be situated

(*Continued on Page 48*)

Architect's Drawing of the New City Hall for Atlanta

Page Three

Fig. 2. "Architect's Drawing for the New City Hall for Atlanta," *City Builder*, March 1928. (Kenan Research Center at the Atlanta History Center)

us in 1864 we have raised a brave and beautiful city" continued to resonate with Atlanta civic leaders in the 1920s. The progressive spirit of the era was manifested as an intense desire to shake off regional stereotypes and show Atlanta as a player in the national arena. Similarly, the Atlanta City Hall represents the architectural manifestation of an important period of civic self-definition expressed through experimentation with architectural forms and styles that had been popularized nationwide, including Skyscraper Gothic. Poised between the decorated neoclassical high-rise blocks of pre–World War I Atlanta and the sleek minimalist towers of the post-Depression age, Preacher's City Hall represents the transposition of Skyscraper Gothic from commercial buildings to a municipal context. This happened at a moment when commercial clients were already turning away from literal Gothic ornamentation and would soon abandon it altogether. But to the aspiring Atlanta city leaders of the 1920s, the Gothic skyscraper remained the ultimate symbol of urban progress and modernity.

The site selected for the city hall was a spacious city block bounded by Mitchell and Washington Streets, and Central and Trinity Avenues, in an underdeveloped section of downtown Atlanta separated from the city's central business district by a major railroad artery. Atlanta's Central Improvement Association had targeted this area for the next phase in the city's growth, for which the new city hall building was to be a major catalyst. Development was further encouraged by the opening in 1929 of the Central and Pryor Street viaducts that greatly improved vehicular access to and from the central business district. The City Hall site was profoundly symbolic as well as practical. Prior to its most recent use for a girls' high school, it was the location of Union general William Tecumseh Sherman's headquarters during the Civil War. Use of this site certainly emphasized the intended image of a city rising from the ashes. It was also directly adjacent to Edbrooke and Burnham's neoclassical Georgia State Capitol (1889), providing an excellent opportunity for the creation of a planned civic precinct, an idea that had long been discussed among city leaders and was a central concept of the City Beautiful movement in urban design (fig. 3).

Fig. 3. Atlanta City Hall at night, Capitol Square, Atlanta, Kenneth Rogers, photographer. (Kenan Research Center at the Atlanta History Center)

Funded by the passage of a $1 million civic improvements bond in 1926 under Mayor I. E. Ragsdale, construction began on the new Atlanta City Hall in March 1929 and was completed in February of the following year, just four months after the devastating stock market crash.[2] Local labor executed Gothic detail in terra-cotta, concentrated at the primary entrances, setbacks, and tower crown. The Gothic theme was extended to the major public spaces of the interior as well, including the lobby and the grand Council Chambers (fig. 4). No expense was spared in the finishing of these interior spaces, which were exe-

Fig. 4. Interior, close-up of elevator door and directory—Atlanta City Hall. (Historic American Buildings Survey, Library of Congress, Prints and Photographs Division, Washington, D.C.)

cuted in imported Roman travertine, Georgia marble, brass, and birch veneer, and elaborately carved and gilt woodwork. When G. Lloyd Preacher's Atlanta City Hall officially opened to the public in February 1930, it was praised by Atlantans as "a beautiful building, well worthy of the city which it officially represents. . . . [I]t is an edifice of which Atlanta may be proud."[3]

Although unfamiliar in southern cities, the adaptation of the commercial skyscraper form to a civic function was more common in newly developed areas of the country such as the Midwest, California, and Florida. When Preacher began work on the project in 1928, the national design community was still fomenting over architects Austin, Martin, and Parkinson's "modern American" Los Angeles City Hall (1927), and Bertram Goodhue's "strikingly modern" Nebraska State Capitol (1932), still under construction.[4] Both buildings received an enormous amount of national attention from architects and laypersons alike, who were reacting to what were among the earliest definitive architectural expressions of modernism in the United States. Such radically modern designs were a reflection of the youthful, vibrant, commercially focused cities of Los Angeles and Lincoln, and of the progressive politics of their civic leaders during the decade following World War I.[5]

The selection of a skyscraper form for these important civic buildings and the use of a modern, minimalist architectural language was in direct opposition to popular conventions. The willingness on the part of civic leaders to break these conventions illustrates the desire to make a powerful statement through architecture: to proclaim the progressive policies of their governments and the spirit of modernity of their citizenry for the purposes of attracting national attention and both reflecting and encouraging economic growth.

Although located within a historically conservative region, the city of Atlanta had much more in common with Lincoln and Los Angeles than with the established cities of the Old South. Founded in 1837 as the terminus of the Western and Atlantic Rail Road and incorporated a decade later in 1847, Atlanta was from the beginning a commercial city of workingmen, entrepreneurs, and land speculators with progressive political, economic, and social attitudes. Still in its infancy at the outbreak of the Civil War, Atlanta did not identify with the culture of the old plantation South that played such an important role in the urban consciousness of such cities as Charleston and Savannah, particularly during the post–Civil War period. And although the city was burned to the ground by Union troops under the command of General Sherman in 1864, Atlantans were remarkably forgiving, choosing to see the event as, in effect, an opportunity that freed the city from any debt it might have owed to the Old South, providing a blank canvas on which to build a new and greater city.[6]

This sentiment was most eloquently expressed in the now famous words of Atlanta businessman and champion of the New South ideology Henry Grady, who in 1886 became the first southerner to address the prestigious New England Society. Speaking on the conditions and aspirations of the reconstructed New South to an all-"Yankee" crowd including General Sherman himself, Grady boldly stated the words that have embodied the spirit and urban identity of the city of Atlanta for over a century: "I want to say to General Sherman, that from the ashes he left us in 1864 we have raised a brave and beautiful city; that somehow or other we have caught the sunshine in the bricks and mortar of our homes, and have builded therein not one ignoble prejudice or memory."[7] Atlanta adopted its current city seal, featuring the rising phoenix, only a year after Henry Grady's speech, firmly identifying itself with the New South vision. Above the phoenix, in between his outspread wings, is the word *resurgens,* meaning "rising again," and below are the dates 1847 and 1865, the former marking the city's incorporation, and the latter, the end of the war and consequently the beginning of the New South's resurrection.

In the decades following the Civil War, while other southern cities struggled to survive in the grip of a crippled agrarian system, Atlanta was quick to rebuild, benefiting economically from a convenient geographical location that made the city a natural transportation hub, and given an additional boost with the relocation there of the Georgia state capital from Milledgeville in 1868. During this period, a new class of progressive-minded young businessmen, a "commercial-civic elite," rose to political and financial prominence in Atlanta.[8] In 1879 the *Atlanta Constitution* described this new class as composed of "live energetic men. They have no long line of ancestry with coat-of-arms to keep up. . . . They live to drive their business[es]."[9] These men were instrumental in the rebuilding of the city following the Civil War, and under their leadership and ambitious commercial agenda, Atlanta became by the 1880s one of the South's largest and most important economic centers. Atlantans, inspired by Henry Grady, declared their city to be the leader of the "New South," a region that had been "reborn intellectually, socially, industrially, agriculturally, financially, and transportation-wise."[10]

The symbol of the phoenix rising could not have been more appropriate for Atlanta during the decade following the end of the First World War. In addition to suffering standard wartime recession, the city had experienced a major fire in 1917, which destroyed close to two thousand buildings in the residential area northeast of the downtown business district. With the end of the war in 1918, however, the city of Atlanta began to climb out of recession and rebuild, much as it had following the Civil War. Atlanta experienced a tremendous economic boom during the 1920s, manifested in the widespread building construction. It was a decade of technological firsts and infrastructural development for Atlanta, including the installation of its first traffic light downtown on busy Peachtree Street, the construction of its first public airstrip, and the city's first transatlantic telephone call. No fewer than 762 new businesses sprang up between 1925 and 1929, prompting the Chicago Association of Commerce to open an office in Atlanta in July 1928, a point of considerable pride to citizens.[11]

The common interest among the commercial-civic elite in the economic growth of the city crystallized in a collective and cooperative civic boosterism under the auspices of the Atlanta Chamber of Commerce. By 1920, the ranks of the Chamber of Commerce had risen to 2,890 members, and in 1925, when the Chamber launched its "Forward Atlanta" campaign to promote economic growth and civic pride, it boasted the sponsorship of 350 commercial and professional organizations.[12]

Through their monthly publication, the *City Builder,* the Chamber of Commerce encouraged the perception of Atlanta as the economic leader of the Southeast, despite concurrent claims for that position made by both Birmingham and Nashville. In 1925, Fred Newell explained in the *City Builder* that Atlanta was the "principle [*sic*] city" in the region due to its "continuation to maintain business supremacy over all cities in Georgia, and, in recent years, over all cities in the South."[13] This view was apparently shared by Louis D. Newton, who wrote in the January 1927 issue that "the history of Atlanta is the history of the railroads entering Atlanta. *Terminus* was the first name given Atlanta and that word signifies the reason for the establishment here of the South's leading city. It is the gateway to the South, the natural crossroads."[14] Cover images from the magazine reinforced this perception through the repeated depiction of Atlanta at the physical center and symbolic focal point of the southern states (fig. 5).

The Atlanta Chamber of Commerce combated negative stereotypes of the South by emphasizing in the *City Builder* magazine industrial and commercial enterprise not only in Atlanta itself but in the region as a whole through articles, editorials, images, and advertisements focusing on the twin progressive themes of building and transportation. Cover images during this period feature maps of the southeastern states with greatly exaggerated clusters of skyscrapers indicating the major cities, connected by a highly developed web of highway and railway lines, a montage of the newest buildings throughout the South, a view of the Atlanta skyline, or a map of the city of Atlanta with the rate of travel between other major cities in the United States. Atlanta and the other

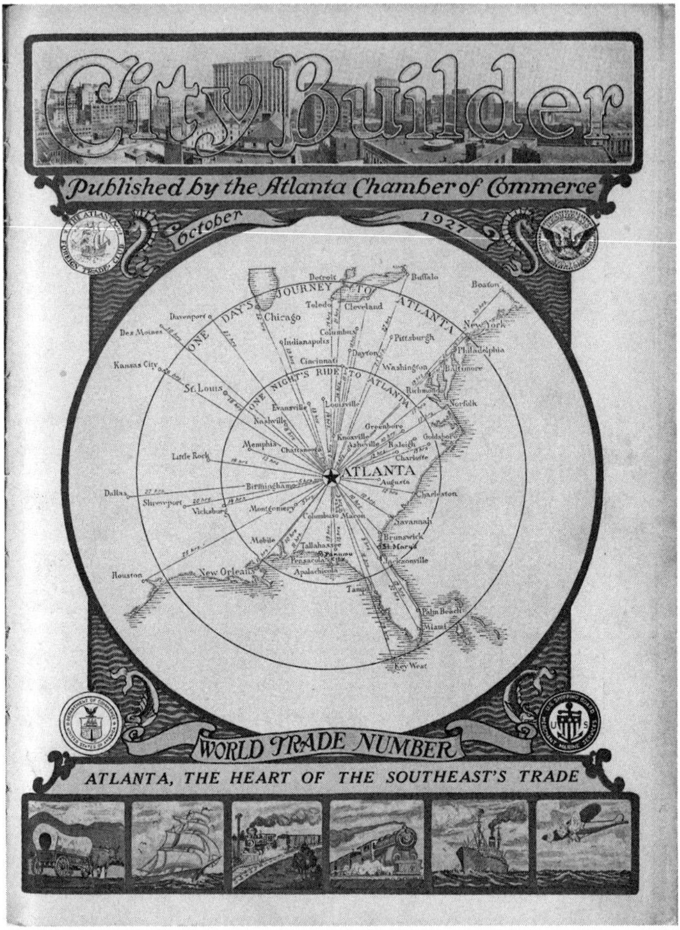

Fig. 5. *City Builder*, cover, November 1927. (Kenan Research Center at the Atlanta History Center)

major southern cities are presented as heavily urbanized, commercially active trade centers like those of the Northeast.

Throughout the *City Builder,* one theme remains constant: that of the skyscraper as the measure of the progressive city. To the urban citizen of the Progressive Era, it was the city's skyline that conveyed its prosperity and success, defined chiefly by the silhouette of the skyscraper—the "outward show of an inward spirit of citizenry."[15] In the still relatively underdeveloped, largely rural, agrarian Southeast, the skyscraper took on particular significance in a region that could boast only a few cities large enough to attract national recognition. Cognizant of this perception, Atlantans took pride in their skyline, which by the 1920s featured several notable skyscrapers, including the New York architect J. E. R. Carpenter's seventeen-story Hurt Building (1913); this was reputed in 1926 to be the "largest office building south of New York City . . . ranked fifteenth largest in the United States."[16] The city's skyscrapers stood out among those of its rival southern cities as "things of beauty and awe . . . made out of Georgia's own bosom."[17] So important was the skyline to urban identity that one proud Atlantan proclaimed in 1926 that "if the question should be asked 'what was the one greatest factor in making Atlanta the city it is today,' the answer should, unhesitatingly be, 'its fine office buildings.' . . . In no other Southern city can be found so many modern, high class office buildings as in Atlanta."[18]

While asserting their superiority among southern cities, Atlantans were aware that their downtown, which in the 1920s featured several of the South's tallest and best-known commercial buildings, lagged far behind the nation's great urban centers in both the number and design of skyscrapers. Since the turn of the twentieth century, commercial buildings in Atlanta had strictly followed the simple formula of the earliest skyscrapers that first appeared in downtown Chicago during the 1880s and 1890s. These buildings rose anywhere from ten to eighteen stories, with a rectangular or triangular plan, and the conventional formula of a highly ornamented, pronounced base of one to three stories, a rising shaft of little architectural distinction, and a crown of one or two stories punctuated with a heavy, overhanging "classical" cornice. The eight-story Equitable Building (1892) was considered Atlanta's first true skyscraper; designed by Chicago school architects and skyscraper pioneers Daniel Burnham and John Wellborn Root, it was one such building, thought to be quite modern at the time of its construction. Over the next three decades, construction in Atlanta's rapidly growing business district would produce several dozen skyscrapers, including Murphy and Stewart's Candler Building (1906), the Gothic-style Healey Building (1913), designed by Morgan & Dillon with W. T. Downing, and Carpenter's Hurt Building (1924). While these subsequent skyscrapers far surpassed the Equitable Building in height and scale, nearly all would adhere to the same predictable architectural format—until the construction of G. Lloyd Preacher's Atlanta City Hall.

The architectural stagnation evident in Atlanta's commercial skyscrapers throughout the first quarter of the twentieth century did not go uncriticized. Atlantans were well aware of the fundamental differences between their own downtown architecture and the new skyscrapers that were appearing in the nation's leading cities, overshadowing the old forms and familiar techniques of the early Chicago skyscrapers. Even Cass Gilbert's iconic Woolworth Building (1913), praised by its contemporaries as representative of the best in skyscraper design, was viewed as dated for its massing and historicized Gothic ornamentation when compared to McKenzie, Voorhees, and Gmelin's nearby Barclay Vesey Building (1923–27).[19]

During the 1920s, the lack of innovation evident in southern skyscraper design was apparent to Atlanta's commercial-civic elite, who looked to New York as the ideal progressive modern city. This attitude is represented by the image of Atlanta on the cover of the September 1927 *City Builder* magazine, designed by Wilbur G. Kurtz and appropriately entitled *Forward Atlanta* after the Chamber's civic booster campaign of the same name (fig. 6).[20] A fascinating representation of the past, present, and future of Atlanta as a vertical progression of five successive tiers from bottom to the top, the image represents the twin themes of building and transportation as the principal manifestations of progress and the underlying belief that progress means bigger, faster, and better.

The story begins at the bottom of the image, a representation of the beginnings of the settlement that would become the great city of Atlanta. The central figure is strapping Stephen Long, a surveyor for the Western and Atlantic Rail Road and the legendary founder of the city, wielding his hammer like a Georgian John Henry, having driven the massive wooden stake into the ground that would determine the terminus of the railroad line and the subsequent location of a new settlement. Also depicted is a covered wagon drawn by a pair of horses, linking Atlanta with America's purportedly hardy, simple pioneering past rather than with the privileged plantation lifestyle of the Old South. Passing on through the depictions of Atlanta in its infancy, then known as Marthasville, and the pre–Civil War city with its street lanterns and horse-drawn trolley, the panorama then gives way to the rapidly growing city of the early twentieth cen-

Fig. 6. *Forward Atlanta, City Builder*, cover, September 1927. (Kenan Research Center at the Atlanta History Center)

tury, represented by a complicated network of railroad lines and the modern downtown skyline beyond. Atlanta's golden future is represented by the towering futuristic skyscrapers that spring from the clouds and rise even above the biplane. These streamlined skyscrapers with setbacks reflected contemporary trends in skyscraper design. Buildings such as these already existed in New York and Chicago, but to Atlantans of the Progressive Era, these buff white towers were ideal skyscrapers, and in direct contrast to the squat, rectangular buildings that punctuated their own skyline. Atlanta city leaders believed that until the city developed a sophisticated, mature skyline it would not be recognized as a competitive, progressive urban center on a national level. But realizing that vision would require a decided break with local architectural convention and a successful demonstration to the general public that modern design aesthetics could be successfully adapted to the southern city.

City leaders and the members of the commercial-civic elite saw the Atlanta City Hall commission as the perfect opportunity to give material form to the newly proclaimed defining characteristics of the Gate City, the capital of the New South: progressivism, modernism, positivism, pride, commercialism, and strength. Atlantans recognized that they could not achieve national status until the perception of the South as a whole was improved, and Atlanta sought to lead by example. For, as one writer in the *City Builder* explained, "if Atlanta can help give the world a better impression of the South through showing the world a great, progressive city, then Atlanta will be serving the South—all of its neighboring cities."[21] The new Atlanta City Hall was intended to contribute to this vision.

The first step toward the realization of Atlanta's ambition for its City Hall was the selection of the local architect G. Lloyd Preacher. An active and influential member of Atlanta's elite class of progressive, civic-minded businessmen and closely associated with New South ideology, Preacher was a logical choice for the commission. Born in 1882 in Fairfax, South Carolina, Preacher graduated from Clemson University in 1904, after which he worked as a draftsman and designer.[22] Preacher's marriage in 1905 to Fannie McDaniel, "a representative of one of the old and prominent families of the state" and the daughter of a man with close ties to the Southern Railroad, one of the largest and wealthiest corporations in the South, immediately placed him within this privileged class.[23] In 1918 Preacher was accepted into the Georgia Chapter of the American Institute of Architects, and in that same year he was appointed to the Georgia AIA Review Board, a position that gave him a great deal of influence within the architectural community.[24] Preacher was also a member of both the York and Scottish Rite Masons, the Mystic Shrine, the Yaareb Temple, and the Benevolent Protective Order of the Elks, as well as the Druid Hills Golf Club and the Atlanta Automobile Club, and the exclusive Capital City Club.[25] As a member of the Atlanta Chamber of Commerce, Preacher strongly supported the

"Forward Atlanta" campaign, toward which his firm, G. Lloyd Preacher and Company, contributed the unusually large sum of $1,560.[26] Through his participation in these social and civic institutions, Preacher demonstrated his affinity with the established social order and with the progressive ideology of Atlanta's commercial-civic elite.

Furthermore, as well as being generally recognized for his creativity and skill as an architect, G. Lloyd Preacher was identified from the very beginning of his career with the building of the New South, an association that the architect cultivated and that proved quite lucrative for his firm during the first two decades of the twentieth century. Preacher began his architectural career in Augusta, Georgia, where he designed the Marion Building (1912), both his own and the city of Augusta's first true skyscraper, and subsequently, the sixteen-story Southern Finance Building (1914). These skyscrapers, unparalleled in height and scale in Augusta, redefined the skyline of that city and earned Preacher the reputation as a progressive architect particularly skilled in the design and execution of the building type. By 1917, *Augusta Magazine* was heralding Preacher as "the leading architect in Augusta and one of the foremost men in his profession in the Southern states," an example of how "genuine talent, united with industry and perseverance, never fails to conquer success."[27]

In 1922 Preacher moved his offices from Augusta to Atlanta, where the unprecedented building boom had created tremendous opportunities for talented young architects. Over the next decade the firm of G. Lloyd Preacher and Company designed and constructed numerous commercial and public office buildings, hotels, theaters, and apartment buildings in Atlanta and throughout the Southeast while maintaining central offices in the English Gothic–inspired Healey Building (1913) in downtown Atlanta. During this period, Preacher and Company became recognized as "a great Southeastern institution rather than a purely local Atlanta business," with an estimated 417 buildings credited to the firm by 1930.[28]

Aware of the potential advantage of such regional associations, Preacher began to market his firm as a progressive builder of the New South. A full-page advertisement from 1924 featured a carefully selected sample of the firm's work within the Southeast under the title of "Modern Southern Buildings," accompanied by the statement: "In the recent tremendous development of the South, the erection of imposing buildings of the most modern character has had a very significant place . . . in every progressive community. . . . [I]t has been the privilege of G. Lloyd Preacher and Company to have a conspicuous part in this huge program during the past several years."[29] This reputation, his experience with the construction of large-scale buildings, and his philosophical and social affinities with Atlanta's commercial-civic elite made G. Lloyd Preacher the ideal architect for the new Atlanta City Hall.

By the mid-1920s a general consensus had developed among city leaders and the local architectural community that the modern skyscraper form for the city's most important civic structure would best communicate the progressive, commercial identity of the city and could become an icon attracting national attention. This was a departure from the prevailing conventions in civic architecture in the Southeast. The Atlanta City Hall rejects traditional civic neoclassical language as well as conventional elements such as the dome, rotunda, and grand stair hall in favor of the architectural lexicon of American business. This aesthetic choice stemmed, at least in part, from a new conception of city government. In Atlanta, a corporate philosophy was applied to the municipal government, as indicated by the *Atlanta Constitution* in 1921, which described the city as "nothing other than a big corporation . . . its affairs must be managed by men who are acquainted with at least the rudimentary elements of business."[30] "The American skyscraper," wrote the scholar R. W. Sexton in 1928, "stands as a noble expression of the high standards and ideals of modern American business. Strength, honesty, and sincerity are features of its design as they are characteristic of commercial enterprise."[31]

The use of the skyscraper form for the Atlanta City Hall may also be seen as an attempt to counteract contemporary anxiety about government corruption, a major issue in Atlanta during the period, by referencing commercial as opposed to earlier civic buildings. Contemporary sources indicate a serious concern that crime and corruption among Atlanta's city officials was widespread and uncontrollable. In 1921, a grand jury investigation into a supposed crime racket involving Atlanta policemen prompted the *Atlanta Constitution* to remark that "Society has reached a point at which human life, to say nothing of property, is not even reasonably safe and secure."[32] Furthermore, the 1920s saw the rise of "keyhole" journalism, which involved digging up as much dirt and scandal on prominent individuals as possible, no doubt feeding existing anxieties on the part of Atlanta citizens.[33] The Atlanta City Hall tower may have been an attempt to refute this perception of municipal corruption by adopting a corporate architectural language.

In addition to its putatively morally superior associations, commercial architecture also invoked the concept of efficiency, which was deemed especially important in both corporate and civic management, as "individual efficiency is the foundation of all constructive effort and when merged with mass-efficiency, whether it be a corporation or a community, the sum total of the result is reflected in achievement."[34] Atlanta's own concerns about municipal inefficiency resulted in the consolidation of many of its departmental divisions in 1922.[35]

In March 1928, the Chamber of Commerce member J. Henson Tatum announced in the *City Builder:* "Another skyscraper will pierce Atlanta's sky line within the next eighteen months when the new city hall building is erected. The structure, of semi-Gothic set-back design, monumental and imposing, will tower fifteen stories above ground, and its walls will enclose twice as much floor area as the present city hall provides."[36] As Tatum suggests, the skyscraper form was a solution to the need for space to accommodate an enlarged municipal staff, but it was also an indication of the increasingly bureaucratic nature of civic government.[37] Tatum went on to assure Atlantans who might have been uncomfortable with the adaptation of an overtly commercial architectural form to their city hall that "according to the architects, monumental type of construction is distinctly American and has gained widely in favor in recent years, much modern construction in the large cities being of this type. Such design of structure lends itself to ample window spacing, it is stated, which is a decided advantage in a public building."[38]

By the mid-1920s, speculation had begun on what a new purpose-built city hall would look like, and architects were already vying for the commission. One early proposal, submitted to the *City Builder* magazine in 1925 under the title "Modern Idea for a New City Hall Whenever Atlanta Can Have One," illustrates a twenty-one-story skyscraper set back at the fourth and seventeenth stories.[39] Although the architect is not named, the design is virtually identical to A. Ten Eyck Brown's Dade County Courthouse and Miami City Hall (1928) in Florida. Brown was a successful Atlanta architect and chief rival of G. Lloyd Preacher. In Brown's informal bid for the Atlanta City Hall commission, the Classical Revival–style building exhibits the stripped-down, monumental Beaux-Arts neoclassicism typical of Brown's civic commissions, including the Fulton County Courthouse and his subsequent Federal Post Office Building (1931), both in Atlanta. By the time Atlanta was ready to select a firm, Brown's proposed design had been realized in Miami, and in any case the City of Atlanta seemed inclined to endorse a more commercial design solution.

Nonetheless, Brown's and Preacher's modern city halls share the same basic approach to skyscraper massing with a shaft rising from a broad, plinth-like base with periodic setbacks. However, Preacher's design presents a more sophisticated and graceful articulation of the setbacks and firmly breaks with conventional civic architecture in the use of Gothic, rather than neoclassical, ornamentation. The set-back skyscraper developed in New York City and proliferated following the passage of the 1916 city zoning ordinance that addressed, among other issues, public anxieties related to the density of downtown skyscraper construction. In other large cities throughout the United States, where architects were not bound by zoning restrictions, the "new silhouette" of the set-back skyscraper appeared and was praised as "one of the most original phases of recent work."[40]

Now recognized as perhaps the most influential set-back skyscraper design of the period, Eliel Saarinen's unexecuted 1922 proposal for the new Chicago Tribune Tower not only incorporated set-back massing but also overtly rejected elaborate applied ornamentation and a bulky projecting cornice in favor of a sleek, simplified, uninterrupted verticality. Though Saarinen's innovative design took second place in the Chicago Tribune Tower Competition behind Hood and Howells's more conventional proposal, thereafter skyscraper design moved steadily toward a more minimalist approach to ornamentation and a pronounced emphasis on aesthetically expressed verticality as seen in such notable examples as Hood and Howells's American Radiator Building (1924), McKenzie, Voorhees, and Gmelin's Barclay Vesey (New York Telephone) Building (1926), Charles Klauder's "Cathedral of Learning" (1926), as well as Preacher's Atlanta City Hall.

Amid widespread acceptance of the setback as an approach to skyscraper massing, the form met with some resistance in the more conservative southern states. Many felt that while the setback made sense in crowded northern cities, the form was antithetical in southern cities, where land was ample, downtown buildings more dispersed, and air and light readily available. As late as 1930, southern architects cautiously urged one another to "look at this movement with open minds to see first if it can be adapted in the South to our best interest."[41] Others argued for the rejection of the setback altogether, so as to "retain such dignity and spaciousness of horizontal dimensions in architectural form as to maintain something of the amplitude and broad hospitality of the Southern tradition."[42]

Preacher's Atlanta City Hall gave no credence to such reservations. On the contrary, it suggests a firm, almost illogical commitment to the set-back skyscraper form as the most important aspect of the design. The building footprint occupied a mere 10 percent of the entire city block on which it was situated, a parcel that could have easily accommodated the 1,044,419 cubic feet of offices in a low-rise building and still left more than enough open land for a dramatic approach befitting a public building and formal green space. The nine-story shaft measures only 82 by 54 feet, which, less the elevator shafts and mechanical spaces, left an area for offices small enough as to border on impractical.[43] The need to maximize office space limited the degree to which the setback could be incorporated in the design, so Preacher responded with true setbacks on the side elevations of the City Hall tower but contained the front and rear elevations entirely on one plane. Through the articulation of the front and rear elevations, Preacher created the illusion of a setback in the projection of Gothic hood ornamentation on the thirteenth floor and the slight recession of the single flanking bays of the fourteenth through the sixteenth floors.

The more progressive among southern architects were receptive to the aesthetic of verticality as exemplified in Saarinen's Chicago Tribune Tower Competition entry, whose "pronounced vertical lines from the base to the top" were heralded by the Atlanta architect Frank P. Smith in 1928 as "the most characteristic features of modern architecture in America."[44] An early sketch of the Atlanta City Hall, printed in the *City Builder* in March 1928, shows the shaft rising from a broad base with Gothic details, as was eventually constructed, with a crown that is ziggurat-like, calling to mind the "wedding-cake" buildings much decried in elite design circles of the day.[45] As built, however, the Atlanta City Hall indicates that Preacher refined his earlier design, bringing it closer to the ideal. It exhibits one fewer setback but the same number of stories, and the setbacks are shallower, with the result that the verticality of the building is more pronounced, giving a greater sense of soaring height. Additionally, the Gothic ornamentation employed on the building is more subdued than suggested in the *City Builder* sketch so as not to detract from the vertical lines of the tower deriving from the steel structural system within. The primary elevations are dominated by two robust buff terra-cotta piers that seem to anchor the building, unifying the three distinct sections of base, shaft, and crown. These dominant piers are reinforced by the slender, respond-like buff terra-cotta bands that define the window bays and counter the bands of Gothic ornamentation, effectively suppressing the horizontality necessarily expressed by the internal structure of stacked floors.

The theme of verticality was extended to the interior of the Atlanta City Hall as well, where the grand public hall and central staircases of the traditional civic building give way to the elevator lobby of the commercial skyscraper. The idea that the elevator could be seen as the union between the ultimate progressive themes of height and speed was expressed in a 1930 issue of the *Southern Architect and Building News,* which describes the elevator not as a functional necessity but as a modern wonder: "We are impressed with the speed at which we move, with the absolute perfection of the mechanical powers of the modern elevator and smoothness of the ascending journey."[46]

Atlanta's complete departure from civic precedent was accomplished through the adoption of Gothic motifs, following the examples of several well-known contemporary skyscrapers. The Atlanta City Hall pays homage to Cass Gilbert's Woolworth Building in its dominant tower rising from a robust base, the use of buff terra-cotta cladding, the rhythm of strong and weak vertical piers, the periodic horizontal bands of Gothic detailing to divide the facade into base, shaft, and crown, and the tabernacle hoods employed at the twelfth story. And like the Woolworth Building and Chicago Tribune Tower, the Atlanta City Hall is embellished with literal Gothic ornamentation. Flamboyant tracery can be seen in the panels between the windows, the parapets at the top stories of the tower and flanking wings, and in the cornice above the doorways of the main entrance. The window panels of the third and eleventh stories display the city seal, with the mythical phoenix rising from the ashes emblazoned upon terra-cotta shields.

Gothic pointed lancet arches are found in the windows and doors of the grand entranceway, alluding to the triple portals of a medieval church west end. The Gothic trefoil graces the third-story corbelling of the central tower and hangs in stalactite drops from the arches over each main portal, together serving to emphasize the elaborate entranceway as the focus of the elevation. The use of corbelling, both stylized and more literal, is found at the third story, the fourteenth-story setback, and the fifteenth story, signaling the termination of the elevation of the building at those levels. Furthermore, the strong verticality of the central tower, with the two structural terra-cotta-clad steel piers dominating the elevation, and the secondary, more slender piers in between, suggest a cathedral nave.

Gothic motifs are applied to the hardware and fixtures of the building, as well as throughout the primary interior spaces of the lobbies, central staircases and hallways, and the council chamber. The central first-floor lobby, clad in travertine and Georgia marble and finished in birch veneer, gilding, and brass, exhibits Gothic detailing in the carved wood and gilt capitals of the structural piers, the balusters of the main marble staircases, the light fixtures, and in the brass elevator casings (see fig. 4). On the second floor, the council chamber takes on the formal characteristics of a medieval hall, with a ceiling of exposed wooden beams elegantly painted in various bright colors and resting on wooden arches springing from stone corbels grounded through the stone piers and responds.

Designed fifteen years after the completion of the Woolworth Building, however, the Atlanta City Hall reflects a transitional period in Skyscraper Gothic during which literal ornament was dissolving into the more abstracted forms characteristic of the Art Deco style. The *Southern Architect and Building News* presented its take on the issue of skyscraper design in 1930, when it proclaimed, "In the simple, truthful expression of the steel shaft and the possibilities for interesting masses lies that path toward which every designer should look with renewed interest."[47] The author hedged his bets with the southern readership, however, with a respectful defense of historicism: "There is still an opportunity to effectively use the basic elements of our traditional styles, and I am not yet convinced that the most refined bits of ornament of the old order cannot be used."[48] Preacher's City Hall exhibits some intriguing abstracted Gothic details in the tapered caps of the four entrance piers and the rocket-like base of the brass lampposts flanking the entranceway, suggesting the influence of Hugh Ferriss's massing studies, reproduced in the landmark publication *The Metropolis of Tomorrow* (1929).

When the Atlanta City Hall opened its doors, Preacher's design was praised as "too magnificent to be called a city hall." "It is a beautiful building, well worthy of the city which it officially represents," the *City Builder* asserted, and "an edifice of which Atlanta may be proud."[49] Shortly after the building opened, city officials held an open house to show off the "most beautiful and modern city hall building in the entire South."[50] Despite this acclaim, the City Hall did not have the profound impact on urban architecture in the region for which civic leaders had hoped. The stock market crash of October 1929 and the ensuing economic depression put an abrupt end to the Chamber of Commerce's ambitious "Forward Atlanta" campaign and permanently altered the course of architectural development in the city and throughout the country. Architecturally obsolete by the time of its completion, the building is the hopeful expression of a city on the rise—a city that could not have imagined the radical changes that would occur in the years ahead.

NOTES

1. During the 1880s, the Georgia native Henry Grady became a part owner of the *Atlanta Constitution* newspaper, which he used as a platform to promote the progressive concept of a New South popularized during the post-Reconstruction period. Grady's idea of the New South rejected the rebellious slavery-based plantation stereotype in favor of an industrialized, commercially minded, urban (in short, more "northern") South fully reconciled with and equal to the North. For additional information on the New South school of thought in the late nineteenth and early twentieth centuries, see Blaine A. Brownell, *The Urban Ethos in the South, 1920–1930* (Baton Rouge: Louisiana State University Press, 1975), 204.

2. Robert M. Craig, *Atlanta Architecture: Art Deco to Modern Classic, 1929–1959* (Gretna, LA: Pelican, 1995), 47.

3. The City Builder Extension Bureau, "Our New Municipal Building," *City Builder,* March 1930, 18.

4. Eldon Huack, *American Capitols* (Jefferson, NC: McFarland, 1991), 14–15; *A Harmony*

of the Arts: The Nebraska State Capitol, ed. Frederick C. Leubke (Lincoln: University of Nebraska Press, 1990), 13.

5. Leubke, ed., *A Harmony of the Arts,* 10.

6. Brownell, *The Urban Ethos in the South,* 204.

7. Ivan Allen, *Atlanta from the Ashes* (Atlanta: Ruralist Press, 1928), 8. The full text of Grady's New South Creed may be found at www.anselm.edu/academic/history/hdubrulle/CivWar/text/documents/doc54.htm.

8. In *The Urban Ethos in the South,* the regional sociologist Blaine Brownell defines the term "commercial-civic elite" as "the business-oriented middle class that asserted itself in southern cities in the late nineteenth century" (47).

9. *Atlanta Constitution,* March 2, 1879.

10. "The Progressive South," *City Builder,* August 1925, 35.

11. Elizabeth Anne Mack Lyon, "Business Buildings in Atlanta: A Study in Urban Growth and Form" (PhD diss., Emory University, 1971), 362–64.

12. Brownell, *The Urban Ethos in the South,* 47.

13. Fred Newell, "Historic Outline of Atlanta," *City Builder,* February 1925, 62.

14. Louis D. Newton, "A Greater City Than We Thought," *City Builder,* January 1927, 9.

15. *Tennessean,* May 26, 1920.

16. Fred Shaefer, "The South's Greatest Office Building City," *City Builder,* March 1926, 22.

17. Craddock Goins, "The Red Old Thrills of Georgia," *City Builder,* January 1925, 20.

18. Shaefer, "The South's Greatest Office Building City," 22.

19. G. H. Edgell, *The American Architecture of To-day* (New York: Charles Scribner's Sons, 1928), 76.

20. "Forward Atlanta," *City Builder,* September 1927, cover.

21. Goins, "The Red Old Thrills of Georgia," 53.

22. Charles Lowe, "Biography of G. Lloyd Preacher," *Augusta Magazine,* Fall 1981, 15.

23. Clark Howell, *A History of Georgia* (1926), 4:25; Lucian L. Knight, *A Standard History of Georgia and Georgians* (Chicago and New York, 1917), 6:3045–46.

24. Lowe, "Biography of G. Lloyd Preacher," 15.

25. Howell, *A History of Georgia* (1926), 4:25

26. Forward Atlanta Commission, *Report of the Forward Atlanta Commission, 1926–1929* (Forward Atlanta Commission, 1930), 32.

27. Knight, *A Standard History of Georgia and Georgians* (1917), 6:3045.

28. Julian Wade Adams, "G. Lloyd Preacher, Southern Architect: A Study of His Career" (master's thesis, Augusta College, 1987), 63, 94.

29. "Modern Southern Buildings," *Manufacturers Record,* December 11, 1924, 655.

30. Qtd. in Brownell, *The Urban Ethos in the South,* 41.

31. Kenneth Turney Gibbs, *Business Architectural Imagery in America, 1870–1930* (Ann Arbor, MI: UMI Research Press, 1984), 1.

32. *Atlanta Constitution,* March 17, 1921.

33. George E. Mowry and Blaine A. Brownell, *The Urban Nation, 1920–1980: The Making of America* (New York: Hill and Wang, 1981), 19.

34. Brownell, *The Urban Ethos in the South,* 141.

35. Ibid., 16.

36. J. Henson Tatum, "Atlanta's Magnificent New City Hall," *City Builder,* March 1928, 3.

37. Craig, *Atlanta Architecture,* 43.

38. Tatum, "Atlanta's Magnificent New City Hall," 3.

39. Craig, *Atlanta Architecture,* 43.

40. Thomas E. Tallmadge, *The Story of Architecture in America* (New York: Norton, 1927), 294.

41. Ernest Ray Denmark, "Are We Going Modern?" *Southern Architect and Building News,* January 1930, 49.

42. Ibid.

43. Tatum, "Atlanta's Magnificent New City Hall," 25.

44. Frank P. Smith, "Modern Architecture in America," *City Builder,* February 1928, 10.

45. Tatum, "Atlanta's Magnificent New City Hall."

46. "Office Building Design," *Southern Architect and Building News,* November 1930, 16.

47. Ibid.

48. Ibid.

49. The City Builder Extension Bureau, 18.

50. *Atlanta Constitution,* February 23, 1930.

GOTHIC WITH AN AMERICAN ACCENT

The Cathedral of Learning

Anke Koeth

In 1928, George H. Edgell stated in *The American Architecture of To-Day* that "most Americans continued their belief that one can worship God properly only in a Gothic building and, for the cloistered atmospheres of the university, Gothic was considered eminently apt."[1] Although he was dean of the architecture faculty at Harvard University,[2] his book about contemporary architecture is explicitly not addressed by a specialist to other experts. Instead, as he writes in the preface. "It is a layman's review for laymen."[3] Edgell's claim that the Gothic was the only proper style for universities reflected a general tendency in educational building that had begun in the nineteenth century with, for example, the campus of Trinity College in Hartford in the early 1870s.[4] The stylistic trend continued through the first several decades of the twentieth century with the traditional Harkness Memorial Quadrangle at Yale (James Gamble Rogers, 1917–21), which, in terms of structure and character, adopts the forms of medieval English universities. However, the increasing acceptance of modernist solutions to a variety of institutions spelled the decline of the Collegiate Gothic at midcentury.[5]

This essay discusses a unique adaptation of modern architecture for the purposes of a university: specifically, the appropriation of the skyscraper for an educational institution. The use of the tall commercial building for an educational purpose offered both opportunities and challenges. The Cathedral of Learning at the University of Pittsburgh demonstrates how the skyscraper building type and the Gothic style could be used conjointly and could provide a new symbolism for metropolitan universities. Gothic as *the* architectural style for universities, illustrating their traditions that went back to medieval cloisters, was so deeply rooted in the general consciousness of the time that a stylistic term had evolved for it: Collegiate Gothic. Yet the choice of a skyscraper for a university campus was controversial because the skyscraper could provide neither a campus in the traditional American university model nor the conventional language of the Collegiate Gothic. This building type could not achieve general acceptance for this particular use. However, Gothic skyscrapers represented a particular and compelling, if fleeting, adaptation of modern architecture to the university. Moreover, they demonstrate the extension of the Gothic skyscraper to a new function, and to new places, well beyond Chicago and New York.

A NEW UNIVERSITY BUILDING FOR PITTSBURGH

In February 1925, the chancellor of the University of Pittsburgh, John Bowman, published *The Cathedral of Learning of the University of Pittsburgh,* presenting the anticipated new building of the university through plans and model photographs as well as in writing. The building was shown as a skyscraper with fifty-two stories and a height of 680 feet; it was intended to contain classrooms, a library, laboratories, and additional spaces required by a university of twelve thousand students (fig. 1).[6] From 1925 to 1937, the building—even though reduced to "only" forty-two stories and 535 feet in height—was built according to the plans of the architect Charles Z. Klauder.[7] It rises in several set-back masses, being additionally monumentalized by the open space around it. It is accompanied by the Heinz Chapel (1934–38) and the Stephen Foster Memorial (1933–37), both of which were also built by Klauder (fig. 2).

The Cathedral of Learning was the tallest of all the buildings in its vicinity at the time of its completion. Being the central building of the University of Pittsburgh, it is located in the Oakland neighborhood, which is characterized by smaller-scale buildings for culture and education, such as the Carnegie Institute and the Carnegie Library (Longfellow, Alden, and Harlow, 1892–95),

Fig. 1. Cathedral of Learning, under construction in 1929. (University of Pittsburgh Historic Photographs, 1884–present, University Archives, University of Pittsburgh)

Carnegie Mellon University (Henry Hornbostel, 1905), the Allegheny County Soldiers' and Sailors' Memorial (Palmer and Hornbostel, 1907–10), and the Masonic Temple (today Alumni Hall [Benno Janssen, 1914]).[8] The central business district of Pittsburgh, the Golden Triangle, is around two-and-a-half miles away from Oakland. Both its site and its height contribute to the building's dominance, which is further emphasized by its urban context. It is aligned with the axis of Forbes Avenue, a major street leading from the Monongahela River up the hill to Oakland, and consequently dominates the view for all traveling by that route to the university. The street axis continues to the entrance

Fig. 2. Klauder's first perspective for the Cathedral of Learning. (Klauder and Day Collection, Architectural Archives, University of Pennsylvania)

of the building. From there, a dramatic double-flight stairway leads to the Commons Room, a cathedral-like space of impressive dimensions that serves as a student lounge. Following the axis further on, one enters the elevator lobby. Leaving the building on the opposite side, the visitor views the Heinz Chapel straight before her. Around the Commons Room and the elevator lobby is a hall that leads to the classrooms.

The building is distinct from its neighbors not just in its height but also in its architectural style. Instead of classicism, predominant in the district and the chosen style for an earlier plan for the university,[9] Gothic was selected for the Cathedral of Learning as well as for its two companion buildings (erected a few years later). The Cathedral of Learning is designed in a contemporary and severe Gothic style: very large pointed arches with a simplified tracery embrace multiple stories of windows, but no flying buttresses relieve the massive structure of the building. By way of contrast, the Heinz Chapel shows an "archaeological" French High Gothic with three-tiered wall structures and Flamboyant tracery. In further contrast, the Stephen Foster Memorial with its rotunda adapts a rather free Gothic with smooth, stark walls crowned with tracery reminiscent of Bertram G. Goodhue's later churches.

THE MEANING OF THE GOTHIC

The Gothic style was not adopted from the buildings in the vicinity, and the skyscraper building type was not necessitated by high real estate costs in the area. Bowman outlines his motivations for adapting the type and style in his publication *The Cathedral of Learning of the University of Pittsburgh* and in several newspaper articles. According to Bowman, the building was emblematic of the fundamental motivating force behind the university: "a spirit of achievement in which energy, intelligence, and spiritual fineness are combined."[10] In his view, this spirit could only be represented by a tall building of singular design, such as a Gothic skyscraper. According to Bowman, this "spirit of achievement" is appropriate for Pittsburgh, a city shaped by its early settlers: "There is a provincial way of thinking here and a provincial way of doing; there is courage, daring, speed of action, and honor, out of which has come the wealth, the manufacturing, and the tonnage production. This spirit was brought here by the pioneers."[11] Bowman tried to make the symbolic connection between the city and the university explicit by announcing the university skyscraper as the materialization of the city's identity: "Pittsburgh is widely known. But its spirit of achievement, its courage, its individualism are nearly undiscovered. The building [the Cathedral of Learning will] be a true symbol of the titanic industrial city."[12] By construing the building as a civic rather than just an educational monument, Bowman raised his potential circle of sponsors together with the notoriety of his building: certificates were even handed out to schoolchildren who contributed money for the building funds.[13]

With the symbolic connection between the city and the university building, Bowman also legitimized the use of the modern skyscraper type. While proponents of the conservative academic architecture of the time, as described by Edgell,[14] would probably not have accepted the "spirit of achievement" as sufficient justification for the use of a skyscraper, it was seen as an appropriate symbol for Pittsburgh, the home of the steel industry. It was in that sense that R. L. Duffus construed the building in the *New York Times Magazine* in 1928, when he wrote of it as "the apotheosis of steel and of a civilization resting on steel."[15] In order to further strengthen the relationship with the city of Pittsburgh, Bowman conceived of the interiors as memorials to the pioneers of the city, as he wrote in his publication in 1925.[16] In the 1930s, this idea was manifested in the "nationality rooms": classrooms furnished in the styles of the settlers' native lands.[17]

Bowman also gave pragmatic reasons for the choice of a skyscraper building type. He identified the huge amount of required space, the flexibility of the building type (which would easily allow changes to the interior if they were necessitated by the university's future development), better lighting in the rooms, and a more effective heating system. Despite the low density of its surrounding neighborhood, Bowman also mentions the value of "saving in land"—an imperative in the cities where the skyscraper had been developed.[18] The expected overload of the elevators, noted by critics, was alleviated by shifting the starting times in the different schools of the university.[19] The main arguments, however, were of a symbolic nature. In physically bringing together the university's different schools and departments under one roof in this building, Bowman attempted to embody his concept of the unity of the university and the unity of education.[20] Still more important to him was the impact that the building would have on the viewer:

> The height to which the buttresses might go seems to be unlimited, undiscovered. They are undefeated. Force, daring, courage, achievement, all are there. . . . Men seem dwarfed beside the structure. The imagination starts. A rush of self-expansion comes and a feeling that we can go beyond our own limits. . . . Force and power, however, are not all that is wanted. Where is the spiritual quality? The answer to this is that at each corner of the tower, conspicuous by its position, occurs Gothic ornamentation. The character of this ornamentation, here in contrast to the otherwise stern simplicity of the building, means to us, through centuries of association with church buildings, a mood of worship and of reverence.[21]

According to Bowman, the awe—elsewhere he even speaks of "sublimity"—evoked by the building creates the atmosphere he considers necessary for good teaching.[22] Again and again Bowman emphasizes the fact that architecture has an "edifying" effect. In this sense, Bowman quoted *The Tempest* in his publication of 1925: "Nothing ill can dwell in such a temple."[23] Bowman stopped short of arguing that the building, "the great symbol," could actually generate positive character traits in its users, but he believed it was able to reinforce them.[24]

For Bowman, the effect of architecture was reliant upon both the architectural style *and* the building type; neither Gothic with its "mood of worship and reverence" nor a skyscraper with its overwhelming height could achieve such an effect independently. Together, however, the style and building type could produce the atmosphere of "sublimity" that Bowman ascribes to his building.[25] Bowman attributed the building's sublimity to its type as well as to the presence of Gothic elements, the latter having been associated with the concept of the sublime since the eighteenth century. Bowman sought to establish a religious atmosphere by means of the architectural style, an intention that finds its expression in the name "Cathedral of Learning," a nickname given to the building in the office of the architect and that Bowman frequently used.[26] In addition, like many of his contemporaries, he was inspired by John Ruskin's interpretations of the Gothic and by the most influential American Gothic Revival architect, Ralph Adams Cram, as Mark McCullough Brown has established.[27]

Nonetheless, Bowman explicitly distanced himself from the traditional Collegiate Gothic in some respects:

> The building breaks [with] tradition; it does this not to be merely different or high, but to express its age—an age of creative, forceful energy directed toward usefulness. Oxford and Cambridge expressed the spirit of the days in which they were built; and a kind of glory has attached to these universities and to England through all these years. . . . A hundred years from now, perhaps a thousand years from now, people may look back, see through history these present days as the beginning of a new age and say, "The first great expression of the creative-spiritual force that changed the world came into being at Pittsburgh." The sincerity of the structure, inside and out, will be like the ring of steel.[28]

Bowman clearly did not wish to copy the atmosphere of the vaunted medieval universities, unlike James Gamble Rogers with his Harkness Memorial Quadrangle at Yale;[29] rather he wished to point toward the future. His Cathedral of Learning superseded the Collegiate Gothic derived from Oxford and Cambridge: "Pittsburgh will be Gothic. . . . But it will be Gothic frankly confessing its steel skeleton, speaking with an American accent in every inch of its tenth-of-a-mile altitude, and looking to the future rather than to the past. It will be the voice of new ideals that are beginning to transform higher education in

America."[30] This modernity could not be embodied by the Gothic style alone—however modernized and Americanized it might be—without its accompanying the new building type, the skyscraper. Further, pure medieval historicism was not adequate for the building to fulfill its lofty functions, or perhaps to satisfy the critics. Bowman makes the important point that despite its Gothic details, the tower will express the steel structure beneath. Not only would that quality satisfy modernist predilections for the frank representation of a building's structural system; it would be even more appropriate in a city that was built on steel production.

SKYSCRAPERS FOR METROPOLITAN UNIVERSITIES

If the Cathedral of Learning were to mark the dawning of a new era, it needed to be as novel as possible. In 1928, the *New York Times Magazine* announced, "It is the first skyscraper ever erected in a cow pasture and the first ever devoted to the use of higher education."[31] But the Cathedral of Learning was not as novel as the *New York Times Magazine* suggests. Already in 1923, two years prior to the commencement of construction in Pittsburgh, the Chicago press depicted the planning of the downtown campus of Northwestern University as a "skyscraper campus."[32] Even if the fourteen-story, 260-foot-high Montgomery Ward Memorial Building (1925–27) dominating the campus remained well below the height of the Cathedral of Learning, it was still recognized as a skyscraper (fig. 3).[33] This is due to its structure: the building (designed, like the entire campus, by James Gamble Rogers) contained Northwestern's School of Medicine as well as the School of Dentistry, with all necessary rooms stacked one upon the other, from lecture halls and a library, operating rooms, laboratories and rooms for the dissection course, up to cold rooms for corpses.[34] As was customary for contemporary skyscrapers, it was erected with a steel skeleton, the latest building equipment, and a stone curtain wall that, like the Pittsburgh example, has Gothic details. Furthermore, also like the Cathedral of Learning, the Northwestern building has setbacks, recalling a New York skyscraper, although they were not required in this area of Chicago.[35]

The Montgomery Ward Memorial Building was considered a novelty at the time of its construction, as the contemporary press made clear. In 1926, the

Fig. 3. Montgomery Ward Memorial Building, Northwestern University, Chicago, 1927. (*Architecture* [New York] 55, no. 6 [1927]: 304)

New York Times reported: "A departure from traditional American college architecture was made here [in Chicago] today with the laying of the cornerstone for a fourteen-story university skyscraper, the $4,000,000 Montgomery Ward Memorial unit of Northwestern University."[36] The modern construction technique of the steel skeleton was admired, for example, in an article in the *American Architect* that focused particularly on the structural character of the campus, and especially the Montgomery Ward Memorial Building, while the discussion of the style was limited to the observation that the influence of Oxford and Cambridge was visible.[37]

Northwestern University, too, claimed its new building as a first, and one that responded to the exigencies of the site: "The very valuable tract of city land in such a sightly and conspicuous location made it necessary to build high into the air and gave the opportunity to erect a group having a monumental building as a landmark, the first educational skyscraper in America."[38] Unlike Pittsburgh, the campus in Chicago is situated in the city center, although not in the densely built commercial heart, the Loop. Nonetheless, the Montgomery Ward Memorial Building was located in the city, and therefore the usual justification for skyscrapers, namely the high cost of real estate and the consequent need to maximize the square footage erected on a given site, applies. While Bowman strives to establish his building as a symbol of the "spirit of Pittsburgh" and to tie it to the city, the integration of the Chicago campus into the metropolis is unavoidable because of its location.

However, the relationship to the city was established not just by the site of the Chicago campus but also by its function. The Montgomery Ward Memorial Building housed the professional schools, whose missions were tied to the city, while the traditional academic departments of the university were left on the bucolic campus in suburban Evanston. Hence the Chicago campus embodies the ideal of a modern urban university, both in terms of function and architecture. It was perceived to be a synthesis of commercial and academic architecture and thus a felicitous solution for its specific location in the center of the metropolis, as noted in the magazine *Chicago Commerce:* "His [Rogers's] tentative drawings show an impressive combination of commercial and university architecture to conform with the peculiar problem of an urban campus, intellectual in spirit, yet closely associated with the skyscrapers in the Loop."[39] This connection of commercial and university architecture was made possible by the simultaneous use of the commercial building type of the skyscraper together with the academic Collegiate Gothic style—just what Bowman attempted in Pittsburgh. The appeal of this synthesis, at least for a time, was so strong that William Harold Lee adopted Gothic forms for the skyscraper planned in 1928–29 for Temple University.[40] It was not until the end of the 1920s that other styles, such as Art Deco, were applied to university skyscrapers.[41] As universities, along with many other institutions, expanded in various city centers during the 1920s and 1930s, the Gothic skyscraper provided a viable approach for new buildings.

THE QUESTION OF THE CAMPUS

Although the Montgomery Ward Memorial Building in Chicago and the Cathedral of Learning in Pittsburgh are similar with respect to the building type and style employed, they do differ in one substantial respect: their campus context. Around 1900, the ideal of a mostly pastoral American campus university was combined with the model of a medieval university like Oxford or Cambridge with their series of cloisters framed by Gothic buildings. For the campus university as well as for the medieval cloister or a combination of both, the grouping of the buildings and the open space between them is of central importance. Although the buildings in Chicago, running along the street, do not convey much of the impression of a traditional campus, in which the buildings are embedded in the landscape, the press nonetheless used the term to describe the complex in which Rogers intended the skyscraper to be the focal element. In contrast, in Pittsburgh there is no campus at all, as the skyscraper incorporates all departments within itself. The previously mentioned Heinz Chapel and Stephen Foster Memorial are later additions, and they have only a loose connection with the university: a church and an archive respectively, they contain no rooms for normal student life.

The absence of a campus in Pittsburgh prompted the *Western Architect* in 1925 to severely criticize the Cathedral of Learning, because the tradition of American college life had been neglected: "In American college architecture there has always been an aim, at least, to preserve a certain rhythm and a romantic sequence in the different structures, all grouped upon a campus which serves as a setting that in the graduate life of the student is remembered with more affection, often, than any or all the buildings in which his 'work' was done."[42] For this author, the idea that the many aspects of university could be integrated into one building meant that it failed to conform to an established model. He was especially opposed to the conversion of the open space of a campus into the closed space of the Commons Room. For him, the intention of the high-rise building in Pittsburgh was wrong and not in accord with the purpose of a university: "To build a 'factory' with no more attraction and with all businesslike conditions of a skyscraper office building, will destroy everything that is known as 'college spirit,' leaving no memories."[43]

This essay sheds light on several aspects of the contemporary reception of the Cathedral of Learning: the desire for novelty and modernity that the building epitomized for Bowman was in itself recognized as "an entirely new and radical change." This shift in the approach to campus building was, however, controversial. At the core of the debate were the skyscraper building type and its commercial connotations. This criticism strikes the Cathedral of Learning more deeply than the Montgomery Ward Memorial Building, which has with its professional schools a close connection to business life. In Pittsburgh, however, all parts of the university are incorporated in the skyscraper, and there is no connection to the city's commercial life that would justify its use. Bowman himself was aware of the fact that transferring the characteristics of "commerce, competition, and contest" into a university setting might not be seen as appropriate or acceptable.[44] Thus he attempted to transform the ideological connotations of the skyscraper into the notions of "an intelligent eagerness" and "individualism, freedom and self-expression."[45] This interpretation, however, was not followed by *Western Architect;* instead, the journal read the building as an expression of the workaday world ruled by the time clock. For his part, Bowman argued for the "edifying" impact of university buildings: they "produce an intimate and 'belonging' impression that, in its mental effect upon the student, is worth more than all his educational gains valuable as they are."[46] Thus, in the patron's estimation, the university's buildings do not just reinforce the learning that takes place within them: they actually supersede it in importance.

At first sight, the defense of the traditional colleges in *Western Architect* is not related to a specific ideal or style: the "cloistered environment" in Oxford, the "democratic freedom of a Yale college yard," Harvard, and the Evanston campus of Northwestern University are all referenced. A hint of a preference for Gothic in universities is mentioned in the title, though: "The Perpendicular in College Architecture." "Perpendicular" as a synonym for "vertical" or "upright" relates to the skyscraper in Pittsburgh, yet at the same time it is the designation of a style in English Gothic architecture, which was often used in Oxford, as at New College or the Divinity School, for instance. In addition, the author emphasizes the important role that a traditional campus will play in the constitution of a student's subsequent memories of her or his college days. The urban skyscraper campus threatens to undermine the formative role played by university education in a student's emotional life.

A CAMPUS FOR PITTSBURGH

The deeply rooted importance of a campus in the period of its construction is also documented by the plans for the Cathedral of Learning. Although it is not part of a campus, one was planned in the beginning and over the years there have been several subsequent efforts to develop one. The very first plan, made by E. P. Mellon in 1922 under Chancellor Bowman, shows a university skyscraper within a campus that covers the entire building site.[47] The campus is designed as three- and four-story groups of buildings around yards, with a central lawn. The campus style is not medieval; rather, it corresponds to American tradition. Yet the large dining hall at the entrance and the auditorium situated in the center at the lawn are of a basilica type with flying buttresses. Dormer windows and buttresses articulate the facades, and the small yards create a picturesque and medieval impression, which, however, is undercut by the uniformity of the facades. The medieval approach is not archaeological: as with the later Cathedral of Learning, the Gothic style is applied in a contemporary way.

When Klauder was chosen as architect in 1924, the planning of a campus in a traditional sense seemed to have come to an end: the book *The Cathedral of Learning of the University of Pittsburgh* from 1925 presents the skyscraper alone on the large site. Internally, however, the debate about a campus did not cease, as is evidenced by Klauder's drawing *Scheme A,* from June 5, 1926, in the Archives Center of the University of Pittsburgh.[48] On this sketch, Klauder places lower, two- or three-story buildings around the Cathedral of Learning; they recall to some degree the yards Mellon had anticipated. The dominant skyscraper nonetheless remains isolated; there is no integration with the rest of the campus. The seriousness of this proposal is evidenced by the building application to the Department of City Planning. The application for approval of the height of the Cathedral of Learning was based on a plan that included a campus. Even though it is explicitly mentioned that the structures surrounding the skyscraper only "might" be erected, they were important enough for those responsible to factor them into the volume calculation of the Zoning Ordinance.[49] A second submitted plan, *Scheme B,* was extended by the Heinz Chapel on axis with the Cathedral of Learning. Between the two buildings a central square stretches, comparable to Mellon's plan.

The idea of a campus persisted, as the archives show, in drawings produced over a series of years.[50] For instance, in a plan from 1932, Klauder visualizes an ensemble consisting of four buildings: the Cathedral of Learning is situated at Bigelow Boulevard; the Heinz Chapel—not yet erected at the time—is opposite it on axis at Bellefield Avenue. Between the two buildings is a large quadrangle, bordered by an elongated library extension building at Fifth Avenue. The building on the opposite side closes the inner square; at the same time it parallels Forbes Street by means of a wing. This last structure is dominated by a rotunda towering above the building. There is no indication on the plan of its function. The Stephen Foster Memorial (fig. 4), erected one year later, adopts neither the location of this planned building at Forbes Street (it stands next to the Cathedral of Learning) nor the layout; yet it does adopt the idea of a rotunda.

In addition to the plan, the buildings are depicted in perspectives and partly in elevation. While the buildings on the site plan are presented as a coherent ensemble connected by walls, they are depicted as solitary buildings in the perspective drawings. The Cathedral of Learning rising high above everything else is not visible in the view of either the library or the building at Forbes Street; the only quadrangle view does not show the central yard but a "secondary" inner yard in front of the rotunda. The drawings thus avoid showing the relationship between the skyscraper and the more traditional aspects of the campus: its quadrangles and low-rise buildings. Although the Cathedral of Learning gestured, in its details, to the Collegiate Gothic, the challenge of integrating it visually into a group of campus buildings may have been insurmountable for Klauder. A photograph of the model for the Cathedral of Learning, the Heinz Chapel, and a planned library makes this problem explicit: the buildings are awkwardly juxtaposed. Even if the library takes up the design and the height of the lowest block of the Cathedral of Learning, there is no harmonious connection between the two buildings. This is perhaps one of the reasons why the plans were not implemented. Besides, it was hard enough to finish just the skyscraper in the middle of the Depression.

With the exception of the Heinz Chapel—with its aforementioned "archae-

Fig. 4. Stephen Foster Memorial, University of Pittsburgh. (University of Pittsburgh Historic Photographs, 1884–present, University Archives, University of Pittsburgh)

ological" High French Gothic style reminiscent in its structure of the Sainte-Chapelle in Paris—there is nothing Gothic about the arrangement of the buildings, their plans, or the structuring of the building masses; however, their details are in the Gothic style. Some views, like that of the quadrangle elevation of the Forbes Street building, are eclectic: next to Gothic pinnacles and Gothic ornamental gables with tracery there are Baroque stairs and Renaissance-inspired arcades. This planning is far from what Bowman imagined in 1925, namely a serious effort to develop an American Gothic that conveys a contemporary sense of style and mirrors the construction method of its buildings.

IMPERMANENCE OF THE SKYSCRAPER

Criticism was leveled not only at the lack of a campus in Pittsburgh but also at the transitory character of the skyscraper building type, as Edgell explains in *The American Architecture of To-Day:*

> A steel building is not merely modern, it suggests impermanence. Steel, we know, is subject to change. . . . At a guess, we might give the Cathedral of Learning a life of two or three hundred years, or even more; one could hardly imagine such a building existing for a thousand. The modernist will retort that this makes no difference; that any building will be obsolete in a thousand years and ought to be pulled down. Practically, this may be so; aesthetically, it is certainly wrong. Granted that the Cathedral of Learning will not be needed a thousand years from now, it ought not to remind us of the fact. . . .The question resolves itself into whether the beauty and the suggestion of American dynamic vitality embodied in Mr. Klauder's building compensate for the impermanence, restlessness, and bustling modernity of his academic building.[51]

Edgell identifies a paradox in the Cathedral of Learning. On the one hand, its Gothic vocabulary lends it venerability; on the other, that suggestion of age and permanence is undermined by the use of the skyscraper type, which is closely connected to what the author sees as a changeful contemporary condition. Edgell's call for Gothic for university buildings was therefore not fulfilled with the use of the historic style alone. For him, the adequate building style for universities would not just be Gothic, much less a contemporary Gothic style; rather, the buildings should represent with their surroundings the unchanged continuation of tradition—they should look like medieval universities. (Edgell did not address the fact that this had not been a continuous tradition in the United States but one that only emerged in the second half of the nineteenth century in the course of the Gothic Revival.)

Edgell's criticism of the "impermanence" of the steel frame is not based on its constructional but rather its aesthetic nature. Edgell was not generally biased against steel construction. He did not find fault with its being applied to the Harkness Memorial Quadrangle (fig. 5), embodying the favored "historic" character and being for him "one of the gems of modern American architecture."[52] There, the steel structure is not made apparent and hence does not disturb the medieval atmosphere of the campus. For the same reason, he rather approved of artificial patina or "caved" doorsteps in the Quadrangle; they contributed

Fig. 5. Harkness Memorial Quadrangle, Yale University. (*Architecture* [New York] 44, no. 4 [1921]: plate 144)

to the image of an "old" campus.[53] He was bothered, though, by the effectively "felt life time" of high-rise buildings as well as of the material steel. Looking at skyscrapers, the steel skeleton is almost imposed upon the beholder, for a structure of such height cannot be erected in masonry. Since neither the building type nor the steel would look "old"—because both have existed a rather short time—the illusion of age cannot plausibly be conveyed, which exactly is what was attempted in the Cathedral of Learning. Bowman certainly was aware of this problem; he addressed it in his publication *The Cathedral of Learning of the University of Pittsburgh,* without resolving the question, though, or being able to assure his readers of the permanence of his building.[54]

However, the "felt life time" of a skyscraper was not merely determined by the steel but primarily by the economic climate in which it was built and continued to stand. In 1929, the architect and critic Francisco Mujica argued that permanence in commercial skyscrapers was not at all necessary. The building had merely to persist over the standard period of amortization, for which thirty years would be more than sufficient.[55] How widespread this notion was is demonstrated by the vision of the architect and city planner Harvey Wiley Corbett of an urbanistic remodeling of New York, which would be feasible in a manageable period of time solely by an extremely short cycle of new building.[56] It was not the actual lifetime of a steel skeleton, two hundred to three hundred years according to Edgell, that influenced the perception of the age of a skyscraper, but the period of about thirty years over which it could be financed. In addition, it can be inferred from Edgell's criticism that skyscrapers of the 1920s, realizing the latest standards in terms of construction technique and equipment, were regarded as symbols of modernity that would not "age in dignity" in the eyes of their contemporaries but would fall out of fashion and potentially become useless. Unlike medieval buildings, patina and old age would give them less value instead of more.

MODERNIST CRITICISM OF THE COLLEGIATE GOTHIC

Even Charles Klauder had conservative ideas about university architecture. Although he exhibited his design for the Cathedral of Learning in Berlin as well as in Paris in 1926,[57] it was only at the end of his book *College Architecture in America,* published in 1929, that he tersely mentioned the project: the academic world should be grateful to the University of Pittsburgh for this "bold experiment."[58] What his ideal for university buildings looked like, however, was put forth in his final sentence: "Therefore, let them [universities and colleges] be reared in the fervent spirit that animated the ancient and worshipful guilds, with bricks and stones of honesty and truth and dedicated to the perennial youth in its search for self-expression and for knowledge."[59] The plates of the publication illustrate most impressively that the styles they employed were to be adopted together with the spirit of the ancient guilds. In this call for "truth" in construction, and the return to some extent to premodern guild practices, Klauder echoed the theories of the nineteenth-century critics John Ruskin and William Morris, who had contributed significantly, in the Anglo-American world, to the Gothic Revival and the Arts and Crafts movement.

"Honesty" and "truth" in university buildings were also called for by later critics such as William Harlan Hale, who as a student at Yale University published his view on university buildings in *Architectural Forum* in 1931: "Our first requirement is a simple one: it [the college building] must be honest. It cannot be built of faked materials, in a fraudulent manner (such as hiding steel girders under enormous buttresses), on a basis of untruth. During some of the most impressionable years of his life, a young man must live among college buildings. And if that environment is of falsity, he soon will breathe that same spirit."[60] Hale's call for truth in materials harkens back to nineteenth-century architectural critics, and like Bowman and Klauder, Hale was convinced that architecture had an impact on students' attitudes. He did not share, though, their belief in the dogma that Gothic was the only adequate style for universities and "the thirteenth century . . . the source of all inspiration."[61] On the contrary, he wanted the buildings to be modern, in a "living style." His priorities for university architecture were the use of "plain materials" and the provision of a "maximum of light and air and freedom,"[62] consistently naming as model buildings the German modernist Weissenhof settlement and the Bauhaus in Dessau, even though he felt the latter was not quite suitable for America.

Bowman, too, embraced the call for contemporary, modern architecture for university buildings. The adoption of the most modern building type, the skyscraper (being at the same time perceived as quintessentially American), plus a refined and Americanized Gothic style for the Cathedral of Learning was his solution. Hale, in turn, had a completely different view on the appropriateness of a historicizing style. For him, the Gothic—however modernized—was a mere copy of the past and thus "dead," and he viewed the facing of modern buildings with Gothic elements negatively. For him, the skyscraper was also not a proper building type for university purposes, despite his general sympathy for modernism: "Nobody would ask for skyscrapers as dormitories, factories as recitation buildings, or grain elevators as recreation halls."[63] Hale's view was typical of American critics at the time who were willing to admit the use of modernist architecture in certain contexts but resisted it as a vocabulary for domestic and other sorts of buildings for which there were already accepted styles.

In 1949, Walter Gropius made an argument very much like Hale's in his article "Not Gothic but Modern for Our Colleges" in the *New York Times Magazine.* Echoing Hale, he asked for a new, contemporary style by reason of the life-shaping character of the college environment, which was supposed to be "the *real* thing," "creative," and not "imitative": "How can we expect our students to become bold and fearless in thought and action if we encase them timidly in sentimental shrines feigning a culture which has long since disappeared?"[64] However, beside this plea for contemporary and modern architecture, he also addressed the subject of tradition in his article, this question certainly being central to his contemporary design for the Harvard Graduate Center (1948–50). He saw tradition in Harvard's "Yard," showing "a sound basic theme of architectural design which has been reverently kept throughout the centuries by almost all architects who have contributed individual buildings." The connection between tradition and modernism that Bowman saw realized in his Cathedral of Learning, to which Gropius even referred in his article, was important for Gropius, too. Like Bowman, he was interested in tradition as a "result of constant growth." What interested Gropius was not so much the style of the buildings, which had concerned Bowman, but rather the basic layout of the traditional campus with quadrangles or yards. However, Gropius was staunchly opposed to imitation in campus design: "New buildings must be invented, not copied."[65]

Although the influence of the modern movement became increasingly visible in the United States during the middle decades of the twentieth century, the solution of a Gothic skyscraper for universities came to seem outmoded. The Cathedral of Learning nonetheless kept on stirring imaginations in this period, as the yearbook of DePaul University of Chicago demonstrates. In 1949, the same year in which Gropius's article was published, it pictured the Cathedral of Learning as DePaul's vision for its own downtown campus of the future. Even if adaptations of the Skyscraper Gothic to educational buildings were

Fig. 6. Cathedral of Learning, University of Pittsburgh, contemporary view. (Author's photograph)

scarce, and to some degree controversial in the estimation of critics, they nonetheless proved memorable in the eyes of viewers and came to define the universities where they appeared, especially at the University of Pittsburgh (fig. 6). Furthermore, these buildings are significant as expressions of the confidence some architects and patrons felt during the interwar period that the formula first developed in the tall commercial structures of downtown Manhattan and Chicago's Loop could be applied to universities across the country. The skyscraper campus building was a unique case, however, for as the Cathedral of Learning shows, the use of Gothic forms connected modern architecture to the traditions of college buildings. This traditionalism was balanced by the simultaneous reference made to the commercial skyscraper, the very epitome of American modernity.

NOTES

1. George H. Edgell, *The American Architecture of To-Day* (1928; repr., New York: AMS, 1970), 159.

2. After 1935, Edgell was director of the Boston Museum of Fine Arts ("G. H. Edgell Dead; Museum Director," *New York Times*, June 30, 1954, 27).

3. Edgell, *The American Architecture of To-Day,* v.

4. Paul Turner, *Campus: An American Planning Tradition,* rev. ed. (Cambridge: MIT Press, 1990). See also Kevin D. Murphy's essay, pages 39–54 in this volume.

5. Margaret M. Grubiak, "Reassessing Yale's Cathedral Orgy: The Ecclesiastical Metaphor and the Sterling Memorial Library," *Winterthur Portfolio* 43, no. 2/3 (Spring/Autumn 2009): 159–84.

6. John G. Bowman, *The Cathedral of Learning of the University of Pittsburgh* (Pittsburgh: University of Pittsburgh Press, 1925), 7.

7. Franklin Toker, *Buildings of Pittsburgh,* Buildings of the United States 11 (Charlottesville: University of Virginia Press, 2007), 48–50. For a building history of the Cathedral of Learning, see Mark McCullough Brown, "The Cathedral of Learning. 1921–1926: A History of an Architectural Design for the University of Pittsburgh" (master's thesis, State University of New York at Binghamton, 1983); and Mark McCullough Brown, *The Cathedral of Learning: Concept, Design, Construction* (Pittsburgh: University of Pittsburgh Press, 1987). For Charles Z. Klauder, see Kurt W. Pitluga, "The Collegiate Architecture of Charles Z. Klauder" (PhD diss., Pennsylvania State University, 1994). For university skyscrapers, see Anke Köth, "Elfenbeintürme mit Stahlskelett: Amerikanische Wolkenkratzeruniversitäten," in *Architektur für Forschung und Lehre: Universität als Bauaufgabe. Beiträge zur Tagung des Kunsthistorischen Instituts der Christian-Albrechts-Universität zu Kiel am 5. bis 7. Juni 2009,* Kieler Kunsthistorische Studien N. F. 11, ed. Klaus Gereon Beuckers (Kiel: Ludwig, 2010), 147–74; and Köth, "Wolkenkratzerkirchen: Ein amerikanischer Bautyp der 1920er Jahre" (PhD diss., Technische Universität Dresden, 2010).

8. For Oakland, see Toker, *Buildings of Pittsburgh,* 41–61.

9. In 1908, Henry Hornbostel won the competition for the new planning of the university with a campus design in the style of an antique acropolis (Turner, *Campus,* 191, figs. 195, 196).

10. Bowman, *Cathedral of Learning,* 5.

11. Ibid., 6.

12. Ibid., 18–19.

13. A certificate of the Cathedral of Learning from May 4, 1925, reprinted 1981, 13/3-A, Box 1, FF1, Archives Service Center, University of Pittsburgh. Additional archival materials concerning the Cathedral of Learning are housed in the Klauder Archive, Carnegie Mellon University Architecture Archives, Pittsburgh.

14. Edgell, *American Architecture of To-Day,* 158–59.

15. R. L. Duffus, "A Tower of Inspiration to a Busy City: Such Will Be the Skyscraper Shaft of the University of Pittsburgh, New Rising above the Smoky Mills," *New York Times Magazine,* June 17, 1928, 23.

16. Bowman, *Cathedral of Learning,* 6.

17. See *Nationality Rooms of the University of Pittsburgh. Seventeen Water Colors and Forty-Six Crayon Drawings by Andrew Avinoff, Two Etchings by Louis Orr. Text by John G. Bowman,*

Ruth Crawford Mitchell and Andrey Avinoff (Pittsburgh: University of Pittsburgh Press, 1947). For a more recent treatment, see Lucia Curta, "'Imagined Communities' in Showcases: The Nationality Rooms Program at the University of Pittsburgh (1926–1945)" (PhD diss., Western Michigan University, 2004).

18. Bowman, *Cathedral of Learning,* 11–12, 14–16.

19. Ibid., 15.

20. Ibid., 11.

21. Ibid., 9–10.

22. "The atmosphere of the room itself should make a boy take off his hat as he enters, leaving all but his best self outside. I think that such a room would renew day by day the courage and the vision of the teacher as well as of the student, and go far to perfect the relationship between master and learner out of which real results in education come" (Bowman qtd. in Duffus, "A Tower of Inspiration," 9). According to Bowman, the building provokes the same reaction—taking off one's hat—in older people, though with the slightly different result: they do not become willing to learn themselves but instead to send their children to this university.

23. Bowman, *Cathedral of Learning,* 8.

24. Ibid., 10.

25. Bowman qtd. in "University Plans a Skyscraper Home: Pittsburgh Will Build a 52-Story 'Cathedral of Learning' Next Year: Mellon Supports Scheme: Authorities Say the New Departure Will 'Express Pittsburgh and Its Spirit,'" *New York Times,* November 7, 1924, 18.

26. John G. Bowman, *Unofficial Notes* (Pittsburgh: privately printed, 1963), 84.

27. Brown, "The Cathedral of Learning," 41–53.

28. Bowman, *Cathedral of Learning,* 19.

29. See "The Harkness Memorial Quadrangle and Memorial Tower, Yale University," *Architecture* 44, no. 4 (1921): 297–98.

30. Duffus, "A Tower of Inspiration," 9.

31. Ibid.

32. "Planning Skyscraper Campus: Rogers Outlines Beauties Sought in N.U. Project: Conforms to City Plan, Architect Says," *Chicago Daily Tribune,* February 22, 1923, 3.

The construction of the campus in Chicago started in May 1925; the commencement in Pittsburgh was in October 1926 (Philip Kinsley, "Break Ground for N.U.'s Huge Chicago Units: $7,000,000 Campus to Add to City Beautiful," *Chicago Daily Tribune,* May 9, 1925; "Board of Trustees: Foundation Excavation to Begin Early Next Month," [a Pittsburgh newspaper], September 22, 1926, 13/3/2 A-E Box 1, 13/3/2 E Buildings—Cathedral of Learning—Newspaper Clippings, Archives Service Center, University of Pittsburgh).

Even the planning started earlier in Chicago than in Pittsburgh: the publicity campaign for the Chicago campus used the term "skyscraper" one year earlier than in Pittsburgh. See the aforementioned article in the *Chicago Daily Tribune;* and "University Plans a Skyscraper Home," 18.

The idea of a university skyscraper for Pittsburgh, however, was developed as early as July to October 1922 (design of E. P. Mellon, in Brown, "Cathedral of Learning," 98, fig. 10); in Chicago, the plans for a university skyscraper were not published until the campaign in 1923, among others in the *Northwestern University Alumni News* (James Gamble Rogers, "What It Means to the Architect," *Northwestern University Alumni News* 2, no. 7 [May 1923], 8).

33. In an article in the *American Architect* in 1927, the year of the inauguration of the building, the general comparability of the two buildings is pointed out, in spite of the lower height of the Chicago building ("The Alexander McKinlock Memorial Campus, Northwestern University, Chicago. James Gamble Rogers and Childs & Smith, Associated Architects," *American Architect*, no. 2525 [July 20, 1927]: 78, 80, 82).

34. Information on the building, including photographs of the rooms taken by the Chicago Architectural Photographing Company—presumably on the occasion of the completion of construction—are available at Special Collections, Galter Health Sciences Library, Northwestern University, Chicago.

35. "Alexander McKinlock Memorial Campus," 80.

36. "Start 14-Story 'Campus,'" *New York Times,* June 12, 1926, 6.

37. "Alexander McKinlock Memorial Campus," 80.

38. "Montgomery Ward Building," *Syllabus* 43 (1928): 206.

39. "Northwestern University Prepares Plan for Fine Campus at Chicago Avenue," *Chicago Commerce,* February 24, 1923, 6.

40. "Temple University. 350-Foot Structure to Dominate Proposed $5,000,000 Group," *Philadelphia Inquirer,* August 15, 1926.

41. Cf., for example, the Mundelein Skyscraper College in Chicago (Nairne W. Fisher and Joseph W. McCarthy, 1929–31) or the DePaul University Building (also 64 East Lake Street Building, Vitzhum and Burns, 1928).

42. "The Perpendicular in College Architecture," *Western Architect* 34, no. 10 (October 1925): 99.

43. Ibid.

44. Bowman, *Cathedral of Learning,* 8.

45. Ibid.; Duffus, "A Tower of Inspiration," 9.

46. "The Perpendicular in College Architecture," 99.

47. *Proposed Expansion of the University of Pittsburgh: Opposite the Carnegie Institute and the Entrance to Schenley Park,* photograph, University Cathedral of Learning, plot plans, 1920s 8–5, Folder 1, 5 items, Archives Service Center, University of Pittsburgh. The figure is also in Brown, "Cathedral of Learning," 98, fig. 10. Edward Purcell Mellon (1875–1953) was the nephew of Andrew Mellon, and although he resided in New York City from 1916, following a period of several years studying architecture in Paris, he executed a number of

important institutional and residential commissions in Pittsburgh (Lu Donnelly, "Architecture Around Us: A Late-Blooming Architect," *Western Pennsylvania History* 95, no. 1 [Spring 2012]: 14–17).

48. *Bird's-Eye View of Proposed Development of Low Buildings around Cathedral of Learning University of Pittsburgh,* Charles Z. Klauder Architect, *Scheme A,* June 5, 1926, photograph, University Cathedral of Learning, plot plans, 1920s 8–5, Folder 1, 5 items, Archives Service Center, University of Pittsburgh. This figure is also in Brown, "Cathedral of Learning," 123, fig. 35. However, Brown does not mention the surrounding campus development in his explanation.

49. This plan was made at the same time as the one described above, as the correspondence from August 1926 shows (Department of City Planning, Letter, August 17, 1926, 2/10 1921/45, Box 11, Chancellor's [John Gabbet Bowman] Office File, board of trustees FF 93, Archives Service Center, University of Pittsburgh).

50. University of Pittsburgh, Development of the Cathedral of Learning Site, n.d., RG 13/3/3, Box 1, FF7, Archives Service Center, University of Pittsburgh. The Architectural Archives at the University of Pennsylvania, Day and Klauder Collection, holds cyanotype prints of additional buildings for the campus around the Cathedral of Learning from the 1930s and 1940s. Some of the prints show the same project for a library as preserved in the University of Pittsburgh Archives Service Center, but others also show an additional project science building near the street: a project for men's dormitories close to the main entrance was planned in 1944 after the erection of the Foster Memorial (069.226 col. 3 Day and Klauder .069).

51. Edgell, *American Architecture of To-Day,* 181, 183.

52. Ibid., 171, 173.

53. Ibid., 173.

54. Bowman, *Cathedral of Learning,* 16–17.

55. Francisco Mujica, *History of the Skyscraper* (1929; repr., New York: Da Capo, 1977), 49.

56. Corbett planned a separation of functions, with the pedestrian area under arcades being transferred into the buildings in order to keep the complete street width free for automobile traffic (Harvey Wiley Corbett, "The Problem of Traffic Congestion and a Solution," *Architectural Forum* 46, no. 3 [1927]: 201–8): "When a block has been rebuilt (not so long a time as one might imagine, when one sees the rate at which buildings change in New York), the temporary cantilever sidewalk is removed, the new arcade is opened."

57. *Ausstellung neuer amerikanischer Baukunst,* ed. Akademie der Künste zu Berlin (Berlin, 1926), 60. A drawing of the building is mentioned in the catalogue, but not all drawings from the catalogue were exhibited. "Skyscraper Style Features Exhibit: Famous Works from Paris Exposition on View Here for the First Time," *New York Times,* February 7, 1926, 14.

58. Charles Z. Klauder and Herbert C. Wise, *College Architecture in America and Its Part in the Development of the Campus* (New York: Charles Scribner's Sons, 1929), 293.

59. Ibid., 294.

60. William Harlan Hale, "Old Castles for New Colleges," *Architectural Forum* 54, no. 6 (June 1931): 720.

61. Ibid., 731.

62. Ibid., 719.

63. Ibid., 731.

64. Walter A. Gropius, "Not Gothic but Modern for Our Colleges," *New York Times Magazine,* October 23, 1949, 16, 18.

65. Ibid.

RADIANT HEAT AND GLOWING LIGHTS

Raymond Hood's American Radiator Building

Christine G. O'Malley

Through the eyes of two fictional pedestrians, a 1925 narrative guidebook to New York City, *New York in Seven Days,* presented its readers with a lively tour of the city's attractions, including its famous skyscrapers. In this book, a man and a woman are recorded walking down West Fortieth Street, where their eyes are "arrested by a tall, black building with gold trimmings," which the man remarks was "supposed to resemble a lump of coal with flames at the top."[1] This tourist-oriented guidebook reveals how rapidly the American Radiator Building (fig. 1), completed just one year earlier in 1924, had emerged as a popular fixture on the New York City skyline. As the book's description makes clear, the skyscraper was symbolically identified with the idea of heat generated by the products of its owner, the American Radiator Company. Designed by Raymond Mathewson Hood (1881–1934) shortly after his success with John Mead Howells (1868–1959) in the 1922 Chicago Tribune Tower Competition, the American Radiator Building was recognized by many of Hood's fellow architects and critics as a key contributor to the skyscraper's development and viewed as an ideal example of the marriage between architecture and advertising. Earlier skyscrapers, including Hood and Howells's winning Tribune Tower entry, were often constructed in eye-catching historical styles that made deliberate ref-

Fig. 1. 40 West Fortieth Street, American Radiator Building, 1933 Wurts Bros. photograph. (Museum of the City of New York)

erences to Italian campaniles or Gothic civic buildings and cathedrals. As many historians have noted, the American Radiator Building's prominence, by contrast, was the result of its unique coloration and nighttime illumination. These two design elements enhanced its advertising value because the Radiator Building could be read as creatively embodying the products displayed in its ground-floor showrooms. This essay offers a closer reading of contemporary responses to this skyscraper to reconstruct how a particular set of interpretations was almost immediately attached to it—interpretations that dwelt little, if at all, on any of its actual medieval features, such as its arched main entrance door with slender pinnacles, finials and colonnettes, or the vaulted interiors.[2] By 1924, the medieval design elements celebrated in earlier skyscrapers such as the Woolworth Building and the Tribune Tower now appeared less compelling to the public. Writers, critics, artists, and the general public all played significant roles in shaping the building's image, and the American Radiator Company capitalized on the direct association with blazing heat for its own promotional purposes. Upon its completion, it emerged as both a commercial monument and an atmospheric urban marvel that was painted, photographed, and praised. The American Radiator Building became a potent advertising tool for the company, generating interest and excitement for a manufacturer of a mundane, functional product. Ultimately, people celebrated the American Radiator Building for what it suggested to them as an embodiment of the company's products, largely ignoring any traces of its historically inspired medieval design motifs.

From the moment it was unveiled, a division existed between the architect's specified sources of inspiration for the American Radiator Building and the public's own reading of it. This disjunction between intention and reception points to the variety of possible meanings assigned to the growing presence of skyscrapers on city skylines in the 1920s, and it also highlights the inability of the architect to definitively control the way in which others would understand a building. Moreover, it appears to mark the end of the general public's desire to comprehend skyscrapers within a strict framework of historical styles and precedents espoused by architects or to appreciate them as simply objects of "civic beauty."[3] Although Hood looked to a late Gothic north European source[4] and the work of other architects for inspiration, the popularity of his American Radiator Building was chiefly generated by its enthusiastic public reception as an imaginative and symbolic expression of the company's products. For the general public, the commercial and advertising connection to the products firmly trumped any other elements of the skyscraper's design.

Hood's commission for the American Radiator Building came immediately after his famous victory with Howells in the highly publicized Chicago Tribune Tower Competition in 1922.[5] Their winning entry catapulted Hood into the spotlight and propelled his career forward in a dramatic fashion. At the time of the Tribune Tower Competition, Hood was working in New York and struggling to find work. He received his architecture degree from MIT in 1903, worked in the Boston offices of Cram, Goodhue, and Ferguson, and then in the New York office set up by Goodhue for the United States Military Academy at West Point commission.[6] Although it is not clear how much of an influence this office exerted on Hood, he was certainly exposed to the medieval spirit permeating the current office projects, which included the Church of St. Thomas in New York and West Point.[7] After a brief stay in this office, Hood traveled to France, where he enrolled in the École des Beaux-Arts in 1905 and then traveled home to the United States several times to work in various offices over the course of his studies before completing the program in 1911.[8] From 1911 until 1914, Hood worked in the office of the Pittsburgh architect Henry Hornbostel, for whom he had worked earlier on one of his many return visits; then, in 1914,

Hood moved back to New York to work on his own while sharing an office with his friend Rayne Adams.[9] For the next few years, Hood received few commissions but often assisted other architects as they prepared competition entries. Ironically, Hood survived on income he made designing radiator covers for the American Radiator Company.[10]

Hood's situation quickly improved with the invitation from Howells to join him in the design competition for the Chicago Tribune Tower. The Tribune Company promoted the competition as a noble quest to erect "the world's most beautiful office building," although as the historian Katherine Solomonson has shown, the competition also revealed the *Tribune*'s multiple desires as it aimed to build both a "public monument" and "corporate trademark."[11] Hood and Howells's victory was a boost for their careers and had a particularly powerful impact on Hood because he had not yet attained the professional stature and reputation that Howells already possessed.[12] Their winning design of a Gothic skyscraper inspired by French and Belgian church towers, including the Butter Tower of Rouen Cathedral, did draw some criticism. Several individuals, including the architects Thomas Tallmadge, Irving K. Pond, and Louis Sullivan, felt that the second-place entry by the Finnish architect Eliel Saarinen (1873–1950) was superior in its expression of soaring verticality and its avoidance of an overtly historical style.[13] At the awards dinner for the competition, Howells defended their design by arguing that Gothic architecture could be most usefully associated with the structural expression and construction needed in a skyscraper.[14] As Solomonson pointed out, the *Tribune* chose instead to see this winning design as representing "the consolidation of beauty and technology, commercialism and spirituality" and as a building that would elevate the city of Chicago into a higher realm.[15]

Despite the *Tribune*'s claims and Howells's defense of the use of a Gothic vocabulary, the interest in Saarinen's second-place design did not disappear. Although it remained unbuilt, the runner-up's design exerted its influence through its portrayal on paper. In 1923 the *Tribune* published almost all of the competition entries in an illustrated volume, *The International Competition for a New Administration Building for the Chicago Tribune,* presenting each of the participating architects with a copy and offering the rest for sale at bookstores.[16] Saarinen's entry, therefore, was accessible to a wide audience through this illustrated volume, and it would prove to be a significant source of inspiration for skyscraper design in the 1920s. Moreover, as will be discussed below, Saarinen's design had a direct impact on Hood when he worked on the American Radiator Building.

Howells and Hood's use of a Gothic design vocabulary for the Tribune Tower was not unprecedented; they were following a well-used design concept for skyscrapers dating back to the turn of the century. According to Sarah Bradford Landau and Carl W. Condit, the Times Building in New York City by Eidlitz and McKenzie (1903–5) initiated the passion for "Skyscraper Gothic."[17] In the early twentieth century, arguments linked the use of the steel frame with the skeletal system of construction found in the Gothic style to justify its use.[18] Other New York skyscrapers inspired by the Gothic period followed, but none was as famous as the Woolworth Building, designed by Cass Gilbert and constructed from 1910 to 1913. Built for Frank Winfield Woolworth, the ambitious businessman behind the popular bargain-store empire, the skyscraper was intended to serve as the company's headquarters and the headquarters of the Irving National Bank, with the remainder designated as speculative office space.[19] It was also planned as the tallest skyscraper in Manhattan and the world.

Woolworth wanted a Gothic-style building, and Gilbert believed that the Gothic was an appropriate model to use for articulating the verticality of the skyscraper tower. For his inspiration, Gilbert looked to northern European Gothic town halls with towers, along with the Perpendicular Gothic of the English Houses of Parliament and the Flamboyant Gothic found on the towers of Reims, Antwerp, and Malines Cathedrals.[20] The Woolworth Building's central tower extended from a lower block to dominate the New York City skyline. Reverend S. Parkes Cadman famously christened the building the "Cathedral of Commerce" at its opening ceremonies, a phrase that both Woolworth and Gilbert disliked; Gilbert, in fact, tried to stress the fact that he had based its main design elements on secular late Gothic town halls rather than cathedrals.[21] The phrase stuck, however, and the Woolworth Building played an important role in elevating the public profile of the company. These types of skyscrapers were a prominent component of the commercial world by this date, and as Gail Fenske and Deryck Holdsworth remark, "the visibility afforded by the towers expressed, and ultimately, legitimized a newly powerful commercial order."[22]

For Woolworth and the Tribune Company, their Gothic style trademark skyscrapers embodied this new commercial order.

Gilbert's Woolworth Building stood as a highly successful example of the promotional possibilities of a trademark skyscraper; it drew thousands of visitors to see it in person while its image was reproduced in countless publications. Undeniably, it was an asset to the public face and advertising needs of the company, and this did not go unnoticed by the American Radiator Company, which hired Hood for his first independent skyscraper commission. The architect pursued the commission with his new engineering partner, J. André Fouilhoux.[23]

American Radiator's rise to prominence in the early twentieth-century heating world underlines the integral role of their skyscraper to the company's business ambitions. American Radiator's president and chairman, Clarence Mott Woolley, may have been a "relatively unknown" individual, as a 1935 *Fortune* magazine article described him, but he was perfectly attuned to the promotional needs of his company.[24] Woolley was born in 1863 to a Detroit iron manufacturer and worked for Michigan Radiator before becoming head of sales for the newly formed American Radiator Company. By 1902, Woolley's keen business sense and salesmanship led him to the position of president. American Radiator experienced a tremendous period of growth under his leadership, and the company emerged as the most powerful company in the world heating market by the time Woolley retired in 1938.[25] The post–World War I economy brought substantial revenues to American Radiator, and by 1924 it was earning $11 million annually.[26] It had sales offices and plants in North America and Europe, and Woolley established a head office and showroom in New York City after the company had outgrown its Chicago office on South Michigan Avenue. Without a doubt, the constant publicity of the Tribune Tower Competition must have attracted Woolley to the idea of building a corporate skyscraper, and he surely knew about the Woolworth Building.

Located on West Fortieth Street, the American Radiator Building's site faces Bryant Park, a green space behind Carrère and Hastings's Beaux-Arts New York Public Library, which opened in 1911. On nearby streets stood Helmle and Corbett's 1918–21 Bush Terminal Building and the narrow Remington Building, two early Gothic-style skyscrapers. In 1923, Hood and Fouilhoux began design work on the Radiator Building by determining the massing using Plasticine models, a method the architect had employed while designing the Tribune Tower. Although the mass of the American Radiator Building shares some similarities with the Tribune Tower's beveled corners and its base, shaft, and crown arrangement, the American Radiator's crown is more fully integrated with the tower's shaft, a feature found on Saarinen's second-place Tribune Tower design.[27] On its upper zones, setbacks were included to accommodate the 1916 New York zoning law, which required these features. When Hood described the American Radiator Building in 1924, he stated that its mass and form were "an honest development of the zoning law" and recounted the design process, noting that the "first step in the design consisted in the shaping of a small plasteline model into the maximum model that the zoning law permitted. This little plasteline model is surprisingly like the building as it was finally developed."[28] Hood and the company only disputed whether or not to carry the building beyond the twentieth floor, and whether courts should be placed on either side of it to give the sides light and enhance its tower form. In the final design, Hood included these courts. The building was completed on a tight schedule, with design and construction conducted during a thirteen-month period.[29]

The sleek and unified profile of the American Radiator Building reveals how Hood reacted to the criticism of the Tribune Tower Competition, as several historians have noted.[30] Hood, in fact, openly stated to his colleagues and his critics that he felt his design was inspired by steps made by others when he published his own evaluation of the American Radiator Building in a lengthy November 1924 article in the *American Architect.* He explained how his design fit into the ongoing history of skyscraper development and noted, "Goodhue, Corbett, Saarinen and the other men who gave impetus to the study of this problem, and reproductions of whose drawings were scattered over our tables as we worked, gave us a lift over many rough places."[31] Hood freely recognized his interest in the work of other architects and indicated, by including Saarinen's name, how the American Radiator Building was partly a response to Saarinen's Tribune Competition entry. Like Saarinen's entry, Hood's Radiator design merges its upper portion with the central mass, allowing the tower to appear as a more complete unit and placing the emphasis on the form of a dynamic, vertically elongated, and tapered building.[32] Inspired by the upper zone of Saarinen's design, the rocket-like forms in the Radiator's pinnacles are a distilled version of the Tribune Tower's Gothic detailing, suggesting the upward thrust of Gothic pinnacles and finials. But the Gothic elements Hood used on the Radiator's crown are abstracted rather than literally reproduced and, as historians have noted, represent a shift from the carefully conceived Gothic details and the more overt historicism of the Tribune Tower. Hood included some of the round-headed windows Saarinen used for its crown, but he avoided Saarinen's use of tall sculptural figures in the upper setbacks, choosing instead to use the abstracted pinnacles.[33]

The skyscraper's massing was heightened by the choice of its exterior sheathing—made from black brick—and its nighttime illumination, a novel combination that, as histories of the building note, formed its reputation in the press and with the general public.[34] Hood selected a golden-colored stone for portions of the lower zone of the building and the uppermost sections of the crown, using it as a contrast to the black brick to create a striking impression. At the base, black granite walls were set around and above the large radiator showroom windows and a central arched entrance door, which contained the few vestiges of Gothic design elements found on its exterior (fig. 2). The metal details of the thin colonnettes and finials formed a highly visible main entrance. Above this street entrance area, Hood included an intermediary zone with golden-colored stone trimming with high-relief sculpted corbel figures by René Paul Chambellan, who would become one of his frequent architectural sculpture collaborators. From this area, the tower rises up as a black brick mass to the first setback zone, where the central portion is stepped back, at which point it extends four more stories again before it tapers and culminates in its lantern-like top. As Hood explained in his 1924 article, the steel frame had to be ordered quickly, leaving the exterior to be worked out while the framework was rising and implying that the exterior ornamentation was a secondary concern. On the choice of color, Hood explained, "The decision to go in for black and gold was not finally made until after the steel frame was partially up, and as a result I must admit that the exterior detailing was done under a constant pressure."[35]

Hood's choice created a dramatic visual effect, and the press interpreted it as a "daring departure from the conventional."[36] According to Hood, the black brick was intended to solve a practical problem, specifically, the black-hole

Fig. 2. Detail of main street-level entrance door, American Radiator Building. (Author's photograph)

effect caused by rows of windows in skyscrapers. He argued that "monotony and ugliness in office building seem to come from the fact that the windows are actually black holes, and the regular spacing of these black holes makes a building look like waffles or doormats hung up to dry."[37] Claiming that the color would make these holes less obvious, Hood contended that in the end he found that the building "struck a very cheerful note."[38] Hood later stated that the owners agreed with him that it should be built of black brick, and he maintained that the chosen material would not require the "cleaning that a lighter color would."[39] The architect, therefore, framed his choice in pragmatic terms and articulated his approach to design as a problem to be solved, a prevailing attitude of Hood's detected in his writings and statements by several historians.[40]

During both day and night, Hood provided the building with a theatrical atmosphere. At night, its unusual coloration was heightened by specially designed illumination, adding another level of visual spectacle to its appearance (fig. 3). The symbolic connection of the black brick and the lighting to the company's products in people's imaginations and in the ensuing descriptions helped shape the building's identity into one that was inflected in a very pro-

Fig. 3. American Radiator Building at night, New York City, exterior, 1926. (Library of Congress, Prints and Photographs Division, Gottscho-Schleisner Collection, LC-G612-T01-05710)

nounced manner by its products. Illuminating skyscrapers became an accepted practice for architects and owners eager to have their buildings stand as glimmering beacons in the city's dark sky. Woolworth and Gilbert created one of the earliest floodlighting schemes for the Woolworth tower so that it could be seen from a distance, "enhancing its quality of monumentality," as the historian Gail Fenske notes.[41] In conjunction with Hood, the theatrical and architectural lighting designer Bassett Jones created a lighting design to distinguish the Radiator Building from the multiple skyscrapers in New York.[42] Hood's interest in illuminating buildings originated with his Tribune Tower project when he and Howells had suggested illumination for the upper part of the building, but this illumination only occurred in 1929, when Jones provided designs for floodlights on the crown.[43] Jones's design for the Radiator allowed the owners to "vary the night appearance of the building from time to time, and to introduce spectacular displays on special occasions."[44] It was strategically lit by a variety of amber lights projecting varying wattage at different points between the twenty-first floor and the roof.[45] At night, this array of lights produced a dazzling and compelling appearance for the American Radiator Building, making its crown glow and float above its dark tower in the city sky. Articles on its exterior lighting system appeared in specialty electrical publications, and as the historian Dietrich Neumann remarks, Hood became extremely interested in nocturnal illumination for buildings, later writing the text for a booklet published by General Electric in 1930, *Architecture of the Night.*[46]

In the months and years after its completion, the American Radiator Building, with its impressive daytime and nighttime appearance, stimulated strong reactions among architectural critics and commentators and stirred imaginative interpretations of its symbolism among artists and writers. American Radiator president and chairman Woolley fully appreciated the commercial and advertising benefits of his company's distinctive skyscraper, and the powerful identification value of a skyscraper with a company or product. In a 1926 article Woolley wrote for the *American Architect* magazine, he straightforwardly asserted his conviction that good architecture was an "economic asset" because it attracted the "best paying tenants."[47] Woolley praised the virtues of American skyscrapers and noted that Europeans were coming to observe and study them. He proclaimed that the "skyscraper with its wealth of aspiring significance has already become the wonder and marvel of connoisseurs, regardless of nationality."[48] For Woolley, an attractive and profitable skyscraper promoted the concept of good architecture, a quality he believed his own American Radiator Building epitomized.

Although Hood limited any lengthy discussion of historical styles in his own commentary on the American Radiator Building, preferring instead to concentrate on the subject of the black brick and the illumination, a closer examination of his early comments about the project reveals, in fact, that he did make reference to a medieval source. As the skyscraper neared completion, Hood stated in the *New York Times* that he found precedents for the effective use of black, noting that it could be found at Pompeii and in France during the Empire. He also explained: "The idea of gold trimming came next and caught the fancy of us all. Precedent, at least in Europe, pointed to other periods of architecture, where black had been used effectively, particularly, for example in the Grande Place of the hôtel de ville, Brussels."[49] Hood had probably seen the Grande Place of the hôtel de ville when he traveled to France and Belgium with Howells as they prepared the Gothic details for the Tribune Tower.[50] Evidently intrigued by the Grande Place, Hood later elaborated on his fascination with it in a 1924 article he prepared for the *American Architect:* "The old buildings surrounding it, black with age, had recently had the ornamental parts brought out in gold, and a group of buildings that had become gloomy and dingy, were completely transformed by the note of golden color. The blacker the stonework of the buildings became, the more brilliant by contrast was the picture."[51]

Curiously, many critics and writers in the 1920s—and even many later historians—overlooked Hood's comment about the connection between the dark buildings and the ornamental gold in this historic context and in his own design. In terms of scenographic effects, the Brussels Grande Place surely exerted an influence on Hood. The location of the Brussels buildings facing onto the open Place itself can be compared to the way in which Hood's skyscraper faces Bryant Park. More importantly, the polished bronze figures and gold ornament against the old, blackened guild houses and buildings surrounding the Place produced a vivid effect. The contrast between the two colors was startling and influenced Hood's design for the Radiator Building. The hôtel de ville, a Flemish Gothic building, was erected between 1402 and 1454 and stands as one of the central buildings in the Grande Place. Hood absorbed the spirit of the Gothic from it in some form: the idea for the small corbel figures on the lower exterior section of the Radiator Building may have come from the hôtel de ville or from the other guild houses around the square, many of which included sculpture on their facades. Perhaps more significantly for Hood's purposes, the civic model of the hôtel de ville also inspired him. Just as Gilbert looked to late Gothic Flemish town halls as his source of inspiration for the Woolworth Building, so Hood appeared to link this type of secular structure with the Radiator Building.[52] The hôtel de ville and the Grande Place were telling symbols of Brussels's mercantile power in the late Gothic period, and therefore they offered relevant commercial associations for Hood as well.

Hood's remark about the historic hôtel de ville and the Grande Place was not the only overlooked aspect of the building's design. Aside from the 1924 *American Architect* article, little critical attention was given to the character of any of the interior spaces of the American Radiator Building. Inside, groin-vaulted public showrooms on the lower level were reached from the ground floor, and other product showrooms were placed near the mezzanine level. In these public showroom areas, the interiors were finished in an ornate, vaguely medieval manner with wrought iron gates featuring the company's initials and functioning much like a rood screen in a medieval church. The low, groin-vaulted ceiling of the lower showroom suggested a medieval crypt, yet these features attracted little commentary. Instead, the exterior fascinated people and became the sole subject of discussion.

Both the architectural press and the public focused almost exclusively on the building's unusual color and its illumination, generating meanings for it based on these striking elements that allowed the building to stand out in the city skyline. Virtually no interest was directed to any of the historical sources Hood mentioned, suggesting that the novelty of merging medieval designs with the skyscraper form had faded considerably. A March 1924 article in *Architecture* magazine commented on the Radiator Building as it neared completion and noted that there "are those who even think that when it is completed it will take its place among the modern towers of commerce with considerable distinction."[53] As the building was readied to receive its first occupants in May 1924, the architect Harvey Wiley Corbett discussed the Radiator Building in a now famous article in *Architectural Record.* He spelled out the link between the building's appearance and its advertising value: "A great black structure with yellow trimmings, now almost completed, does it not seem to express the spirit of commercialism? It is self advertising."[54] Although Corbett did not explicitly state that the building resembled any of the company's products, he believed that it was successful because it advertised the company itself. *Architectural Record* drew attention to the building's unique coloration by featuring a color image of it to accompany Corbett's article, a rare step for a magazine that still presented the majority of its subjects in black and white.

When the American Radiator Building opened in the spring of 1924, numerous articles in architectural journals, popular periodicals, and newspapers provided extensive coverage. Even in an age of prolific skyscraper construction, it provoked considerable excitement. The Fifth Avenue Association and the New York Chapter of the American Institute of Architects awarded it the second prize for new building design in 1925. In an article recognizing this achievement, the editors of *Architecture* magazine mentioned that the general style was a combination of Romanesque and Gothic elements, but they stressed what they considered to be the distinguishing feature of the building: "Built for a company which manufactures heat appliances, its very atmosphere is symbolic of its function—the black of the main structure suggesting a huge coal pile, and the gold and yellow of its higher points the glow of flames of an unbanked fire."[55] In effect, the magazine portrayed it as an example of *architecture parlante,* or "speaking architecture," which embodies its function in its very form. The imagery of the glowing flames was prompted by the nighttime illumination of its upper zones. If Hood is to be believed, it was a type of accidental *architecture parlante;* despite the attempts of many critics and writers to claim that the building was designed deliberately to resemble a lump of coal with its top ablaze, Hood denied any intention to suggest the heating products of its owners, emphatically stating that his design was merely a solution to the problem at hand.[56] The popular press and the general public, in fact, persisted in attaching this particular reading to the company's products, and it circulated widely and consistently until it became accepted as fact. As a result, the imagery flourished in the popular imagination, as this essay's opening comments from the 1925 narrative guidebook demonstrate, and the American Radiator Company avidly embraced this portrayal of its skyscraper.

Perhaps in response to the fascination with the black brick, Hood himself quickly tried to downplay any of the medieval elements in a September 1924 article in *Architectural Forum* and offered his own explanation for the Radiator Building's appearance: "My experience, which in reality consists of designing only two skyscrapers, does not justify my expressing an opinion as to whether a building should be treated vertically, horizontally or in a cubist fashion." Hood further stated that he felt it was better to "not have a definite opinion" and claimed that both the Tribune Tower and the Radiator Building were in "the 'vertical' style or what is called 'Gothic,' simply because I happened to make them so." He concluded, "If at the time of designing them I had been under the spell of Italian campaniles or Chinese pagodas, I suppose the resulting compositions would have been 'horizontal.'"[57] Hood's comments disclose his steadfast refusal to formulate a firm opinion about the appropriate design for a skyscraper; instead, he declared that only his current interests guided him.

While his comments may have been directed at any lingering criticisms of the Tribune Tower, Hood's words expressed his reluctance to attach his practice to any single design vocabulary. His statements also point, perhaps, to his growing realization that he could not dictate the way in which the general public would interpret a building. Once completed, a skyscraper could be accepted and transfigured by the public in ways that the architect could not control. Very few architectural critics and writers at the time mentioned any of the historically inspired details of the building at all, directing their attention instead to its black brick, evening illumination, and appropriately symbolic commercial appearance.[58] Even Hood's fellow architect Ely Jacques Kahn baldly stated in 1926 that the building's "gothic detail seems quite incidental compared to the basic conception of a dark mass in which darker holes, the windows, do not disturb the block of the building."[59] In the end, material and technological innovations garnered much more interest than the historical vocabulary of the medieval past, and the power of the expanding consumer culture prevailed over all.

Part of Hood's problem in dealing with people's perceptions of the Radiator Building may have stemmed from his only previous experience with a skyscraper commission. A high level of carefully orchestrated publicity accompanied the Tribune Tower project before its actual completion, including a public display of the winning design and those of the runners-up. Countless publications featured it as construction progressed, easily allowing Howells and Hood to gauge the public reaction to their design. When the Tribune Tower was completed in 1925, the public, therefore, was fully prepared for the final result, and, indeed, the nonstop publicity from the *Tribune* newspaper itself largely shaped the public's understanding of it throughout its construction, efficiently steering them on how exactly to view the building.[60] This was not the case with the American Radiator Building, which was built quickly, making its completion more of a surprise unveiling. Without the elaborate preamble that the Tribune Tower received, critics and the public readily established their own interpretations of the skyscraper, making Hood less prepared for the insistent symbolic reading attached to it.

Like the architectural press, many artists were also fascinated by the American Radiator Building's striking presence and mysterious nighttime illumination, taking little note of any of its medieval design motifs. Absorbed by the atmosphere created by the building's coloration and illumination, they frequently described it in imaginative ways. The German architect Erich Mendelsohn featured it in his 1926 book *Amerika: Bilderbuch eines Architekten,* a summary of his architectural travels in the United States. In his section on "garish" or "grotesque" architecture, he included a photograph of the building and referred to its startling presence as something that grew like an unusual plant in its city environment: "The American Radiator Corp. shot up suddenly like an exotic flower. Black with gold ornament that gleams in the evening."[61] Ben Judah Lubschez included a photograph of its powerful night image in his 1927 book *Manhattan: The Magical Island.* Calling his photograph *The Great Lantern, Bryant Park,* Lubschez echoed Mendelsohn's reading of it as exotic or foreign, describing the building as "a stone garden lantern of the Orient, but of unheard, gigantic size."[62] The vision of the lit skyscraper against the night sky entranced the artist Georgia O'Keeffe, who painted it in 1927 with its glowing nighttime illumination in her *Radiator Building—Night, New York* (fig. 4). First shown in a 1928 exhibition in New York, the painting was reproduced in various newspapers and magazines in subsequent years, including the 1935 *Fortune* magazine article on American Radiator's Woolley.[63] Both Lubschez's photograph and O'Keeffe's painting capture the building's sensational, luminous presence against the night sky. O'Keeffe deliberately avoided presenting an exact depiction of the building, and, as the historian Mary Woods observed, the artist added extra windows across the facade to enhance the image of light windows against the dark background and gave it eight more stories to accentuate its verticality.[64]

Writers also offered unique and sometimes rhapsodic descriptions in various publications. The French author Paul Morand conveyed a sense of the building's elegant originality in a description of an evening stroll in his 1930 book *New York:* "On my left, the American Radiator Building, the color of dark grapes, is crowned with a tiara of gold like that of some modern Kremlin; lit from beneath, its head merges with the mist and makes the darkness glow."[65] By evoking the Kremlin, Morand conjured up images of this skyscraper beyond the New York commercial metropolis, seeing it as something with a foreign touch. Other writers accepted the building's appearance, even if they found it harsh, like the anonymous author of an article that originally appeared in the *Villager*

Fig. 4. *Radiator Building–Night, New York,* 1927, by Georgia O'Keeffe. (Alfred Stieglitz Collection, co-owned by Fisk University, Nashville, Tennessee, and Crystal Bridges Museum of American Art, Bentonville, Arkansas; photography by Edward C. Robinson III; © 2015 Georgia O'Keeffe Museum/Artists Rights Society [ARS], New York)

and was reprinted in the *American Architect.* The author claimed that the building represented the city itself: "The Radiator Building does not cross the city's grain; no, it is sprung out of the city's very heart! No fair fancies here, no sentimental dreams; no sugariness; no subtlety; no majesty or peace; no friendliness; no lovingness; power without vitality; beauty without grace and kindness; it is New York. . . . New York has a meaning, and Radiator gathers it up and distills it."[66]

Without a doubt, it became part of the "spectacle" of 1920s New York by calling attention to itself in a city that Elizabeth Dean described as "conscious of being seen," noting that the city's skyscrapers generated a "self-consciousness" and the buildings were "the show."[67] According to Fenske, the Woolworth Building was an important component of New York's new "signature skyline," one that was invested with connotations of American progress and possibilities.[68] Hood's Radiator Building was also part of this emerging skyline and metropolitan dynamism, demanding recognition as a piece of the larger city ensemble, what Dean called an "icon of glamorous Gotham."[69]

As Robert A. M. Stern noted, G. H. Edgell highlighted its dual attributes as both a commercial icon and a visual wonder in his 1928 book *The American Architecture of To-day,* in which he included it as one of the "latest and most sensational skyscrapers."[70] Although Edgell explained that the "effect is theatrical to a degree that opens it to the charge of vulgarity," he found much to praise in the building, calling it a "magnificent piece of work" whose design at night has "a dreamlike beauty." He defended it by stating, "And if we think it a trifle crude, remember that it is designed to house a radiator company and not to commemorate a war hero nor glorify a saint."[71] Yet Edgell's comments reveal an important distinction between this commercial skyscraper and others that had preceded it in New York. Frank Woolworth intended the Woolworth Building to be an object of civic beauty, evoking noble associations through its Gothic design vocabulary, and, of course, serving as a highly visible form of advertising. Although Woolworth planned his skyscraper to be, as Fenske stated, the company's "imperial capital," it had a different connection to Woolworth's retail enterprises.[72] There was no Woolworth store in the building, and the company headquarters occupied less than two stories out of fifty because the building was planned for speculative office purposes.[73] In contrast, the American Radiator Building was much more integral to the company's operations and identity: over a third of the usable space was taken over by the executive offices and the New York sales branch of the company, and the ground floor and lower levels featured extensive company showrooms that were regularly available for consumers to view the company's products.[74] Visitors to the Radiator Building were able to inspect the company's products in the showroom and stand in its basement to see these products in use, while admiring its heating system under the groin vaults.

The American Radiator Company fully exploited the reception the American Radiator Building received by incorporating both its outright advertising and spectacular elements into their own company literature and trade catalogues. There is every indication that the company knew the building would be the talk of the city from its opening: the 1924 American Radiator annual report, the

Fig. 5. *The Ideal Fitter*, 1925, American Radiator Company. (Courtesy of Hagley Museum and Library)

first to appear after the building's completion, displayed it on its opening pages with day and night images, confirming its commercial role and urban theatricality.[75] In many of American Radiator's trade catalogues and promotional booklets, images of the skyscraper figured prominently, exposing suppliers and consumers to the new commercial headquarters. On the title page of the 1925 catalogue for *The Ideal Fitter,* a color reproduction of an original rendering by Birch Burdette Long was included (fig. 5). Directed at both sales staff and customers, this catalogue clearly intended to bring the aura of the building's architectural innovations to its heating products as its black shaft stands out against its pale and sedate neighbors. This same image had appeared in the May 1924 issue of *Architectural Record* as a full-page illustration to accompany Corbett's article, demonstrating a remarkable continuity of images from periodicals to company literature. In the 1925 trade catalogue *Ideal Type "A" Heat Machine,* the building is shown complete with an image of the heaters in the vaulted showroom basement. The text is revealing because it adopts the very language that people had used to describe the building from its unveiling: "That greatest of all forces, heat, the control of which has made possible the development of civilization in all parts of the world, has found an appropriate and artistic interpretation in this new American Radiator building—a Modern Cathedral of Commerce."[76] Within this passage, two important themes are conveyed. First, although Hood denied the symbolic function of the building's appearance, the American Radiator Company seized the power of this connection, largely made by writers and the public. Heat, they concurred, was truly embodied by this novel building that was, in turn, heated by the very products it sold. In addition, the copywriters for this catalogue astutely picked up the well-known phrase first applied to the Woolworth Building, "Cathedral of Commerce," suggesting that the American Radiator Building was the new heir to this moniker.[77]

The company's understanding of its new skyscraper as an artistic success is also evident in its publications as they skillfully conflated commerce and art in the illustrations used in their trade catalogues. O'Keeffe's 1927 painting had a formal influence on the 1931 cover of the catalogue for American Radiator and Standard Sanitary Corporation and Subsidiary Companies, showing how the company utilized the extraordinary appearance of the building (fig. 6) to its advantage. Its black and gold elements are depicted in a stylized and abstracted manner against the black cover paper to emphasize its sensational nighttime qualities, taking its cue from O'Keeffe's painting. Here, the exchange between the company's skyscraper and the artist bounced back to the company as it seized upon the artist's stunning representation of its own building.

The popular success of the American Radiator Building allowed the company to maximize the advertising value of its new skyscraper, introducing the company's name to a very broad audience. Hood, too, eventually realized the benefits of its fame, and, over the years, appeared to adjust to the gap between his stated intentions for the building and its actual reception. In the end, it served as a type of litmus test for assessing the rising level of consumer culture

Fig. 6. Cover of catalogue for the American Radiator and Standard Sanitary Corporation and Subsidiary Companies, 1931. (Courtesy of Smithsonian Institution Libraries, Washington, DC)

in American society by revealing the readiness of the general public to actively read commercial imagery into the building. Hood received attention from the architectural periodicals and from his professional peers as it was highlighted in countless articles, some of which Hood was asked to write or comment on himself, and in a number of architectural books about skyscrapers and the history of American architecture. Around 1929, Hood was asked to design an extension to the Radiator Building, which he envisioned as a tall, pointed spire-like tower, a largely fantastical design that still bore traces of Gothic verticality. Instead, the company opted for a much smaller showroom extension of a few stories completed by Hood and Godley and Fouilhoux, expanding the original building's base for a few bays.

The fame of the American Radiator Building, however, remained with Hood throughout his career. When Arthur Strawn wrote about the architect in a 1930 article, "Skyrocket," in the *Outlook and Independent,* it was not the Daily News Building or the Chicago Tribune Tower that served as the accompanying illustration for the article but the American Radiator Building. By this date, any interest in the medieval or historically inspired details of this skyscraper had long disappeared as the symbolic commercial associations tightly adhered to it. Perhaps most tellingly, Hood kept his architectural office on the fourteenth floor in the American Radiator Building until his death in 1934, a decision that allowed his clients to be constantly reminded of his most unusual building each time they passed through his door. For the American Radiator Company, the building remained an important component of its corporate life and identity, even after the company's 1929 merger with Standard Sanitary Corporation. The company remained in the building until the late 1980s, when American Standard, as it became known, moved its headquarters to Piscataway, New Jersey.[78] Yet the identification of building, company, and products created one of the most successful commercial architectural efforts of the interwar years, living up to the ambitions of American Radiator, who could safely claim in a 1936 brochure the "leadership" role of their building as both an advertising triumph and an impressive, creative addition to the skyline of New York City.[79]

NOTES

1. Helena Smith Dayton and Louise Bascom Barratt, *New York in Seven Days* (New York: Robert M. McBride, 1925), 10.

2. In Robert A. M. Stern, Gregory Gilmartin, and Thomas Mellins, *New York 1930* (New York: Rizzoli, 1987), the authors refer to various contemporary accounts of the building after its completion. This list provided me with a departure point for considering these articles along with others in order to specifically reexamine Hood's own descriptions of the Radiator Building and, in particular, any discussion of medieval design sources or motifs. See pages 576–77 and 813–14n132 for Stern, Gilmartin, and Mellins's list of selected press and newspaper coverage.

3. Gail Fenske, in *The Skyscraper and the City: The Woolworth Building in the Making of Modern New York* (Chicago: University of Chicago Press, 2008), 99–119, discusses Cass Gilbert's Woolworth Building in terms of Beaux-Arts ideals and the "urban picturesque."

4. "Black Brick Building for New York City," *New York Times,* January 20, 1924, RE1.

5. The story of the Chicago Tribune Tower Competition is comprehensively studied by Katherine Solomonson in her book *The Chicago Tribune Tower Competition: Skyscraper Design and Cultural Change in the 1920s* (Cambridge: Cambridge University Press, 2003).

6. Walter H. Kilham, *Raymond Hood, Architect: Form through Function in the American Skyscraper* (New York: Architectural Book Publishing, 1973), 30.

7. Hood's biographers are divided over the Gothic impact of Cram and Goodhue. Walter H. Kilham, who worked in Hood's office, stated that he did not know to "what degree Hood was influenced in his feeling for Gothic architecture" while in the employ of Cram and Goodhue (see ibid., 30–32). The 1935 appreciation of Hood's life in *Architectural Forum* suggests that Hood learned about Gothic architecture in this office (see "Hood," *Architectural Forum,* February 1935, 127). Robert A. M. Stern considered Hood's arrival in Cram and Goodhue's office as the next logical step after his senior thesis project at MIT, a church designed in the French Gothic style (see Robert A. M. Stern, *Raymond M. Hood* [New York: Rizzoli and Institute for Architecture and Urban Studies, 1982], 3).

8. Kilham notes that Hood was not admitted in 1904 on his first try (see Kilham, *Raymond Hood, Architect,* 32–49; see also Robert A. M. Stern, *Raymond M. Hood*, 3–4, on Hood's time in Paris).

9. Kilham, *Raymond Hood, Architect,* 50–51.

10. It is not clear how Hood received this commission, but the *Architectural Forum* appreciation of his life noted that he was paid five hundred dollars a month for this work in about 1920 ("Hood," 130; Kilham, *Raymond Hood, Architect*, 56; Stern, *Raymond M. Hood*, 6). Biographical information on Hood's life comes from Stern; *Raymond M. Hood;* Kilham, *Raymond Hood, Architect;* and *Architectural Forum.*

11. Solomonson, *Chicago Tribune Competition,* 8; see esp. chaps. 1 and 2 for a discussion of the competition's planning and how the *Tribune* presented it to the public. Solomonson notes that they transformed a "publicity stunt" into "what it characterized as an educational campaign combining the idealism of high culture with advertising strategies" (10).

12. See Solomonson, *Chicago Tribune Competition,* 79, for the various accounts explaining how Howells and Hood paired up for the project.

13. See ibid., 171–72. She notes Sullivan's objections in particular, remarking that he saw Saarinen as a "master of ideas."

14. Ibid., 172.

15. Ibid., 182. Credit for the design of the Tribune Tower was an issue of some confusion after the competition. Hood was in charge of the drafting room and worked on most of the massing and detail drawings. While Howells stayed in New York, Hood worked in their spe-

cial Chicago office and exchanged sketches and drawings with him. By the time the project was completed, it was presented as a collaboration between the two men (see ibid., 253).

16. Ibid., 94–97. Solomonson points out that publication provided an opportunity to study the detailed drawings of the winning design and the other prizewinners along with the drawings of most of the other competitors. The winning entries and the prizewinners also appeared in architectural periodicals and other magazines.

17. Sarah Bradford Landau and Carl W. Condit, *Rise of the New York Skyscraper: 1863–1913* (New Haven: Yale University Press, 1996), 312.

18. Solomonson, *Chicago Tribune Competition,* 174; see also Fenske, *The Skyscraper and the City*.

19. Gail Fenske and Deryck Holdsworth, "Corporate Identity and the New York Office Building: 1885–1915," in *Landscapes of Modernity: Essays on New York City, 1900–1940,* ed. David Ward and Olivier Zunz (New York: Russell Sage Foundation, 1992), 143. The story of the Woolworth Building is the subject of Fenske's book *The Skyscraper and the City*.

20. Fenske and Holdsworth, "Corporate Identity and the New York Office Building," 146. See Fenske, *The Skyscraper and the City,* 120–60, for Gilbert's myriad Gothic sources of inspiration.

21. Landau and Condit, *Rise of the New York Skyscraper,* 387. See Fenske, *The Skyscraper and the City*, 268–69, on Gilbert's efforts to emphasize his secular Gothic sources.

22. Fenske and Holdsworth, "Corporate Identity and the New York Office Building," 154. See also Solomonson, *Chicago Tribune Competition,* chap. 4 ("Design for Advertising") on the vast advertising potential of skyscrapers; and Kenneth Turney Gibbs, *Business Architectural Imagery in America 1870–1930* (Ann Arbor: UMI Research Press, 1984).

23. In 1924, Frederick A. Godley joined Hood and Fouilhoux, and the partnership became known as Raymond Hood, Godley, and Fouilhoux. Godley largely worked on his own projects rather than those of Hood, retiring in 1931 (Kilham, *Raymond Hood, Architect,* 73).

24. "Heating Man," *Fortune* 11, no. 4 (April 1935): 81.

25. For information on Clarence Mott Woolley and the history of the American Radiator Company and its merger with American Standard, see *International Directory of Company Histories,* vol. 3, ed. Adele Hast (Chicago: St. James, 1991), 663, entry for American Standard Inc.; "Heating Man," 80–83, 161–64, 188; "American Radiator & Standard Sanitary Corp," *Fortune* 21, no. 3 (March 1940): 57–61, 154–62; and "C. M. Woolley Dies, Manufacturer, 92," *New York Times,* July 20, 1956.

26. American Radiator Company, *Thirty-Third Annual Report of American Radiator Company,* 1924.

27. In *Raymond M. Hood,* Stern notes that Hood's "tower interlocked with its base" (8).

28. Raymond M. Hood, "The American Radiator Company Building, New York," *American Architect* 126 (November 19, 1924): 472. Hood's ideas and descriptions of the American Radiator Building were largely expressed in this article and others he prepared for

architectural periodicals. Letters between Hood and the American Radiator Company, if they exist, would perhaps reveal more about his intentions, but they are not among Hood's surviving papers.

29. Hood, "The American Radiator Company Building, New York," 470. Hood stated that his clients were "sanely enthusiasts" who were willing to do their part in the development of the skyscraper.

30. See, for example, Solomonson, *Chicago Tribune Competition,* 247.

31. Hood, "The American Radiator Company Building, New York," 472. Stern, Gilmartin, and Mellins, *New York 1930,* 576, also makes reference to this famous quote by Hood.

32. Stern, Gilmartin, and Mellins, *New York 1930,* 576, sees the inspiration from the "telescoping setbacks of Saarinen's Chicago Tribune proposal."

33. Hood was not alone in utilizing Saarinen's Tribune entry as a point of departure; the influence of Saarinen's design reached beyond Hood's office, and traces of it could be seen in other skyscrapers built in the 1920s (see Solomonson, *Chicago Tribune Competition,* 247, where she notes that Thomas E. Tallmadge named the New York Telephone Building, the Book Tower in Detroit, and the Pacific Telephone Building in San Francisco as examples in his 1927 book *The Story of Architecture in America*).

34. See, for example, Kilham, *Raymond Hood, Architect;* Stern, *Raymond M. Hood*; and Stern, Gilmartin, and Mellins, *New York 1930*, 576–77.

35. Hood, "The American Radiator Company Building, New York," 470.

36. See "Black Brick Building for New York City." In Stern, Gilmartin, and Mellins, *New York 1930,* 576–77, the authors refer to many of the immediate press responses to it.

37. "Black Brick Building for New York City."

38. Ibid.

39. Raymond M. Hood, "Attempting to Build with Black Brick," *Architecture* 56 (July 1927): 59.

40. For a further investigation of Hood's penchant for emphasizing practicality as an operating principle, see Mario Canato, "Pragmatic Thinking in the Ideas of the Skyscraper Architects of the 1920s" (PhD diss., University of Pennsylvania, 1992), 63. Kilham states that Hood did not have an intellectual philosophy to define his approach to architecture and defined Hood as "a doer, not a theorist" (see Kilham, *Raymond Hood, Architect,* 185). Stern, in *Raymond M. Hood*, 10, and in Stern, Gilmartin, and Mellins, *New York 1930*, 576, also points out Hood's pragmatic approach.

41. Fenske, *The Skyscraper and the City,* 283–84.

42. A survey of the history of illuminated buildings can be found in *Architecture of the Night: The Illuminated Building,* ed. Dietrich Neumann (Munich: Prestel, 2002). See 114–15 for a discussion of the American Radiator Building.

43. Ibid., 142. Neumann notes that Jones had earlier devised a different plan for the illumination of the Tribune Tower that was not executed. It was a theatrical scheme that involved

colored filters and targeted illuminations. For special events, Jones suggested that steam could be released from the upper tower and illuminated by "fire-color" lights.

44. Meyer, Strong, and Jones, "Heating, Ventilating, Electric and Elevator Equipment for the American Radiator Building," *American Architect* 126 (November 19, 1924): 482.

45. "Electricity Adds Night Brilliance to Bold Architecture," *Electrical World* 85, no. 4 (January 24, 1925): 219.

46. See Neumann, *Architecture of the Night,* 58.

47. Clarence M. Woolley, "Good Architecture a Commercial Asset," *American Architect* 129 (January 5, 1926): 56.

48. Ibid.

49. "Black Brick Building for New York City."

50. Solomonson discusses this trip to France and Belgium in *Chicago Tribune Competition,* 260.

51. Hood, "The American Radiator Company Building, New York," *American Architect* 126 (November 19, 1924): 468.

52. Fenske, *The Skyscraper and the City,* 106–10, discusses Cass Gilbert's interest in these "free-trading" Flemish cities.

53. "Our Set-Back Architecture," *Architecture* 49, no. 3 (March 1924): 77.

54. Harvey Wiley Corbett, "The American Radiator Building New York City," *Architectural Record* 55 (May 1924): 477. For later historians referring to this article, see, for example, Stern, Gilmartin, and Mellins, *New York 1930*, 576.

55. "Prizes Awarded for the Best Recent Buildings in the Fifth Avenue Section, New York," *Architecture* 51 (January 1925): 23.

56. I make this distinction that it was the press and others who pushed this concept and not Hood because it reveals much about the reception of the building in a highly commercialized city atmosphere. While Neumann writes in his book *Architecture of the Night* that it was a "serious" attempt at *architecture parlante*, contemporary articles indicate that it was not an attempt originally generated by the architect but rather was one created by those "reading" the building after its completion.

57. Raymond M. Hood, "Exterior Architecture of Office Buildings," *Architectural Forum* 41, no. 3 (September 1924): 97. Historians like Stern and Canato refer to this often quoted statement by Hood to stress Hood's pragmatic approach to design.

58. There is little or no discussion of the medieval or Gothic elements in many of the articles and books that featured the Radiator Building in the 1920s and 1930s. Compare, for example, the descriptions in "Our Set-Back Architecture," 77; Harvey Wiley Corbett, "The American Radiator Building New York City," *Architectural Record* 55 (May 1924): 473–77; "Living Architecture" *Pencil Points* 6 (January 1925): 37; C. H. Blackall, "American Architecture since the War," *American Architect* 133, no. 2536 (January 5, 1928): 1–11; G. H. Edgell, *The American Architecture of To-Day* (New York: Charles Scribner's Sons, 1928); and Hugh Ferriss, *The Metropolis of Tomorrow* (New York: Ives Washburn, 1929).

59. Ely Jacques Kahn, “Our Skyscrapers Take Simple Forms,” *New York Times,* May 2, 1926, M11.

60. Solomonson, *Chicago Tribune Competition,* 251, notes that the newspaper actively reported on the stages of construction.

61. Erich Mendelsohn, *Amerika: Bilderbuch eines Architekten* (Berlin: Rudolf Mosse, 1926), 55.

62. As qtd. in Stern, Gilmartin, and Mellins, *New York 1930,* 66. The authors also reproduce Lubschez’s photograph.

63. For a complete exhibition and publication history, see Barbara Buhler Lynes, *Georgia O’Keeffe Catalogue Raisonné,* vol. 1 (New Haven: Yale University Press with the National Gallery of Art, Washington, D.C., and the Georgia O’Keeffe Foundation, 1999), 333. More recently, Vivien Green Fryd has interpreted this painting as a type of emblematic portrait (see “Georgia O’Keeffe’s Radiator Building: Gender, Sexuality, Modernism, and Urban Imagery,” *Winterthur Portfolio* 35 [Winter 2000]: 269–89). For a general discussion of the skyscraper in art, see also Anna C. Chave, “‘Who Will Paint New York?’ The World’s New Art Center and the Skyscraper Paintings of Georgia O’Keeffe,” *American Art* 5 (Winter/Spring 1991): 87–106; and Merrill Schleier, *The Skyscraper in American Art 1890–1931* (New York: Da Capo, 1986).

64. Mary Woods notes these alterations in her essay “Photography of the Night: Skyscraper Nocturne and Skyscraper Noir in New York,” in Neumann, *Architecture of the Night,* 74.

65. Paul Morand, *New York* (New York: Book League of America, 1930), 146–47. I thank Kevin D. Murphy for directing me to Morand’s writings on New York.

66. “The Radiator Building,” as reprinted from the *Villager* in *American Architect* 126 (November 19, 1924): 483. Stern interpreted this article as offering “unconditional praise” for the building (see Stern, Gilmartin, and Mellins, *New York 1930*, 577).

67. Elizabeth Dean, “Georgia O’Keeffe’s Radiator Building: Icon of Glamorous Gotham,” *Revue Française d’Etudes Américaines,* no. 11 (April 1981): 82.

68. See Fenske, *The Skyscraper and the City,* 302–9.

69. Dean, “Georgia O’Keeffe’s Radiator Building,” 81.

70. Stern, *Raymond M. Hood,* 10.

71. Edgell, *The American Architecture of To-day,* 363.

72. Fenske, *The Skyscraper and the City,* 245.

73. Fenske and Holdsworth, “Corporate Identity and the New York Office Building,” 143. See Fenske, *The Skyscraper and the City,* 246–57, for a discussion of the office interiors and the tenants.

74. “Black Brick Building for New York City” lists the space usage.

75. See the photographs placed on the opening facing pages of American Radiator Company, *Thirty-Third Annual Report of American Radiator Company,* 1924. Stern emphasizes the post–World War I period in New York architecture as working in service of “corporate identity” (Stern, Gilmartin, and Mellins, *New York 1930*, 30). Here, with the American

Radiator Building, the building itself was discussed in contemporary accounts as more than a billboard and as actually embodying the key attributes of the company's products.

76. American Radiator Company, *Ideal Type "A" Heat Machine* (New York: American Radiator Company, 1925), 30.

77. Both drawings and photographs of the building appeared regularly in the company's trade literature. In the 1932 catalogue for Arco Radiator Enclosures, for example, the American Radiator Building and other skyscrapers that used the heating equipment were featured on its pages.

78. In February 2001, the building began a new life as the Bryant Park Hotel.

79. Back cover image of *This New Comfort: A Book for Home-owners Describing a New Method of Assuring Perfect Indoor Comfort* (New York: American Radiator Company, 1936).

SELECTED BIBLIOGRAPHY OF PUBLISHED SOURCES

"The American Skyscraper: The Giant in Architecture: Its Purpose, Beauty and Development." *Craftsman* 24 (April 1913): 3–10.

"The American Tall Building from a European Point of View." *Inland Architect* 30 (November 1897): 38–40.

"Ante-bellum Skyscraper." *American Society of Architectural Historians Journal* 9 (October 1950): 27–28.

Behrendt, Walter Curt. *Modern Building. Its Nature, Problems, and Forms.* New York: Harcourt Brace, 1937.

Bennett, David. *Skyscrapers: Form and Function.* New York: Simon and Schuster, 1995.

Billington, David P. *The Tower and the Bridge: The New Art of Structural Engineering.* Princeton: Princeton University Press, 1983.

Bletter, Rosemarie Haag. "Invention of the Skyscraper: Notes on Its Diverse Histories." *Assemblage,* no. 2 (February 1987): 110–17.

Bluestone, Daniel. *Constructing Chicago.* New Haven: Yale University Press, 1991.

Bonshek, Jane. "The Skyscraper: A Catalyst of Change in the Chicago Construction Industries, 1882–1892." *Construction History* 4 (1988): 53–74.

Bossom, Alfred C. *Building to the Skies: The Romance of the Skyscraper.* New York: The Studio, 1934.

Bowman, John G. *The Cathedral of Learning of the University of Pittsburgh.* Pittsburgh: University of Pittsburgh, 1925.

Bragdon, Claude. *Architecture and Democracy.* New York: Knopf, 1918.

———. "Architecture in the United States: Part 3, Skyscraper." *Architecture Record* 20 (August 1909): 84–96, 122.
Brooks, Michael W. *John Ruskin and Victorian Architecture.* New Brunswick, NJ: Rutgers University Press, 1987.
Canato, Mario. "Pragmatic Thinking in the Ideas of the Skyscraper Architects of the 1920s." PhD diss., University of Pennsylvania, 1992.
Capam, H. "The Riddle of the Tall Building: Has the Skyscraper a Place in Modern Architecture?" *Craftsman* 10 (1906): 477–88.
Chave, Anna C. "'Who Will Paint New York?' The World's New Art Center and the Skyscraper Paintings of Georgia O'Keeffe." *American Art* 5 (Winter/Spring 1991): 87–106.
Chicago Tribune Company. *The International Competition for a New Administration Building for the Chicago Tribune MCMXXII.* Chicago: The Tribune Company, 1923.
Condit, Carl. *American Building Art: The Twentieth Century.* Oxford: Oxford University Press, 1981.
———. *The Rise of the Skyscraper.* Chicago: University of Chicago Press, 1952.
Corbett, Harvey Wiley. "The Birth and Development of the Tall Building." *American Architect* 129 (January 5, 1926): 37–40.
———. "The Bush Building." In *Masterpieces of Architecture in the United States: Memorials, Museums, Libraries, Churches, Public Buildings, Hotels and Office Buildings,* edited by Warren Hoak and Willis Humphry Church, 195. New York: Charles Scribner's Sons, 1930.
———. "The Skyscraper and the Automobile Have Made the Modern City." In *Studies in the Arts and Architecture,* edited by Carl W. Blegen, 107–13. Philadelphia: University of Pennsylvania Press, 1941.
Cram, Ralph Adams. *The Substance of Gothic.* Boston: Marshall Jones, 1917.
Cressey, Charles. "The Crown of the Skyscraper." *Architectural Record* 27, no. 5 (May 1910): 430–35.
Des Jardins, S. E. "The Gallic Ancestry of the Skyscraper." *Western Architect* 12 (November 1908): 56–59.
Domosh, Mona. "The Symbolism of the Skyscraper: Case Studies of New York's First Tall Buildings." *Journal of Urban History* 14, no. 4 (May 1988): 320–45.
Douglas, George H. *Skyscrapers: A Social History of the Very Tall Building in America.* Jefferson, NC: McFarland, 1996.
Drexler, Arthur. *Transformations in Modern Architecture.* New York: Museum of Modern Art, 1979.
Duvert, Elizabeth. "Georgia O'Keeffe's Radiator Building: Icon of Glorious Gotham." *Places* 2, no. 2 (1984): 3–16.
Edgell, George. *The American Architecture of To-Day.* New York: Charles Scribner's Sons, 1928.
"The Evolution of the Skyscraper." *Architectural Record* 14 (November 1903): 329–43.

Fenske, Gail. *The Skyscraper and the City: The Woolworth Building in the Making of Modern New York.* Chicago: University of Chicago Press, 2008.

Fenske, Gail, and Deryck Holdsworth. "Corporate Identity and the New York Office Building: 1895–1915." In *Landscape of Modernity: New York City, 1900–1940,* edited by David Ward and Olivier Zunz, 129–59. 1992. Paperback edition. Baltimore: Johns Hopkins University Press, 1997.

Ferree, Barr. "The Art of the High Building." *Architectural Record* 15 (May 1904): 445–66.

Ferriss, Hugh. *The Metropolis of Tomorrow.* 1929. Reprint, New York: Princeton Architectural Press, 1986.

Fitch, James Marston. *Architecture and the Aesthetics of Plenty.* New York: Columbia University Press, 1961.

Flagg, Ernest. "The Dangers of Tall Buildings." *Cosmopolitan* 21 (May 1896): 70–74.

Fleming, Robins. "A Half Century of the Skyscraper: Tracing the Expansion and Refinement of a Brilliant American Achievement." *Civil Engineering* 4, no. 12 (October 1934): 634–38.

Flowers, Benjamin. *Skyscraper: The Politics and Power of Building New York City in the Twentieth Century.* Philadelphia: University of Pennsylvania Press, 2009.

Fryd, Vivien Green. "Georgia O'Keeffe's Radiator Building: Gender, Sexuality, Modernism, and Urban Imagery." *Winterthur Portfolio* 35 (Winter 2000): 269–89.

Gallo, Emmanuelle. "Skyscrapers and District Heating, An Inter-related History, 1876–1933." *Construction History* 19 (2003): 87–106.

Gibbs, Kenneth Turney. *Business Architecture Imagery in America, 1870–1930.* Ann Arbor: UMI Research Press, 1984.

Giedion, Sigfried. *Space, Time and Architecture: The Growth of a New Tradition.* 5th ed. Cambridge: Harvard University Press, 1977.

Gillespie, H[arriet] S[isson]. "The Bush Terminal Sales Building." *Architecture* 39, no. 1 (January 1919): 1–4.

———. "A New Gothic Skyscraper." *International Studio* 67, no. 265 (March 1919): xx–xxiii.

Goebel, Stefan. *The Great War and Medieval Memory: War, Remembrance and Medievalism in Britain and Germany, 1914–1940.* New York: Cambridge University Press, 2009.

Goldberger, Paul. *The Skyscraper.* New York: Knopf, 1981.

Gordon, F. "The Skyscraper." *American Architect and Building News* 46 (December 1894): 100–101.

Gould, Stephen Jay. "Restoration and the Woolworth Building." *Natural History* 110, no. 10A (Winter 2001/2002): 96–97.

Gournay, Isabelle. "France Discovers America, 1917–1939 (French Writings on American Architecture)." PhD diss., Yale University, 1989.

Gray, Christopher. *New York Streetscapes: Tales of Manhattan's Significant Buildings and Landmarks.* New York: Abrams, 2003.

Grubiak, Margaret M. "Reassessing Yale's Cathedral Orgy: The Ecclesiastical Metaphor and the Sterling Memorial Library." *Winterthur Portfolio* 43, no. 2/3 (Spring/Autumn 2009): 159–84.

Hamlin, A. D. F. "The Battle of the Styles." *Architectural Record* 1 (January/March 1892): 265–75.

———. "Twenty-Five Years of American Architecture." *Architectural Record* 40 (June 1916): 1–14.

Hamlin, Talbot. *The American Spirit in Architecture.* New Haven: Yale University Press, 1926.

Heilbrun, Margaret, ed. *Inventing the Skyline: The Architecture of Cass Gilbert.* New York: Columbia University Press, 2000.

Hitchcock, Henry-Russell. *Modern Architecture: Romanticism and Reintegration.* New York: Da Capo, 1993.

Holliday, Kathryn E. *Leopold Eidlitz: Architecture and Idealism in the Gilded Age.* New York: Norton, 2008.

Hood, Raymond M. "The American Radiator Company Building, New York." *American Architect* 126 (November 19, 1924): 466–74.

Huxtable, Ada Louise. *The Tall Office Building Artistically Reconsidered.* New York: Pantheon, 1984.

Jordy, William, and Ralph Coe, eds. *American Architecture and Other Writings by Montgomery Schuyler.* Cambridge: Belknap Press of Harvard University Press, 1961.

Kilham, Walter. *Raymond Hood, Architect: Form through Function in the American Skyscraper.* New York: Architectural Book Publishing, 1973.

Lamb, Frederick Stymetz. "Modern Use of the Gothic: The Possibilities of New Architectural Style." *Craftsman* 8 (May 1905): 150–70.

Landau, Sarah Bradford, and Carl Condit. *Rise of the New York Skyscraper, 1865–1913.* New Haven: Yale University Press, 1996.

Lears, Jackson. *No Place of Grace: Antimodernism and the Transformation of American Culture, 1880–1920.* New York: Pantheon, 1981.

Leslie, Thomas. "'Built Mostly of Itself': The Chicago Brick Industry and the Masonry Skyscraper in the Late 19th Century." *Construction History* 25 (2010): 69–84.

Lorne, Francis. "The New Architecture of a Flamboyant Civilization." *Arts and Decoration* 24 (November 1925): 58–59, 90.

Merwood-Salisbury, Joanna. *Chicago 1890: The Skyscraper and the City.* Chicago: University of Chicago Press, 2009.

———. "The First Chicago School and the Ideology of the Skyscraper." In *Architecture and Capitalism, 1845 to the Present,* edited by Peggy Deamer, 25–47. New York: Routledge, 2014.

Morshed, Adnan. *Impossible Heights: Skyscrapers, Flight, and the Master Builder.* Minneapolis: University of Minnesota Press, 2015.

Moudry, Roberta, ed. *The American Skyscraper: Cultural Histories.* New York: Cambridge University Press, 2005.

Mujica, Francisco. *History of the Skyscraper.* New York: Da Capo, 1977.

Mumford, Lewis. "High Buildings: An American View." *American Architect* 126, no. 2458 (November 5, 1924): 423–24.

Neumann, Dietrich, ed. *Architecture of the Night: The Illuminated Building.* Munich: Prestel, 2002.

Newcomb, R. "The Trend of Skyscraper Design." *Western Architect* 35 (March 1926): 31–33.

"The Newest Thing in Skyscrapers." *Architectural Record* 19 (May 1906): 398–400.

Newton, Roger Hale. "New Evidence on the Evolution of the Skyscraper." *Art Quarterly* 4, no. 1 (Winter 1941): 56–70.

"A Picturesque Skyscraper." *Architectural Record* 5 (January/March 1896): 299–302.

Radstone, Susannah, and Bill Schwar, eds. *Memory: Histories, Theories, Debates.* New York: Fordham University Press, 2010.

"Rearticulating the Skyscraper: New York, Kansas City and Minneapolis." *Architectural Record* 172 (May 1984): 22–23, 36.

"The Rise of the Skyscraper: A Study in the Origins of Modern Form." *Arts and Architecture* 69 (January 1952): 22–23.

Rowe, Colin. "The Chicago Frame" (1956). Reprinted in *The Mathematics of the Ideal Villa and Other Essays.* Cambridge: MIT Press, 1976.

Schleier, Merrill. *The Image of the Skyscraper in American Art, 1890–1931.* Ann Arbor: UMI Research Press, 1986.

Schuyler, Montgomery. "The Evolution of a Skyscraper." *Architectural Record* 14 (November 1903): 329–43.

———. "The Evolution of the Skyscraper." *Scribner's* 46 (September 1909): 257.

———. "The Skyscraper Problem." *Scribner's* 34 (August 1903): 253–56.

———. "The Skyscraper Up to Date." *Architectural Review* 8 (January/March 1899): 231–57.

———. "Some Recent Skyscrapers." *Architectural Record* 22, no. 3 (September 1907): 161–76.

———. "The Works of Francis H. Kimball and Kimball & Thompson." *Architectural Record* 7, no. 4 (June 1898): 479–518.

Scully, Vincent. *American Architecture and Urbanism.* New York: George Braziller, 1961.

Shand-Tucci, Douglass. *Ralph Adams Cram: An Architect's Four Quests: Medieval, Modernist, American, Ecumenical.* Amherst: University of Massachusetts Press, 2005.

Shepherd, Roger, ed. *Skyscraper: The Search for an American Style, 1891–1941: Annotated Extracts from the First 50 Years of "Architectural Record."* New York: McGraw-Hill, 2003.

Simmons, G.C. "Skyscrapers in America." *A.I.A. Journal* 11 (September 1923): 370–72.

Siry, Joseph. "Wright's Price Tower: Context, Clients, and Construction." In *Prairie Skyscraper: Frank Lloyd Wright's Price Tower,* edited by Anthony Alofsin. New York: Rizzoli, 2005.

Stamper, John W. *Chicago's North Michigan Avenue: Planning and Development, 1900–1930.* Chicago: University of Chicago Press, 1991.

Stern, Robert A. M. *Raymond M. Hood.* New York: Rizzoli and Institute for Architecture and Urban Studies, 1982.

Stern, Robert A. M., Gregory Gilmartin, and Thomas Mellins. *New York 1930.* New York: Rizzoli, 1987.

Sullivan, Louis. "The Chicago Tribune Competition." *Architectural Record* 53 (February 1923): 151–57.

———. "The Tall Office Building Artistically Considered." In *Kindergarten Chats and Other Writings.* 1918. Reprint, New York: Dover, 1979. (First published in *Lippincott's,* March 1896.)

Tallmadge, Thomas. *The Story of Architecture in America.* New York: Norton, 1927.

United States Travel Service. *Skyscrapers.* Washington, D.C.: Department of Commerce, 1976.

Van Leeuwen, Thomas A. P. *The Skyward Trend of Thought: The Metaphysics of the American Skyscraper.* Cambridge: MIT Press, 1988.

Van Trump, James D. "The Skyscraper as a Monument." *Charette* 43 (April 1963): 10–13, 21.

Van Zanten, David. "'Twenties Gothic." *New Mexico Studies in the Fine Arts* 7 (1982): 19–23.

Weingarden, Lauren S. "Naturalized Naturalism: A Ruskinian Discourse on the Search for an American Style of Architecture." *Winterthur Portfolio* 24, no. 1 (Spring 1989): 43–68.

Weisman, Winston. "A New View of Skyscraper History." In *Rise of American Architecture,* edited by Edgar Kaufmann Jr., 113–60, New York: Metropolitan Museum of Art, 1970.

———. "New York and the Problem of the First Skyscraper." *Journal of the Society of Architectural Historians* 12, no. 1 (March 1953): 13–21.

———. "Philadelphia Functionalism and Sullivan." *Journal of the Society of Architectural Historians* 20, no. 1 (March 1961): 3–19.

Wharton, Annabelle. "The Tribune Tower: *Spolia* as Despoliation." In *Reuse Value: Spolia and Appropriation in Art and Architecture from Constantine to Sherrie Levine,* edited by Richard Brilliant and Dale Kinney, 179–97. Farnham, UK: Ashgate, 2011.

Willis, Carol. *Form Follows Finance.* New York: Princeton Architectural Press, 1995.

Wright, Frank Lloyd. "The Tyranny of the Skyscraper" (1930). In *Frank Lloyd Wright: The Future of Architecture.* New York: Horizon, 1953.

Wright, Gwendolyn, and Janet Parks, eds. *The History of History in American Schools of Architecture, 1865–1975.* New York: Temple Hoyne Buell Center for the Study of American Architecture and Princeton Architectural Press, 1990.

Wright, Henry N. "The Case for the Skyscraper." *Architectural Forum* 72 (December 1939): 463–64.

Zukowsky, John. "Cathedrals of Commerce: America's Gothic Skyscrapers." *Art and Antiques* 11 (January/February 1979): 106–13.

CONTRIBUTORS

CARRIE ALBEE is an architectural historian and historic preservation consultant with nineteen years of experience documenting historic properties in the mid-Atlantic, Southeast, and throughout the United States. She is a resident of Frederick, Maryland, where she serves on the local Historic Preservation Commission, and a member of the Board of Directors of the Frederick County Landmarks Foundation.

GAIL FENSKE is author of *The Skyscraper and the City: The Woolworth Building and the Making of Modern New York* (2008) and coeditor of *Aalto and America* (2012). She has contributed essays to several books, among them *The American Skyscraper: Cultural Histories* (2005), *The Landscape of Modernity* (1997), and *The Education of the Architect* (1997). She is Professor of Architecture in the School of Architecture, Art and Historic Preservation at Roger Williams University.

ANKE KOETH examined skyscraper churches in America in her doctoral thesis, "Wolkenkratzerkirchen: Ein amerikanischer Bautyp der 1920er Jahre" (2010). A former member of the academic staff at the Technische Universität Dresden and an adjunct lecturer in the School of Architecture at the University of Arizona, she currently works as a monument conservation expert for the city of Zürich, Switzerland.

JOANNA MERWOOD-SALISBURY is Professor and Head of the School of Architecture at Victoria University of Wellington, New Zealand. She has published widely on the Chicago school of architecture, including *Chicago 1890: The Skyscraper and the Modern City* (2009); scholarly essays in *Architecture and Capitalism* (2013); *Chicagoisms: The City as Catalyst for Architectural Speculation* (2013); and *Chicago Architecture: Histories, Revisions, Alternatives* (2005). She is the recipient of grants from the Graham Foundation and the National Endowment for the Humanities.

KEVIN D. MURPHY is Andrew W. Mellon Chair in the Humanities, and Professor and Chair in the Department of History of Art at Vanderbilt University. He has been a faculty member in the Ph.D. Program in Art History at the CUNY Graduate Center, where he was Executive Officer, and in the School of Architecture at the University of Virginia. Professor Murphy has published articles in the *Journal of the Society of Architectural Historians,* the *Journal of Urban History,* and the *Winterthur Portfolio,* among other scholarly publications. In addition, he has published books and edited volumes on European and American architecture and visual culture, most recently, *The Tudor Home* (2015).

CHRISTINE G. O'MALLEY is an architectural historian and serves as the Preservation Services Coordinator for Historic Ithaca. She previously taught art and architectural history at Ithaca College, Carleton College, and St. Olaf College. She is a former member of the Ithaca Landmarks Preservation Commission and a former board member of the Vernacular Architecture Forum.

LISA REILLY is Associate Professor and Chair of the Department of Architectural History at the University of Virginia. The author, with Karen Van Lengen, of *Campus Guide: Vassar College,* she has also published a monograph on Peterborough Cathedral. A former editor of *Gesta* (2009–12), she is a Fellow of the Society of Antiquaries of London. In 2015, she was the Fulbright Fellow in the History of Art at the University of York, and in 2014 she was the Bonnie

Wheeler Fellow. Her recent articles and essays discuss the notion of the Gothic, digital humanities, and the role of inscriptions in medieval stained glass.

KATHERINE M. SOLOMONSON is Associate Professor in the School of Architecture at the University of Minnesota. In addition to teaching courses in architectural history, she cochaired the planning task force for the university's new College of Design and then contributed to bringing it to fruition as the college's Associate Dean for Academic Affairs. Her publications include *The Chicago Tribune Tower Competition: Skyscraper Design and Cultural Change in the 1920s* (2003) and the coedited anthology *Making Suburbia: New Histories of Everyday America* (2015). She also coedits the book series "Architecture, Landscape and American Culture.

INDEX

Italicized page numbers refer to illustrations.